T0316880

New Lithuania in Old Hands

New Lithuania in Old Hands

Effects and Outcomes of EUropeanization in Rural Lithuania

Ida Harboe Knudsen

ANTHEM PRESS
LONDON · NEW YORK · DELHI

Anthem Press
An imprint of Wimbledon Publishing Company
www.anthempress.com

This edition first published in UK and USA 2012
by ANTHEM PRESS
75-76 Blackfriars Road, London SE1 8HA, UK
or PO Box 9779, London SW19 7ZG, UK
and
244 Madison Ave. #116, New York, NY 10016, USA

British Library Cataloguing-in-Publication Data
A catalogue record for this book is available from the British Library.

Library of Congress Cataloging-in-Publication Data
Knudsen, Ida Harboe.
New Lithuania in old hands : effects and outcomes of Europeanization in rural
Lithuania / Ida Harboe Knudsen.
p. cm.
Includes bibliographical references and index.
ISBN 978-0-85728-453-2 (hardback : alk. paper)
1. Farms, Small–Lithuania. 2. Lithuania–Social conditions–21st century.
3. Social stratification–Lithuania. 4. European Union–Lithuania.
5. European Union–Membership–Lithuania. 6. Lithuania–Politics
and government–21st century. I. Title.
HD1476.L58K58 2012
330.94793–dc23
2012007677

ISBN-13: 978 0 85728 453 2 (Hbk)
ISBN-10: 0 85728 453 3 (Hbk)

This title is also available as an eBook.

CONTENTS

Acknowledgments   vii

Lithuania: An Overview   ix

List of Tables and Figures   xi

Chapter 1   Introduction   1

Chapter 2   Small-Scale Farmers at the Geopolitical Return
            to Europe, 1990–2004   33

Chapter 3   Paradoxes of Aging: On Aging Farmers and
            Aging Politicians   63

Chapter 4   Effects of and Responses to the EU Programs
            in the Countryside   87

Chapter 5   The Insiders and the Outsiders: EUropeanization of
            Products and People in the Marketplace   111

Chapter 6   "If you wish your son bad luck, give him your land":
            EUropeanization, Demographic Change and Social Security 135

Chapter 7   "They told us we would be getting up on the high mountain":
            Concluding Remarks   163

Bibliography   173

Index   185

ACKNOWLEDGMENTS

This book is based upon my PhD dissertation at the Max Planck Institute for Social Anthropology (MPISA) in Germany. The research has been funded by the EU under the Marie Curie Programme for Social Anthropology – a project established to promote anthropology in and about Central and Eastern Europe. I received a further six months' writing stipend from the Graduate School, "Society and Culture in Motion" at the Martin-Luther-Universität Halle-Wittenberg in Germany. Thanks to the postdoctoral grant I received afterwards from the Danish Independent Research Council (FKK), I have been able to transform my doctoral dissertation into the current book.

I would like to thank the Lithuanians who let me into their houses and lives. I value how they patiently answered my many questions and made me aware of conditions in Lithuania that I had not taken into consideration beforehand. Thanks to their efforts, I got a "hands on" feeling for rural life, as I was taught how to work in the fields, in the stables and how to milk cows (luckily the Lithuanian cows showed the needed patience with me too – I send them warm thoughts). I am particularly grateful to my host families for their help and guidance and for making the research possible.

Special thanks to my previous supervisors, Prof. Dr. Keebet von Benda-Beckmann and Prof. Dr. Franz von Benda-Beckmann from the MPISA for their continuous support, their constructive critiques and for their encouragement when I faced difficulties both during the fieldwork and while writing my material. I would furthermore like to thank Dr. Michael Stewart from University College London, who set the Marie Curie SocAnth Program in motion. Likewise, thanks to my external supervisor, Dr. Frances Pine of Goldsmiths University, London, whose critique and suggestions helped me improve my analysis. I also thank my previous supervisor at Aarhus University, Denmark, Dr. Poul Pedersen, for arranging for me to go to Lithuania as a master student and for inspiring me to continue in academia and Dr. Vytis Čiubrinskas from the Vytautas Magnus University in Kaunas, Lithuania, for having me in his department.

Special thanks to Anthem Press, and in particular to my editor, Janka Romero, for making the publishing process swift and smooth. I appreciate my two anonymous reviewers' valuable comments and suggestions.

Last, but certainly not least, very special thanks to Eugenijus Liutkevičius for his careful and critical reading of every version of the book's manuscript and for his tireless efforts in alerting me to specific Soviet and Lithuanian conditions at different epochs. This book is dedicated to him.

Many other people have helped me through critical discussions of the material, by sharing their thoughts and generally supporting me in the process of research and writing. I will not be able to mention you all here, but I have not forgotten any of you. The responsibility for any inaccuracies or flaws in this book remains solely with the author.

LITHUANIA: AN OVERVIEW[1]

Geographical Location

The Republic of Lithuania (Lietuvos Respublika) is a country in Northeastern Europe. Lithuania, together with Latvia and Estonia, constitute the three Baltic states. The country shares borders with Latvia to the north, Belarus to the east and south, Poland to the south, and the Russian exclave (Kaliningrad Oblast) to the southwest.

Geopolitical History in Brief

During the fourteenth century, Lithuania was the largest country in Europe, existing under the name the Grand Duchy of Lithuania. It consisted of present-day Belarus, Ukraine and parts of Poland and Russia. In 1569 Poland and Lithuania formed a new state, the Polish–Lithuanian Commonwealth. The commonwealth lasted for more than two centuries. From 1772 to 1792 it was slowly dismantled by the neighboring countries. Hereafter, the Russian Empire took over most of Lithuania's territory.

In the aftermath of World War I, Lithuania's Act of Independence was signed on 16 February 1918 declaring the reestablishment of a sovereign state. Independence lasted a brief time. Starting in 1940 Lithuania was occupied first by the Soviet Union and then by Nazi Germany. As the Germans retreated toward the end of World War II in 1944, the Soviet Union reoccupied Lithuania. On 11 March 1990, after 50 years of Soviet occupation, Lithuania became the first Soviet republic to declare independence. Lithuania entered NATO on 29 March 2004 and the EU on 1 May 2004.

Country, People, Economy

Country area: 65,200 km^2

Capital: Vilnius

---

1 See http://lt.wikipedia.org/wiki/Lietuva (accessed 24 November 2004).

Currency: Litas (Ltl.)

Language: Lithuanian (*lietuvių kalba*) – one of the most conservative Indo-European languages extant

Governance: Parliamentary republic

Independence days: 16 February and 11 March

National hymn: "Lietuva, Tėvyne mūsų" ("Lithuania, Our Fatherland")

National flag: Horizontal tricolor of yellow, green and red

Ethnic groups: Lithuanians 83.9%, Poles 6.6%, Russians 5.4%, Belarusians 1.3%, Ukrainians 0.6%, other 2.9%

Population in Lithuania (2011): 3.2 million

Religion: Roman Catholic 79.0%, Orthodox 4.8%, Protestant 1.9%, other 4.8, non-religious 9.5%

GDP per capita 2010: $16,000 (ranking number 70 in the world). Prior to the global economic crisis of 2007–2010, Lithuania had one of the fastest-growing economies in the EU

GDP composition per sector: Agriculture 3.4%, industry 27.9%, services 68.7%

Unemployment rate (2010): 17.8%

Life expectancy (2009): 66 years for males and 78 for females (the largest gender difference and the lowest male life expectancy in the EU)

Suicide rate (2009): 31.5 suicides per 100,000 inhabitants per year (highest suicide rate in the world). In 1995 Lithuania had the highest suicide rate in recorded world history with 45.6 per 100,000 people.

LIST OF TABLES AND FIGURES

Tables

Table 4. 1   Changes in land under cultivation, 2007 (compared to 2002).   94

Table 4. 2   Changes in cattle stocks, 2007.   95

Table 4. 3   Reasons for not applying for funds.   97

Table 6. 1   Age distribution, Lithuania 2007.   139

Table 6. 2   Age distribution, Bilvytis and Straigiai, 25% of all households.   139

Table 6. 3   Age and gender distribution in Straigiai and Bilvytis, 2007.   141

Figures

Figure 1. 1   Lithuania and the field sites. © Max Planck Institute for
               Social Anthropology.   9

Figure 1. 2   The photograph from the Barcelona conference.
               Lithuania 2007. © Harboe Knudsen.   15

Figure 2. 1   Milkmaids at the collective farm in Straigiai in the 1970s.
               Private photo.   34

Figure 3. 1   Horses having a short break at a celebration for the
               Valstiečių Sąjunga. Lithuania 2007. © Harboe Knudsen.   83

Figure 4. 1   Lithuanian farmer, 2007. © Harboe Knudsen.   100

Figure 5. 1   Cow. Lithuania 2007. © Harboe Knudsen.   119

Figure 6. 1   Lithuanian wedding around 1970. Private photo.   145

CHAPTER 1

Introduction

After every liberation there seems to be a backlash. So we believe, oh yes, we do believe there is change all around us. But we do not believe in change, for we cannot trust it.

—Mary Catherine Bateson

As Lithuania entered the EU on 1 May 2004, large-scale celebrations were held in the capital, Vilnius, with concerts, speeches and fireworks. Banners hung in the city center with slogans such as *Būkime Europiečiais!* (Let's be Europeans!) and *Mes Europoje!* (We are in Europe!). Seven other formerly socialist countries joined the EU on the very same day together with Malta and Cyprus, and historical change was vibrating in the Vilnius festivities. Or so I was told, at least. I myself was not in Vilnius that day, but was residing in a village in southwest Lithuania. Looking out from my window in the evening, I saw nothing but empty streets. It was dark outside and except for a few barking dogs, it was quiet.

The silence hardly surprised me. From conversations about experiences and perceptions of the dissolution of the Soviet Union, I knew that the rural denizens had a rather practical take on "great events." They had referred to the regained Lithuanian independence with such statements as "What changed for us? We still had to work," "We thought there would be fewer alcoholics – but we only got more of them" or the metaphorical reflection "Before 1990, we had a piece of shit in one hand, now we have it in the other."[1] The rural residents had been struck hard by the breakdown of socialist societal structure and were now anticipating the EU with anxiety, as it was uncertain what impact it would have on their daily life and farm production.

Intrigued by the anticipation of EU membership and the consequences this would have for the small-scale farmers, I returned to Lithuania approximately two years later, in autumn 2006, in order to research the transformative process in the Lithuanian agricultural sector in the years leading up to and since the EU membership. My research included the neighboring regions in southwest

---

1 Quotation from my field notes 2006–2007; my translation from Lithuanian.

Lithuania, Dzūkija and Suvalkija. Here, I carried out research in two villages, Bilvytis and Straigiai,[2] and in order to grasp the changes on the administrative level, in the two municipal administrations to which the villages belonged.

From the outset my focus was on small family farms, as this farm type constituted the majority of agricultural enterprises in Lithuania after the regained independence. The reestablishment of private farms had been set into motion for different reasons: First, privatization had been recommended by the EU and the World Bank, as the smaller, privately owned farms were the only way to secure sustainable development in the future (Spoor and Visser 2001; Alanen 2004; Gorton, Lowe and Zellei 2005). Second, privatization was driven by strong political and economic motives, signaling Western Europe that Lithuania was ready to undergo a rapid de-Sovietization and adapt to liberal democracy and market economy. And third, the reestablishment of family farms was perceived as a solution to the immanent problem of environmental pollution in Lithuania – a result of Soviet industrialization and the giant collective farms in the countryside (Mincyte 2006, 2011).

While different reasons and motives stimulated the process of privatization, the outcome turned out to be dissatisfying. The approximately 300,000 newly established family farms were based on unspecialized, diversified production, lacked proper equipment and were run by people close to or above retirement age who lacked knowledge and options for investment. These farmers would not be able to compete in, let alone produce for, the EU market.[3] This led EU's agricultural advisory boards to undo what was seen as the mistake of the 1990s: aging small-scale farmers were now encouraged to withdraw from production altogether, and sell or lease their land. After a stressful process of division, the land would be consolidated into large fields and transferred to younger, educated farmers.

The problem was that the aging farmers were unwilling to cooperate. Indeed, the many confusing, contradicting and rapid changes throughout the 1990s in areas of the economy and politics, a number of corruption scandals among the political elite involving money and property, not to mention the severe social changes, had evoked a general feeling of insecurity and taught people not to rely on any institutional solution. No one knew if a promise would be kept, how long a law would last, how fast a decision would change or if money would keep its value. However, all knew that a piece of land and a few cows, pigs and chickens could provide a family with the necessities. The result was that the creation of an EU-shaped agricultural sector to a large extend remained in the hands of an aging rural population.

---

2 Pseudonyms.
3 See Lithuanian Ministry of Agriculture, *Agriculture and Rural Development Plan 2000–2006*; *Rural Development Plan 2004–2006 Lithuania*; and *Lithuanian Rural Development Program 2007–2013*.

The situation among aging small-scale farmers raised the following key questions for my research: To what extent do previous and existing social, political and economic structures limit or direct the implementation of EU policy, and to what extent are new structures emerging at the local level? What new opportunities emerge for the farmers, and how do they make use of them? In which ways do laws made in the anticipation of EU membership and EU laws affect demography, family structures and patterns of care and social security? And taking the wide impact of the development projects into consideration, how can we understand and conceptualize processes of EU-supervised change in the former socialist countries? I considered how new legal influences were understood, reshaped and integrated into already existing modes of local regulation and practice and how it affected the economic and social situation of the farmers.

Coining EUropeanization

The themes of development and change that I address evolve from long-standing debates, as the breakup of the Soviet Union triggered a range of scholarly responses and gave rise to ideas and speculations about the future development of the previously socialist countries. It was commonly assumed that they would enter into a phase of transition, during which they would smooth out political and economic deficits and catch up with the "modern West," as liberal democracies were considered to provide the optimal political framework for the future. In EU reports from the 1990s, it was suggested that the prospect of EU membership itself would marginalize "illiberal" domestic politics and facilitate the adoption of liberal constitutionalism and the rule of law in the accession countries during the transformation phase (Schöpflin 2000; Lange 2007; Priban 2007; Vonderau 2007). Such ideas of transition were not only nurtured by economic and political experts in Western Europe, but also by their Eastern European counterparts (Abrahams 1996). Although economists and political scientists recognized that the process of change would be difficult, it was still assumed that, given the right conditions, capitalism would be the inevitable outcome of change (Bridger and Pine 1998). Such linear approaches to the development are commonly known as instrumentalism, that is, the idea that law can fulfill specific functions in terms of change and adjustment of human behavior, because all are supposed to work for the wanted effects. It is thus assumed that law functions as a primary instrument of controlling social relationships (Lange 2007).

The anthropological responses were embedded in what became known as postsocialist literature. This wave of writings emphasized that such linear understandings as seen in the instrumentalist contributions gloss over inherent contradictions and complexes imbedded in transition in terms of economy, politics and social relations, not to mention daily life in both urban and rural areas

(Verdery 1991, 1996, 2002b, 2003; Hann 1994, 2002, 2003; Swain 1992, 1996; Anderson and Pine 1995; Bridger and Pine 1998; Humphrey 1995, [1998] 2001, 2002; Kalb 2002; Lampland 2002; Thelen 2003a). One concern the postsocialist scholars evoked was that both terminology and models used to describe the transition phase emerged from Western European countries and were thus adapted to the situation in the former Soviet countries without taking the influence of the previous system into closer consideration. Furthermore, the idea of transition was subject to much scholarly uneasiness due to its implicit understanding of a development between two fixed points, which was unfit to describe the situation in Central and Eastern Europe (Hann 1994, 2002, 2003; Anderson and Pine 1995; Kaneff 1996; Bridger and Pine 1998; Humphrey 1998, 2002). The writings under the label of postsocialism have therefore pervasively stressed the continuations from the past, arguing that there cannot be any development of capitalism similar to the one known in Western Europe. Without disagreeing, I would add that for a part of these countries, the course was already fixated on what would eventually be integration into the EU. For these Central and Eastern European countries, the outcomes were contradictory and unequal processes of disintegration from the Soviet Union, while early steps of integration into the EU were already taken. What we see today is a hybrid of what was and what was supposed to be, not fitting any form, neither socialism nor liberal democracy. The processes of change prior to and after the EU accession, which I accordingly set out to analyze, I refer to as "EUropeanization." This concept embeds a geographical location (the changing area of the EU), which we can refer to as "EUrope" and an analytical approach. In order to clarify the latter, I will present four points that serve as analytical guidelines.

The first point is that the EU is not a recent phenomenon in the accession countries, as they actually started their integration and preparation only a few years after they gained independence. Indeed, the EU entered the stage and introduced the earliest preparations for obtaining membership at the same time as the previously socialist countries struggled to undo the Soviet dominion over their societies. I therefore suggest considering and analyzing the disintegration from the Soviet Union and the integration into the EU as coexisting processes, as the one hardly preceded the other.

The second point is that EUropeanization entails a new class of marginalized citizens; the geopolitical belonging that came about with the membership not only fueled political and economic processes, but likewise forged a reconceptualization of recent history and national identity. In Lithuania, citizens were expected to arise from the Soviet breakup as no longer Soviet-minded citizens, but internationally minded "New Lithuanians." The rejection of the immediate past through a change of identity was a highly politicized project, which both merged with and reinforced the ideas for the development of the rural areas, as aging farmers were seen as the antithesis to both the national remaking of identity and the future development of the agricultural sector.

The third point stresses developmental outcomes of EUropeanization. The enlargement of the EU was, ideally, to be created through the spread of specific technoscientific forms, through which the individual countries were to turn into metonyms for the larger entity. However, embedded in the idea of EUropeanization is the idea that these very processes aiming at greater harmonization and compatibility between the old and the new member states inevitably become flawed as their implementation largely depends on the local adjustment of law. Rather than the desired outcome of member states as metonyms for the EU, it would be sensible to speak of the emergence of "locally processed EUs."

The fourth point underlines that the EU development programs often affect other aspects of life than originally aimed for and intended. EUropeanization likewise leads to changes in patterns of obtaining social security, affects family structures and relations between genders and generations. An interconnected argument is that it is often those who are the furthest from the decision-making, people who might not even recognize themselves as a part of the current changes, who have to deal with the greater consequences following the long process of restructuring after the breakdown of the Soviet Union.

As the above-mentioned points suggest, EUropeanization refers to socioeconomic and legal outcomes and changes of self-perception targeting the population at large and resulting from the coexistence of old Soviet structures and goal-oriented EU influence, even when the consequences turn out to be in opposition to the intended goals as set by the EU. Embedded in EUropeanization lies the idea that EU programs often do not fit into the local environment and people's way of doing things, and thus, people are bound to change them and adjust them to their daily life. In the scope of this interpretation, bending, ignoring and changing rules, an increased illegal sale of farm products, alienation from the EU project and state institutions, a blurred coexistence between increased individualism and persisting kinship obligations, mass-scale emigration and changes in the family structures are all coming to grips with processes of EUropeanization.

Europeanizing Europe?

The term EUropeanization should not be confused with "Europeanization," which frequently has been used to analyze the EU influences on the former socialist countries and the implementation of EU-policies (Ågh 1993; Grabbe 2005; Hugh, Sasse and Gordon 2005; Schimmelfennig and Sedelmeyer 2005; Bafoil 2009). As the anthropologists John Borneman and Nick Fowler have rightly observed, Europeanization has commonly been viewed as an outgoing movement, where (old) Europe exercises its influence over either colonies or socialist countries.

In this perspective, Europeanization takes form of a strategy of self-representation and a device of power through which territory and peoplehood are fundamentally reorganized (Borneman and Fowler 1997). This approach is, for one example, seen in the contribution of the political scientist Heather Grabbe, who uses Europeanization as a way to analyze the political and economic changes the former socialist countries went through in order to achieve membership in the EU, a process which is characterized by the candidate countries' "downloading" of EU policies (Grabbe 2005). The political scientist François Bafoil goes even further in his contribution to the debate, as he sees Europeanization alone as the impact of the EU legislation. In his words:

> [W]e can only speak in terms of Europeanization when the [European] Union showed itself to be the decisive actor; that is to say, when its pressure turned out to be irresistible, namely in late 1997 and early 1998 when it made adoption by the candidate countries of the entire *Acquis Communautaire*, the absolute precondition for membership. (Bafoil 2009, 9)

One of the problems I encounter with this and similar approaches is the implicit understanding of Europe in accordance with the Cold War's Iron Curtain. In order to explain this, it becomes pertinent to take a look back in time. During the Cold War the first attempts were made to heal the wounds of Europe after World War II by securing alliances between the European countries, thereby preventing future warfare in Europe. The first initiative was the establishment of the European Coal and Steel Community (ECSC) in 1951, which in 1957 changed into the European Economic Community (EEC), which consisted of the "Inner Six" countries, Belgium, France, Italy, Luxembourg, the Netherlands and West Germany. In 1973 the EEC expanded with Denmark, Ireland and the United Kingdom, in 1981 with Greece and in 1986 with Spain and Portugal.

From the outset, the EEC was constructed on the basis of what was perceived as a common European heritage of Christianity and Enlightenment, and was thought to create the basis for an ideal European unity (Heffernan 1998; Hudson 2000). It was the intention that this unity with time would transform to an actual economic and political union. This happened with the Maastricht Treaty, which was signed on 7 February 1992. Now the EEC had become the EU, a union that forged closer political, economic and legal cooperation within the member states. Thus, we see that the actual union (EU) is a relatively new geopolitical construction that was even predated by *die Wende* in Germany in 1989.

The consolidation of the EU with the Maastricht Treaty coincided with the challenge of a future expansion with the former socialist countries. The goal was to smooth out differences and work towards greater harmonization within the EU and thus, to diminish inequalities in Europe (Hudson 2000). The enlargement was not an unwanted challenge, as it was the first cause which gave the EU a political justification for its very existence. By setting standards for the former socialist countries, EU came to define the "right" European criteria and values and thereby legitimized its own political, economic and legal power. The result was that the EU to an increasing extent has come to represent Europe. With the words of the geographer Ray Hudson:

> [E]ven at national level the European space has been – and continues to be – subject to complex processes of (re)partitioning that have re-drawn the political-economic map with some frequency and increasingly this has been associated with an extension of the boundaries of the EU itself and a consequent re-definition of the meaning of Europe. (Hudson 2000, 412)

But is the EU the definition of Europe? Or is this a self-ascribed attribution to justify the political influence of the union – which has had the effect that even the former Soviet countries speak about the membership as a "return to Europe." If we take a second look at the banners in Vilnius on May 1, 2004, the fusion of the EU and Europe worked well in Lithuania as the slogan was "we are in Europe" and *not* "we are in the EU." The understandings of EU as equalizing Europe and the power exercised by the EU as Europeanization are, in my perception, misleading and inaccurate. This comes down to my geographical understanding of Europe as going far beyond the changing borders of the union; at the time the EU opened up for membership for the former socialist countries, there were 15 member countries. In comparison, there were 34 countries that geographically were a part of Europe, yet were not members of the EU. At the time of writing (2011), the EU has expanded greatly and consists of 27 member states; yet there are still 22 European countries that are not members.[4] Thereby, an approach that focuses on "core" European values as defined by (old) EU member states presents a flawed picture of Europe, as it leaves out the perspective of multiple European countries that are not EU members, and to a great extent approaches from former socialist countries and other late-joiners that had to encapsulate the predefined values, laws and EU-defined ways of governance.

---

4 Albania, Andorra, Armenia, Azerbaijan, Belarus, Bosnia and Herzegovina, Georgia, Lichtenstein, Moldova, Monaco, Norway, Russia, San Marino, Serbia, Switzerland, Ukraine and the Vatican City State belong geographically to Europe but are not members of the EU. Croatia, the Former Yugoslav Republic of Macedonia, Iceland, Montenegro and Turkey likewise belong to geographical Europe and are currently candidate states to the EU but not yet members (2011). Austria, Finland and Sweden only joined in 1995, Cyprus, the Czech Republic, Estonia, Hungary, Latvia, Lithuania, Malta, Poland and Slovenia joined in 2004, and Bulgaria and Romania in 2007.

Returning to the actual processes of EU influence, which has been stressed by the scholars of Europeanization, I agree that for political and economic reasons the candidate countries had little space for negotiation in the last phases before obtaining membership. However, when looking at the "ground level," that is, when looking at the actual workings and outcomes of the EU programs, local actors seemed to have plenty of space for negotiating, bending and even breaking EU rules in order to make the larger umbrella models fit realistically into their everyday lives. It is this dialectic relationship between EU models and local responses that I seek to capture by framing the term, EUropeanization.

Fieldwork and Field Sites

The findings of the research are based on all in all one and a half years of participant observation in two regions of rural Lithuania. The majority of my informants were small-scale farmers, meaning they had 1–10 hectares. This included two of my host families, one in Straigiai and one in Bilvytis. Part of my informants were middle-size farmers with a more specialized production with 11–20 hectares. This included my second landlord in Bilvytis. I carried out several interviews with large-scale farmers, but kept my focus on the destiny of small-scale farmers.

My first stay was half a year in 2004, where I lived and worked together with people from a village in rural Lithuania, which I here call Straigiai. This was followed by one year of intense research from 2006 to 2007 that I expanded with an additional village, Bilvytis, in the neighboring region. During the periods of research, I carried out around seventy interviews with farmers, politicians, agricultural advisors and other employees from the municipal administrations. Towards the end of my second field trip, I made a comparative household survey in the two villages of my research, the result of which will be presented in Chapters 3 and 7. The main part of the material was gathered through participant observation in the two villages of research. In order to carry out the research, learning the language was a necessity. Before going to the field, I took part in two language courses in the capital Vilnius, where I was taught the basics. However, upon my arrival in the countryside, the actual "language courses" began, as people in the two villages became my enthusiastic teachers. In this way, I achieved my abilities in the Lithuanian language using the principle of learning by doing.

As I went back to Straigiai to conduct fieldwork in 2006, it was a return to a village where I had previously lived in 2004. I lived with the Jankauskas family,[5] whom I knew from my first fieldwork in Lithuania. Although I spent most of my time on their farm, I often visited other families in the village. My approach

---

5 Pseudonym. All following names and surnames referring to people from my field sites will likewise be pseudonyms.

Figure 1.1. Lithuania and the field sites. © Max Planck Institute for Social Anthropology.

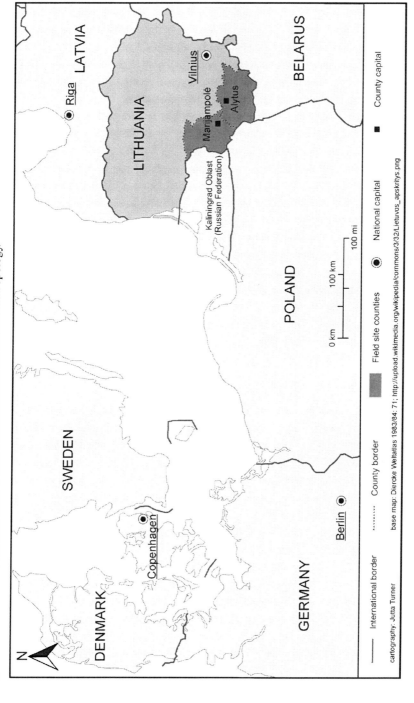

was to take part in the daily work on the farms and thus gain access to the daily routines and talks. Work was mainly centered on the cultivation and harvest of cabbages, beets, carrots, potatoes and lettuce. In the evenings I went to the stables with an older woman and helped her milk her cows. On Saturdays I went with the village women to the marketplace, where they sold their various dairy products. I expanded my research by trips to the regional capital of Marijampolė, where I carried out interviews at the municipal administration.

Not long after I had returned to village life in Straigiai, I was invited to go to a town of about 5,000 citizens in the region of Dzūkija, where they would hold a seminar about new EU regulations. As I came to the seminar, a group of politicians from Graižiūnai immediately spotted me as a possible asset for the local branch of the Lithuanian Peasants' Union (Valstiečių Sąjunga). The stronger connections with the municipal administration in Graižiūnai eventually resulted in an expansion of my research, as I now included a new region and soon moved to the small village of Bilvytis, situated close to Graižiūnai. Here I lived with two different families: the family Kaminskas, the wealthy dairy farmer Kostas and his wife Vida; and the family Kazlauskas, the older semi-subsistence farmers Daiva and Kazys. This expansion of my research meant that I was now able to conduct a more comparative research about EU influences on rural life and the municipal administrations the villages belonged to in Marijampolė and Graižiūnai.

Lithuania and the regions

Lithuania is divided into five regions: Aukštaitija, Žemaitija, Dzūkija, Suvalkija and Mažoji Lietuva. The regions do not have any administrative function, but are kept for historical and ethnographic reasons. These five regions are divided into ten different administrative counties, which again are divided into 60 municipalities. People in the areas where I conducted research always referred to the historical region as their place of belonging and saw themselves as *suvalkiečiai* (people from Suvalkija) or *dzūkai* (people from Dzūkija).

The names of the villages have been changed. Regarding the cities of the municipalities the villages belonged to, I found a combined solution. In the case of Suvalkija, I have chosen not to change the name of the city, since it would be obvious which city I talk about, anyway: Marijampolė is the capital of Suvalkija. This is, however, not the case of the town in the other region, Dzūkija, where the region's capital Alytus is located far away from the area where I did my research. Here I use a pseudonym, Graižiūnai, for the town where I did my research. The reason for this choice is that I had much closer connections with people from this municipal administration, which meant that the information I gathered was more detailed and personal.

Suvalkija

The village of Straigiai is located in the region of Suvalkija, a region known for its strong agricultural center. The soil is known to be the most fertile in Lithuania and the landscape is flat and level, which makes the cultivation of the land easy. Even though much of the land lays fallow in Lithuania, this is not that common in the region of Suvalkija. The traditional crops are rye, wheat, barley, peas, sugar beets, potatoes and various other vegetables. The fieldwork in Suvalkija was done in Marijampolė County. The area connected to the county covers 755 km² of land, 72 percent of which is agricultural land, 12.3 percent covered by forest, 4.2 percent by towns and villages, and 6.9 percent used for other purposes. Suvalkija is known for being one of the richest regions in the country.[6]

The municipal administration is located in Marijampolė, the "capital" of Suvalkija. The name of the city derives from the Catholic monastic order of the Marijonai (Marijonų Vienuolynas), whose monastery had been built in the area in 1750. During Soviet times the city was renamed Kapsukas after the Lithuanian founder of the Communist Party, Vincas Mickevičius-Kapsukas. Shortly before 1990, the name was changed once again to the original Marijampolė. Marijampolė is an industrial city with about 50,000 inhabitants. In and around Marijampolė, various enterprises process all the main agricultural products: AB Marijampolės konservai (processing and canning fruits, berries and vegetables), AB Marijampolės pieno konservai (producing dairy products, milk powder, coffee, refreshing drinks), AB Marijampolės cukrus (sugar), AB Marijampolės grūdai (combined forage, corn). Furthermore, Marijampolė is known for its big outdoor market for used cars. The salespeople drive to Germany, where they buy used and sometimes damaged cars for a low price, whereafter they fix them and sell them for a higher price in Lithuania.

The village of Straigiai belongs to Marijampolė County and is situated at the crossroads of two highways, Via Baltica that connects Helsinki with central and Southern Europe and as such is the most important highway for export and import in Lithuania, and the old highway running on the other side of the village, connecting the city of Kaliningrad in the Russian Kaliningrad Oblast bordering Lithuania, to Minsk, the capital of Belarus. There are 290 households in the village with a total of 685 inhabitants.[7] Straigiai has its own school with about 150 pupils. The pupils are not only from Straigiai; they also come from the surrounding villages to attend school there. Straigiai has its own *seniūnija* – the central administration of the village – its own library that also functions as a cultural center for Straigiai and the surrounding villages, a small medical clinic and a church. The church is the

---

6 Information from the municipal administration in Marijampolė.
7 Information from the central administration in Straigiai, 2007.

biggest one in the area and attracts churchgoers from all the surrounding villages as well. There is a kiosk close to the school, and a small store where people can buy the necessary food and non-food products. For bigger shopping, however, people have to go to Marijampolė. Due to its location between two highways, public transportation connections are good in Straigiai, with several buses a day going both to Marijampolė and, in the other direction, to Kaunas, the second largest city in Lithuania.

Although farming is an important income, not all citizens in Straigiai are employed in agriculture. There is a truck company, owned by a couple from Straigiai that transports food to various food chains both in Lithuania and abroad. In Straigiai, there is also a small factory producing sausages, and a small agricultural company employing about twenty men. The school, the library and the medical clinic also offer workplaces for the local people. A few people from Marijampolė are also employed here. Other people commute from Straigiai to Marijampolė every day to work, leaving in the early morning and coming home in the evening.

Dzūkija

Dzūkija is one of the poorer regions in Lithuania. Whereas the region has a well-developed industrial center around the region's capital, Alytus, it becomes more rural towards the west. Bilvytis is located in Graižiūnai County, which covers an area of 1,309 km² and has a population of about 24,800 citizens. In this part of Dzūkija, around 60 percent of the population lives in the rural areas. Forty-four percent of the land in Dzūkija is covered by forest, which makes forestry a quite important industry in the area. As a bonus, the forests offer the locals an opportunity to collect mushrooms and berries. Agricultural land in the region comprises 34.9 percent of the area. Dzūkija is not a region very suitable for agriculture, as the soil is sandy and the landscape hilly, all of which hinders efficient agricultural production. The farms in the region are mainly cattle farms and crops are mostly various grains and potatoes. Buckwheat is popular in Dzūkija, as it is a crop that can grow on the sandy soil. Cattle and dairy farmers often cultivate maize on their land as fodder for their animals. Dzūkija tries to boost the tourist industry in the region, as the countryside and the more than 200 lakes make the area attractive for tourists.

The municipal administration is located in Graižiūnai, a town of about 5,000 inhabitants. Except for some options for working in the service sector, there are few job opportunities outside agriculture. Bilvytis is located on the very border with Poland with a scattered settlement pattern. There are about 100 households with approximately 260 citizens in the village and the surrounding area. It is hard to mark the borders of Bilvytis, since many people live outside the actual village and houses are scattered around. In Bilvytis many houses are in bad condition and there are no proper sanitary conditions (especially regarding the small, outdoor, falling-apart toilets). In the village, empty vodka, beer and soft drink bottles, cigarette packages and similar garbage is spread around, mostly close to the lake and the small bus stop, both of which are favorite places for the youth to gather. Except for the weekends, the village is almost abandoned by the youth, as there are no opportunities for work other than in agriculture. Most of the fields around the village are not cultivated. Either they lie fallow or they are used for grazing.

Bilvytis has a small shop in the center where people can buy various food and non-food products. For more extensive shopping, however, they must go to the town of Graižiūnai, either by car or, if they do not have a car, by public transport. There is a bus twice a day, in the early morning and in the afternoon. A small lake behind the shop is the gathering point for the youth on the weekends. The church in the village also attracts people from the surrounding areas, who come for mass on Sunday. In addition, there is the small House of Culture (Kultūros Namai), where festivities and local gatherings are held. Bilvytis likewise has its own school where children from the surrounding countryside also come. About 70 pupils attend the school, which offers classes up to seventh grade. After that, pupils have to continue their education in the neighboring town or drive to Graižiūnai. Except farming, the only job opportunities in Bilvytis are to work in the local store or to teach in the school. The majority are semi-subsistence farmers, many of whom are retired and live on a combination of farming and state pension. There are five bigger farms in or close to the village. Young people commute to the cities to work. In the areas close to the regional capital of Alytus, most people go there in search of work. In the area around Graižiūnai, which borders right up to Suvalkija, many young people go to Marijampolė.

On Conducting Unpopular Research

In the Soviet state there were people such as the deportees, who were considered the class enemies of the Soviet state, people of religious faith, and others who were publicly marginalized. In the post-Soviet state there are the poor villagers and former industrial town workers who are among the public outcasts. (Klumbytė 2006, 10)

The reactions to my research in Lithuania have been multifold and diverse. While people in the countryside welcomed my attempts to explore both past and current changes from their perspective, my research findings were frequently challenged when I left the villages. Objections to my research came from politicians, political co-workers and not the least from Lithuanian scholars who resided in the larger cities or abroad. The main critique of my study was that the people I set focus on were not "representative" of Lithuania, the narratives I collected were "too rural" and "too Soviet" and did therefore not provide any valuable insights, as poorly educated residents from the countryside did not have the ability to rightly formulate the attachment to the EU nor adequately reflect upon Lithuania's past during the Soviet regime. Additionally, because I am not Lithuanian, my ability to rightly interpret experiences and conditions was questioned, as I did not have an embodied understanding of the national sufferings during the past regime. We can consider three of the incidents I experienced during and after my fieldwork.

In the region of Dzūkija, a local politician welcomed my attempts to write a book about farmers from his region. However, his idea was that my work would be a booklet similar to those local writers had published, showing pictures of (prominent) farmers in front of their houses, stating how much land they had, how many cows, what they cultivated and how heavily they had been subsidized by the EU. My own attempts to pursue the destiny of small-scale farmers were met with critique, as this group did not count as "real farmers" and therefore did not adequately represent rural Lithuania. In order to guide my research in the "right" direction, he made sure that I was picked up by car and transported directly to the large-scale farmers in the region. Thus, we would pass by 30 to 40 small farms in order to reach one big farm, which was seen as "representative."

Once, I visited the city of Kaunas and was interviewed by a Lithuanian journalist about my research. During our talk, I said that many rural citizens voiced positive sentiments for the Soviet times. I further argued that this was not just a matter of what was popularly labeled "Soviet nostalgia," as many rural residents' living conditions indeed had decreased after independence. The reactions to this interview were 576 mainly angry, online comments. It appeared to the readers that I, by referencing such statements, favored the Soviet regime above the present. On this behalf, some of them bluntly classified my findings as "shitty." Others argued that I, as a foreigner, could not adequately judge the implications of such statements, as I had no prerequisites for understanding the Lithuanian sufferings during the Soviet occupation.[8]

The last incident I will mention took place after a conference in Barcelona in 2009. Here a young Lithuanian scholar who studied at the London School of Economics came across a poster about my research. On the poster I had inserted a picture from my fieldwork of two men who were cleaning the body of a pig they just had slaughtered. The Lithuanian scholar wrote me several heated emails in

---

8 "Danų antropologė: Lietuvos kaimo žmones charakterizuoja kančia ir skundas, kad sovietmečiu buvo geriau." http://www.delfi.lt/news/daily/lithuania/article.php?id= 11011434 (accessed 27 September 2011).

order to bring to my attention that the picture was misrepresenting Lithuania as a "backward" country. The picture, he stated, was "Soviet" and what it showed had not taken place in Lithuania for decades; pigs today are sent to the butcher, not slaughtered at home. The picture, which I took in Bilvytis in 2007, was one of the many cases of pig slaughtering I experienced during my time in the two villages and in Lithuania as such.

The incidents and critiques I encountered helped me understand the highly politicized ground I was walking on. In my attempt to tell a story about small-scale farmers in present day Lithuania, I opposed popular discourse about the Lithuanian national transformation from a (backward) Soviet state to a (modern) EU country. The objections to my research topic taught me the forcefulness of the present constructions of social history and alerted me to treat the geopolitical rewriting of social history and the reconfigurations of the images of rural citizens in greater detail. In addition, I believe that because I am not Lithuanian, I can present rural voices without embedding them in my own predefined constructions, of which social narratives about the Soviet past and about present day Lithuania are "reliable" or "socially acceptable."

Figure 1.2. The photograph from the Barcelona conference. Lithuania 2007. © Harboe Knudsen.

Early Influences from the EU

In the remaining part of the introduction I will return to my conceptualization of EUropeanization and treat my previously outlined four points in greater detail. The first point I wish to call attention to may be a simple yet still important observation: while the formal enlargements of the EU took place in 2004 and 2007, the EU had in reality been an active part of society in the former socialist countries since the early 1990s.

The EU closely followed and directed development in the future member countries and was thus engaged in making change happen in a particular and strictly defined way. Already from the early 1990s the candidate countries were persuaded to implement legislation from the *Acquis Communautaire*,[9] and processes of privatization and the implementation of market reforms were undertaken extremely quickly. At the time of the referendums for the EU, all necessary steps were taken in order to secure political, economic and legal compatibility between the applicant states and the rest of the EU (Senior Nello 2002). The EU thus entered the stage and introduced the earliest preparations for obtaining membership at the same time as the previously socialist countries struggled to undo Soviet structures in society.

Farming was an important part of this, as the applicant states were largely dependent on their agricultural sectors (Fernandez 2002; Senior Nello 2002). Therefore, the EU, together with the World Bank, the IMF and the OECD played a central role in supervising the further development of the agricultural sectors in the previously socialist countries (Spoor and Visser 2001; Alanen 2004; Gorton, Lowe and Zellei 2005). All of these organizations pushed for the creation of privately owned enterprises, as it was believed that these would be more efficient than collectively owned farms. Developments thereby rested on the idea that family farms could thus revive the agricultural sectors (Abrahams 1996; Alanen, Nikula, Põder and Ruutsoo 2001; Alanen 2004). However, in the eagerness to privatize the agricultural sectors in the previously socialist countries, many factors had not been taken into consideration. We can here mention the reproduction of old Soviet power structures which led to a highly uneven division of the land, the people's lack of experience as private farmers, their lack of technique and not least the aging farmers and landowners (Lerman 1998; Cartwright 2003; Kaneff and Yalcin-Heckmann 2003). Throughout the 1990s it became evident that rather than pushing the modernization of the agricultural sectors, the result of privatization had rather been a return to peasant forms of agriculture (Cartwright 2003). Consequently, when the EU in the early 2000s started to focus on land consolidation processes and the establishment of large-scale farms, these initiatives did not target the

---

9 *Acquis Communautaire*: the entire body of EU law, subsequently referred to as the *Acquis.*

reminiscence of a Soviet agricultural system. Rather, they targeted the outcome of privatization after 1990 that the union itself was partly responsible for.

In Lithuania we see how the shifting governments had aimed at establishing a model for agriculture that resembled the Western European system of private farming. Breaking down the big collective production units from Soviet times sent an important political message at the time, as it signaled determination in doing away with the Soviet societal structures in order to (re)establish geopolitical and economic relations with Western Europe. However, the hardships of rapid privatization and implementation of Western reforms made people reelect the former communists at the first given opportunity. Thus, while the political framework had changed greatly, the administrative setup of society remained by and large the same, just as many "Soviet" economic practices of favors, bribes and exchange were incorporated into the new system. This EUropeanization of the former socialist countries emerged as hybrid constellations of socialist and liberalist thoughts and practices in an interplay between past and present systems. This coexistence of the two unions, and thus, of conflicting ideologies and practices in everyday life, is thereby the founding aspect of the uneven outcomes. This, however, is covered by the apparent unambiguous political ambition to do away with the past and build a "new nation." The following point in my comprehension of EUropeanization is therefore targeting the rewriting of social history and change of national identity.

Reconstructions of the National Identity

Paul Connerton ([1989] 1998), in his work about social memory, shows us how present factors may influence, or even distort, our recollections of the past, just as past factors influence or distort our conceptualization of the present. This is typically seen in the remaking (rewriting) of history where a certain presentation of the past is preferred above another, and can become the only accepted history at all. Thus, through the reconstruction of history, certain aspects are highlighted while others are repressed or neglected, all of which establishes a new way of remembering in a given society (Connerton [1989] 1998). Giordiano and Kostova (2002) refer to such reconceptualizations of the past as "actualized history," that is, the past is intentionally or unintentionally mobilized in the light of the present. Actualized history is not linked to chronological timeframes, as different parts of the past may be used to serve specific goals. With specific reference to Soviet and post-Soviet context Giordano and Kostova elaborate on two kinds of actualized history. The first kind is the "annihilation of the past" that characterized the Soviet regime. Here "new history" was created by changing national holidays, festivities, by renaming cities, and by destroying symbols and social practices that belonged to Tsarist Russia. The second kind, the "reversibility of events," characterizes the early post-Soviet regimes. This idea entails both retrospective and prospective tendencies. The retrospective aspects are seen in the ambition to return to a status quo ante, and thus, to reestablish pre-Soviet history, while the Soviet past is done away with as a "fatal mistake" that distorted the "natural" historical flow, while the prospective aspects are seen in the ambition to build the future upon this historical re-creation (Giordano and Kostova 2002). Thus, similar discourses are intentionally used in actualized history in order to serve specific goals at specific times; the past is selected, modified and circumvented according to the current discourse in society. In Lithuania, we see such aspects of historical remaking within the context of the EU membership.

The national image of Lithuania was consciously changed during the presidencies of Valdas Adamkus (1998–2003, 2004–2009),[10] when the popular self-victimization based on historical interpretations of the oppressive Soviet regime was replaced with an image of Lithuania as a modern, self-governing and self-conscious nation, ready to enter the EU. The idea was that more than just becoming Europeans again, the Lithuanians should set out to teach the existing member countries a lesson about Europeanness, because they, together with other citizens from previous socialist countries, had had to fight so hard for their European belonging (Klumbytė 2006; see also Čiubrinskas 2000). Such tendencies were also reflected in the nationalist revivals (Roepstorff and Simoniukštytė 2005), while new books were written with focus on freedom fighters (*partizanai*) and Soviet resistance, which is seen in literature of both the Baltic states and Lithuania, more specifically (see, for example, Senn [1990] 2002; Clemens 1991; Kuodytė, Peikštenis and Žygelis 2007; Kuodytė 2009; Veliutė 2009). In this re-creation of the nation and its citizens, the role of the EU was to bring Lithuania back and forward all at the same time; *back* to the geopolitical roots, which was promoted as a "return" to the Europe Lithuania rightfully belonged to, and, at the same time, *forward*, away from the Soviet past, towards modernity, towards influence and welfare. The EU membership thus played an important role in defining and redefining Lithuania and served as an image of wealth and overabundance (De Munck 2008), whereas the Soviet past was more than ever depicted as "archaic," resembling a repressive system, and reconceptualized as the "evil force" (Vonderau 2007; Klumbytė 2010; Harboe Knudsen 2010a), while attachment to the past was characterized as a "disease" of Soviet nostalgia (Klumbytė 2008).

---

10 From February 2003 to April 2004 Rolandas Paksas was the president of Lithuania. However, soon after his presidency had begun, he was dismissed from office as he was accused of having illegal relations with the Russians and taken to court. After Paksas had been dismissed, Adamkus was reelected as president of the Republic of Lithuania and served until 18 July 2009, when Dalia Grybauskaitė was sworn into office, becoming the first female president in Lithuanian history.

Along with the geopolitical reconceptualization of Lithuania, a popular expression popped up: "New Lithuania," and in companion with that, "New Lithuanians." "New" with regard to persons is referring to the modern and cosmopolitan citizen, who can easily navigate in Europe and succeed and gain from the "Westernization" of the society (De Munck 2008). These New Lithuanians became central in the project of redefining Lithuanian identity and showing a new outer face of the country. Indeed, with a slight rewriting of British author George Orwell, it seemed like all Lithuanians were European, but some Lithuanians were more European than others,[11] since the European identity and the imaginations surrounding it were assumed to be more easily embodied by some than by others. If we correspond this to Orwell's idea, these "more Europeans" appeared to be the better-educated people with international experience who led a better life than the majority. The ideas of generations furthermore played into national attempts to restructure history, as young people were supposed to embody Europe, as opposed to the older generations that were assumed to embody the "archaic past."

"The Man of the Future" and *Homo Sovieticus*

It is curious that this discursive form of communication was not so "new" in Lithuania, as many features appeared to be similar to approaches made under the Soviet regime. During Soviet times, the key concepts had also been the establishment of a "new society" and a "new man," both of which were contrasting what was viewed as the archaic capitalistic societies in the West. The "New Soviet Man,"[12] based on early ideas of Soviet communism, was, for example, described in the book *Literature and Revolution* by the revolutionist and political thinker Lev Trotskij ([1924] 1957). Trotskij referred to him as "The Man of the Future" and described him as healthy and hardworking, a man who works for the common good and sets aside individual wishes and gains for society's sake (Trotskij [1924] 1957). In this process of change, the goal was to do away with the pre-Soviet past as quickly as possible in order to make room for the new history. Today, the previous image of the (modern) "New Soviet Man" contrasting (archaic) capitalism is used the other way around. Now it is the (capitalistic) "New Lithuanian" who contrasts the (archaic) "Soviet Man," while the Soviet past is what people should do away with as quickly as possible. The difference is that the "New Soviet Man" was meant to apply to all citizens, whereas the "New Lithuanian" is only applicable to a minority. Additionally, the ideas of Soviet man have been circumvented and

---

11 The original quote from George Orwell's *Animal Farm* is: "All animals are equal, but some animals are more equal than others" (Orwell [1945] 2003, 92).

12 *Naujas Tarybinis Žmogus*, in present day Lithuania, most often referred to as *Naujas Sovietinis Žmogus*.

flourish in society as a negative image of the Lithuanian who does not embrace and embody the "new Europeanism." Rather, s/he is now classified as a *Homo Sovieticus*. This concept is in itself worth a closer investigation as the current use of it as a "backward" citizen actually is a misinterpretation – or we could say at the very least – a simplification of the original meaning of it.

The person who first coined the concept was Russian writer, sociologist and émigré Aleksandr Zinoviev, who in 1982 published a sociological novel, called *Homo Sovieticus*. The book, with its pseudo-Latin title, served as a genuine critique of the Soviet police state, while it in the same breath exposed the foibles of the Western capitalist systems without mercy. Additionally, the book was meant as a critical and sarcastic remark to Trotskij's descriptions of "The Man of the Future." *Homo Sovieticus*, which Zinoviev shortens to *Homosos* (Ru. *Гомосос*), is thus described as indifferent to labor and common property, incapable of taking responsibility and ever ready to shift his moral position to suit his circumstances (Zinoviev [1982] 1985). Zinoviev embedded an additional and subtle meaning in the concept through his play with words. In Russian, *Homosos* is more than an abbreviation of *Homo Sovieticus*; the mere shortening creates yet another term, which in English translates into *Homo Suck(er)*. Zinoviev turned Trotskij's concept upside down: instead of the man who sacrifices himself for society's sake, we now have *Homosos* – the "man sucker," a parasite-like individual who lives off society's fruits without contributing anything himself.

Zinoviev, however, was not solely negative towards Soviet man, but depicted the ambiguous relationship he had to his *Homosos* whom he loved and hated, admired and despised, was attracted to and appalled by – all at the same time. "I myself am a Homosos," Zinoviev conveys (Zinoviev [1982] 1985, foreword).[13] The *Homosos* in Zinoviev's analysis is thus also described as a hardy, cunning and resourceful individual who has learned to survive even when exposed to the toughest circumstances (in contrast to the soft and whiny Westerners), and while the *Homosos* has been deprived of all his convictions and does not trust the authorities, the naïve Western Europeans and Americans still get fooled by theirs. As for his flaws of self-interest, indifference, his shifting moral positions, his high opinions of himself and judgment of others, Zinoviev writes:

> Gentle reader, look into yourself and you will see there at least an embryo of this crown of creation. For you yourself are human. You yourself are Homosos. (Zinoviev [1982] 1985, 199–200)

These ambiguities and dualities so essential to the analysis, the love and wit in the descriptions as well as the statement that there is something deeply human

---

13 This page of the book cited is unnumbered.

and universal about the *Homosos*, features that were but further cultivated under Soviet communism, disappeared in the daily use of the concept, and left was only an unambiguous and one-sided understanding of the concept as a way to characterize the "backwards" Soviet man.

The Changing Image of the Lithuanian Farmer

The reason I go to such length explaining the current transformations of identity and the specificities of a single concept is because it corresponds to the views and perceptions of small-scale farmers in present day Lithuania. In a period when yet another "new man" is invented and yet another "new society" created, aging farmers' voices contradict the current tale. It appears to me that the radical attempts to dismiss the Soviet past and disqualify certain parts of the population for not being "representative," as I experienced during my period of research, bear witness to the inner battles these "New Lithuanians'" fight against their own embryo of the *Homosos*.

In her research about the New Lithuanian elite, the Lithuanian anthropologist Asta Vonderau confirms my impressions of the present-day Lithuanian discourse where we find the distinctions between *Homo Sovieticus* (a term she uses without the Zinovievian ambiguity) and *Homo Europaeus* (Vonderau 2008). While the latter is depicted in present day Lithuania as success orientated, flexible and self-responsible, the former is "[...] becoming increasingly focused on older, socially weak [and] less educated members of society." (Vonderau 2008, 118). More than that, this perception has especially been tied to the rural dwellers who are seen as "backwards," indulging in nostalgia for the past and voting for populist parties, also referred to as *runkeliai* (turnips) (Vonderau 2007, 2008).[14] It appears as if the perception of the farmers has suffered the same destiny as the concept of *Homo Sovieticus* – it has turned into a one-dimensional stereotype. Whether the simplified concept further simplified the image of the rural dwellers, or the simplified image of the rural dwellers further simplified the concept, I am not able to say, but the result is that they today have become linked together in a way that does neither of them justice.

To find this negative perception tied to the rural population is particularly remarkable, as the rural citizens earlier had represented the romanticized image of the Lithuanians in pre-Soviet times as having a close relation to the soil of the fatherland (*tėvynė*), upholding valued national traditions and thereby symbolizing the country's agronational identity (Mincyte 2006). Returning to the ideas of Giordano and Kostova, the farmers had played a particular role after the Soviet

---

14 *Runkeliai* is a highly negative term, commonly used as a reference to rural denizens in Lithuania.

breakup as a way to re-create the order of events according to the ideas of reversible history where a pre-Soviet past should be re-created in order to pave way for a prospective future (Giordano and Kostova 2002). In Lithuania it was believed that land privatization would reestablish previous agricultural and national traditions and break away from the inhuman Soviet "agricultural gigantism" (Mincyte 2011). This tendency is also found in Bulgaria, where the re-creation of the small-scale farmers likewise played a central role in restoring the "natural order" after the Soviet distortions (Giordano and Kostova 2002). Such ideas were again evoked upon independence, as Lithuanians – as had the Bulgarians – at first reattached hope to the farmers as the people who should "carry" the country through the hard times with a revived private farm production. This peasant myth went hand in hand with the rebuilding of the nation (Giordano and Kostova 2002; Mincyte 2006, 2011). As it became clear that the small-scale farmers faced serious difficulties under the changed circumstances, such hopes and expectations failed to materialize. Now, being a farmer was no longer portrayed in such honorable terms and the distorted and solely negative image of the *Homo Sovieticus* had replaced their former glory.

The farmers now found themselves on a battlefield between Soviet practices, post-Soviet modes of cultivating the land, and challenging EU law and requirements for agricultural production. In the EU development reports, we consequently find an explicit focus on generational change in the agricultural sector. In this light, I argue that the aim to replace the aging farmers was not only a way to modernize Lithuanian agriculture, it was likewise an institutional production of anti-Soviet categories in line with the new political waves in society. As has been argued by the anthropologist James Ferguson, aid and development programs are never apolitical; rather, the goal is always to make development happen in a certain and strictly defined way that corresponds with the political models of Western liberal capitalism (Ferguson [1990] 2003).

Taking this argumentation further, I suggest that the national re-creations of the Lithuanian image and the EU development plans found common ground in their persistence on generational change. Aging farmers are obstacles in the way to achieve these goals, putting them in a delicate and vulnerable situation and furthermore, questioning their positions as farmers. Thus, it is safe to conclude that although promoted as an unambiguous way to improve conditions in the rural areas, the EU development reports were highly political in promoting a "right path" for the agricultural sector deeply embedded in a liberal capitalist framework. After having encouraged the reestablishment of private farms in the beginning of the 1990s, the EU in the mid-1990s started to construct the small-scale farmer as the obstacle for the planned development due to their small-scale, autonomous and often unregistered production, which made their farms incompatible with the standardization policies practiced by the EU (Harboe Knudsen 2010b; Mincyte 2006, 2011).

What was most curious was that the age values and the focus on generational change were ideas implemented by aging state representatives, who, just like the farmers they tried to remove, had lived the majority of their lives during the Soviet system. The inherent contradiction appeared that the aging state representatives were not subjected to the same policies of generational change as a way to combat the Soviet features in society. Quite to the contrary, they now experienced their political prime, reaping the benefits of the membership. Indeed, despite the anti-Soviet rhetoric and politics this cannot be viewed as a straightforward and undisputed desire to outdo the recent past, since the disqualification based on age would apply to the people in administrative posts as well.

Harmonization and Inconsistencies

The third point of EUropeanization I wish to call attention to is what I frame as the emergence of "Local EUs." While the EU has been an important factor in the restructuring of production, the national image and self-awareness in the candidate countries, the very process of enlargement has also been a process of restructuring and self-definition for the EU. As previously emphasized, the EU played an important role in defining and directing the way previously socialist countries had to go in order to reintegrate in Europe. In this sense, the EU achieved the function of a "suprastate," working through what Ferguson and Gupta have referred to as "vertical encompassment," being both "above" society and "encompassing" its localities (2002). Working through such premises, the EU legitimizes power by the use of space, especially so for the new member countries, which first had to fulfill requirements in the areas of law, economy and democracy (verticality) before they could geopolitically return to Europe (encompassment). The EU, despite its internal differences, multiethnic societies, complexities and contradictions, was presented to the accession countries as a coherent unit with unifying capacities, a new form of "supersociety." Whereas the previous "imagined community" was national (Anderson 1982), the new imagination evolved around the imagination of Europe, and thus in reality, the EU (Hudson 2000).

This definition of the space and the aim to create compatibility between the member states has popularly been described as "Europe-building," the process of expanding the territory of the EU and strengthening institutional power in the member countries through the rule of law (Bellier and Wilson 2000). Here we see how the imagined community once again is confused with the task of building Europe in the picture of the EU. Elizabeth Dunn took this argumentation of Europe-building a step further as she points to the fact that the EU aimed at the political construction of a single geographical area. This zone has been referred to as the "techno-zone,"[15] meaning a modern and competitive zone of capitalistic industry (Dunn 2005). As Andrew Barry has argued in his contribution to the debate, the EU consequently seeks self-definition through the circulation of specific technological practices and expert knowledge, which comes to characterize the otherwise complex constellation of member countries (2001). Hence, through certain forms of production, specific standards and regulations, the EU should ideally be recognized in every member state submitting to these practices, making each state a "little EU" that mirrors the general ideological principles on which the union is built. As suggested by Ong and Collier, the implementation of EU standards was meant to function as what Bruno Latour has called an "immutable mobile," a technoscientific form that aims to produce functionally comparable results in diverse places and is thus meant to be adapted in various places without changing itself (Ong and Collier 2005).

Dunn (2005) explored this aspect of the EU accession with reference to the EU harmonization process, for which products and production should be ranked on a single scale in all member countries. By evoking a common scale of quality and production, diverse units had to be made comparable. This meant that products from the new member states were expected to become the same as their Western European counterparts, referring back to the argumentation of Barry (2001) of the creation of a specific technical form as the trademark of the EU. However, the scale of measurement was based on Western European industrialized production, which is in many ways incompatible with unspecialized small-scale production. Standardizing measurements revealed the inconsistencies in the existing system, as the EU market could not encompass that which was truly foreign from the onset (Dunn 2005). As emphasized by Diana Mincyte (2006), the EU, rather than creating a niche for small-scale production as a way to protect farmers in vulnerable situations, instead identified the small-scale farmers as the key problem of integration. The consequence was that people who could not comply also could not become part of the (official) EU market. EU requirements thus created new divisions in the agricultural sector. As Giddens (2007) emphasizes, viewing the acceptance of new members in terms of integration and inclusion alone, as normally done in official EU rhetoric, would therefore be to gloss over some fundamental processes within Europe-building. Rather, the underlying premise for the proclaimed improvements was that big parts of the populations in the new member states were excluded from production by the very standardization processes that were originally meant to integrate eastern European producers. As suggested by Dunn (2005) with reference to Poland, the standardization processes consequently impel farmers to bend the rules and find ways around legal procedures; hence, we witness a statistical rise in illegal sales after the entrance.

---

15 "Techno" in this context refers to "technology" and not to a certain music genre.

The farmers did not suddenly decide to engage in illegal activities or change their production methods, but produced in the same way as prior to the entrance. The difference was that such production was now classified as illegal.

Legal Pluralities in Everyday Life

Discussing the legal effects of the EU entrance on the Lithuanian countryside, it becomes pertinent to clarify the concept of law. In my approach, law is not limited to formal laws such as state law or EU law, but applies to different constellations of normative orders in society. In this sense, law becomes an umbrella term for different orders and regulations (F. von Benda-Beckmann 1997; F. and K. von Benda-Beckmann 2006). This is consistent with the analysis of Moore, who works from the point of view that law is not above society. She adopts a point of view that is close to that of Ehrlich ([1936] 2002),[16] as she states that law should not be condensed into one term, abstracted from the social context in which it exists. Law and the social context in which it operates must be inspected together (Moore [1978] 2000). This approach takes into consideration not only formal law, but aims at an understanding of how other (unwritten) local norms for behavior may influence people's decisions and regulate their behavior, even such normative rules that guide behaviors that are against official law. Two aspects of law in particular are of importance in my writings, one being a plurality of laws in the sense that laws from the past continue to make an impact on the present. This also falls in line and overlaps with the first mentioned premise of EUropeanization, namely, the coexistence between the two unions. The other aspect targets an actor-oriented approach to the coexistence of different laws and orders within the same sociopolitical space.

Concerning the first aspect, previous laws from the socialist regime, although no longer existing, still have an impact on the present-day society. This is due to two phenomena. First, the long-time perspective. During the Soviet system, people made decisions and entered into legal arrangements with the idea that the socialist society would last, and rural citizens believed that they would work and later retire, all within the frame of the collective farm. Hence, although a largely overlooked phenomenon in the EU integration process, understandings of and practical arrangements from the previous legal systems continue to shape current responses to new (EU) law. The second phenomenon relates to the distrust in the law and goes back to the unruly 1990s, when many rapidly changing laws made the legal system diffuse, abstract and unreliable for the long term, as no

---

16 Ehrlich differentiated between what he called the state law and the living law, where the state law referred to the rules of society, and the living law was the social reality in which the subjects were engaged.

one could keep up with the plurality of emerging laws and their rapid change or adjustment. This left ordinary citizens at the mercy of those people who could keep up or who were in position to influence the rules according to their own interests (Bridger and Pine 1998; Verdery 2003). Past experiences influenced people's choices with regard to the EU. People had gotten used to laws being unreliable and apparently changing overnight. Furthermore, as they witnessed how laws were interpreted and used by people in central positions to further their own goals, they had no reason to believe that this should be much different under the EU.

This leads me to the second aspect, the existence of normative laws in the environment and how they influence the *Acquis* in daily matters. As F. von Benda-Beckmann (1992) argues, it is unhelpful to classify some legal orders as superior to others, because it prevents us from understanding the influence of complex normative orders in a given setting. I suggest that because local (unwritten) norms are embedded in the close social environment, they have equal or even greater impact on people's daily practices than the more distanced national law or supranational law. People navigate according to different sets of rules in their everyday lives, some of which are complementary, some of which overlap, and some of which contradict each other. Indeed, when farmers make decisions about their production in their everyday lives, the EU law is but one aspect they must take into consideration. In fact, farmers appear more willing to go around EU rules than to enter into a potential conflict with their neighbors if following EU law means violating local normative orders. Or, to give another example, the politician who needs goodwill from his potential voters sees no obstacles to using EU funds to throw a big party, albeit this is clearly a violation of EU rules. In this sense it becomes arbitrary to speak about a hierarchy of laws as this may not be applicable to the villagers' – or politicians' – everyday life. Thus, when discussing the generational issues and the related demographic changes, we must take into account that it is not always possible to reach the objectives of the law (F. von Benda-Beckmann, 1992).

Practical Negotiations

The interactions between EU law and normative rules link up to discussions about structure and behavior, also known as practice theory (Bourdieu [1977] 2000; Giddens [1979] 2003). In his work, Giddens emphasizes the duality of structures, whereby he means that structures shape human behavior and human behavior shapes and reproduces structures. According to Giddens' approach, structure and practice do not function as each other's contradictions; rather, they presuppose each other. And while structures can be restricting, they are not necessarily restricting, and they are not only restricting. Structures can in themselves entail new possibilities. Bourdieu evokes the argument that structures are in many instances unreflectively reproduced by actors, as they have incorporated ways of thinking and behaving and thus take them "for granted." However, in terms of radical changes, such consciousness is forced into establishing new ways of acting and responding. If we relate these thoughts to my study of changes in Lithuanian rural areas, we can see how changes in legal structures for production, for example, evoke a new consciousness of what has hitherto been taken for granted, because such things are no longer obvious and cannot be reproduced in the same way as heretofore. In my approach, structure and actors are bound together in an interrelated dynamic of options and limitations through which agency is expressed.

My understanding of agency emerges from the ideas of anthropologist Talal Asad. In his work, Asad develops a cautious approach to the notion of agency, emphasizing that agency does not equalize a conscious will to self-liberation and self-empowerment. Rather, the agent is hardly free to write his own history, to resist power, or to change his own identity (Asad 2003). Saba Mahmood, who deals with the concept of agency in her study of Muslim women, further adds the concern that agency could be misattributed as resistance to power structures. For Mahmood, agency instead applies to a person working on herself in order to more appropriately fit into an already established order or tradition. My reasons for evoking these two contributions are that I likewise share a concern with interpretations of people's actions as ways of expressing resistance or opposing power. These ideas have been freely ascribed to studies of rural communities ever since Scott (1985, 1990) evoked his idea of "weapons of the weak" as a term to phrase the everyday resistance among peasants and what he phrases "hidden transcripts" – a way to describe how resistance is a predominant feature in all subordinate groups, albeit cleverly hidden in acts and discourses, making it not a direct confrontation, but an indirect opposition. Scott noted that even in apparent casual acts of farmers, we find aspects of resistance against hegemony and power. I, however, share the view of Mahmood, as she suggests that agency could be seen as a way to mobilize one's options for fitting into the structure rather than opposing it. This also leads to a more careful elaboration of the extent to which people can or will act when facing structures (here we are back to Bourdieu and Giddens), as agency is far from uniform. It can vary a great deal both in kind and extent (H. Sewell 1992).

In the context of my research, farmers may break or circumvent EU legislation in their everyday life, and knowingly do so, while still being supportive of the union in general. Explanations may thus be found on a less ideological level than resistance to structures, as people are bound by practicalities of everyday life. I refer to these as *practical negotiations* of the situation. Many farmers from my field sites literally cannot afford to follow the rules because they do not have the financial resources to upgrade their modes of farming; however, they cannot afford to stop producing, either, as they would then lose the main foundation of their income. It is not my intention to reduce agency to mere practicalities, but to evoke an understanding of the restraints people are under when they explore their new opportunities.

Social Security and Change

This brings me to the fourth and final guiding point, namely, how the EU not only affected certain targets for change, but also affected the family setup and premises for obtaining social security in everyday life. The planned modernization of the agricultural sector by enlarging and specializing farms meant that the future prospects for small-scale family farms were meager. While the older generation has come to terms with this situation by finding intermediate solutions, the young people started to leave the countryside in search of jobs in the cities or abroad, as there are no or only very few alternatives to agriculture in the rural areas. This tendency for emigration entails two problematic issues. First, it appears to be counterproductive to the goals set for the future of the agricultural sector, as it proves increasingly difficult to modernize the agricultural sector if the young people leave. The second and related problematic aspect is that the emigration from the countryside likewise affects family structures, because young people leave the villages in great numbers. In this sense it proves equally hard for aging parents to maintain their households. These fundamental changes affect existing systems of social security in the rural areas. This concept is here understood as arrangements through which people obtain food, shelter, care, medical treatment and education, but also and just as important, arrangements that provide people with emotional support and a mere sense of security. In many cases, social security may be nothing more than an unrealized potential that is never put into action, and yet the mere awareness of a potential guarantee gives people a feeling of being safeguarded in the long run (F. and K. von Benda-Beckmann [1994] 2000; Thelen, Cartwright and Sikor 2005; Leutloff-Grandits, Peleikis and Thelen 2009).

Pinning down aspects of social security relates equally to *insecurity*. Indeed, when looking back at the past years in Lithuania as well as other postsocialist countries, the aspect of *in*security played a dominant role as governments, politics and socioeconomic circumstances changed continuously. As has been shown by Hann (2002), the collective farms functioned as a total social factor that cared for its members from cradle to grave. Although the household functioned as the core of the family, people still depended on the provisions and social security arrangements provided by the collective farms (Haukanes and Pine 2005; Leutloff-Grandits, Peleikis and Thelen 2009). After the breakup of the Soviet Union and the privatization of the collective farms, the local networks regained importance in order to provide for one's family (for comparison with Ukraine and Azerbaijan, see

Kaneff and Yalcin-Heckmann 2002; for comparison with Poland, see Pine 2002). Indeed, the emotional aspect is important, as F. and K. von Benda-Beckmann have argued that

> [b]oth repetitive unfulfilled promises in the past and expectations of profound change in the future may undermine the sense of security, even though at present the situation may be quite satisfactory. (F. and K. von Benda-Beckmann [1994] 2000, 17)

This also relates to the fact that the continuously unstable situation marked by unfulfilled promises in the 1990s has reinforced a general feeling of insecurity and distrust of the system, leading people to approach institutional solutions and options with skepticism (Torsello 2003). If we pair this with the large-scale emigration from the countryside as experienced in recent years, we find a situation where people are, on one hand, reluctant to turn to institutions for support and yet, on the other hand, cannot rely on their children to stay at home and take care of their parents when they grow old. Furthermore, we see how children do not want to stay in the rural areas but still feel obligated toward their parents in terms of helping and supporting them. As observed by Haukanes and Pine, can we not automatically assume that the introduction of liberal capitalism leads to more individualized lifestyles in the formerly socialist countries; we are rather

> [...] witnessing a simultaneous development of individualism and associated lifestyles, on the one hand, and entrenchment of patterns of economic and emotional reliance on extended kin relations, on the other. (Haukanes and Pine 2005, 9)

This leads us to explore how generational and demographic restructurings thus become central elements in determining new (old) ways of providing social security in the aftermath of the EU entrance, with a profound impact on everyday life arrangements for work, care and kin-based responsibilities.

Who Participates in EUrope?

To summarize the four points of EUropeanization, I suggest that it often is the people who are furthest from the decision-making institutions and who may not even view themselves as a part of the current modernization processes who have to deal with the greater consequences in their everyday lives.

Political scientist Gabriele Ilonszki has contributed to the debate about influences on the former socialist countries. Ilonszki, by use of surveys, looks at the perception of citizenship in the new EU member states. She distinguishes between what she frames "the economical and political elite," and "the mass." Albeit she thoroughly clarifies who people in "the elite" are, the reader is left to guess as to whom "the mass" could be (Ilonszki 2009). Ilonszki ends up looking almost solely at the elite's responses to her survey, because they are the ones who have the appropriate language to formulate, knowledge to conceptualize, and emotional engagement to consider themselves EU citizens. This is even more problematic, as her original question was whether the EU can continue to function as a purely elite project, if "the mass" cannot be actively engaged. Hence, the analysis contradicts the very aim of the study.

I would like to advocate that there is no "either/or" with reference to European engagement; rather, there are different ways and different degrees of engagement. In accordance with my definition and understanding of EUropeanization, *everybody* is inevitably engaged in the EU project, and especially the rural population that has been subjected to so many and so pervasive restructurings of daily life in the light of the EU preparations and the EU entrance. Thus, young rural citizens may respond by becoming labor migrants in Western EU countries and thus in a very concrete "hands-on manner," make use of the new possibilities that came along with the EU entrance (Vonderau 2007; Liubinienė 2009). In a similar way, other young people from the rural areas move to the cities to find work because the kind of small-scale agricultural production their parents engage in no longer pays off and because the countryside offers no alternative jobs. This is also EUropeanization and their response to this situation deeply embeds them in obstacles they face in the aftermath of the EU integration. Even when working in the cities they still have to adhere to their parents' need for support, as the expectations of the youth did not change despite the changed practical circumstances. Thus, only when refraining from persistently formulating the EU as an elite project and from setting specific requirements for what kind of engagements and activities count as "active participation in Europe" are we able to analyze how those people, who are otherwise excluded or alienated, actively correspond to and implement the changes. They might not always do it in the ways they were supposed to, but in the ways they find possible. Despite massive campaigns, the "return to Europe" has not only been fueled by an undisputed desire to become European. Rather, as argued by Haukanes and Pine (2005), in their contribution to the debate, people do embrace some aspects of the Westernization with enthusiasm, while they only reluctantly comply with others. And, we could add, other aspects they do not comply with at all. In this sense, EU membership had different meanings both symbolically and practically. Only by viewing the various and sometimes ambivalent aspects will we see a broader and more nuanced picture of the consequences of EU integration.

Aspects of Analysis

Apart from this introductory chapter, the book consists of five analytical and empirical chapters and one concluding chapter. Each chapter touches upon the effects of the ongoing process of EUropeanization and how people in the two villages of research understand and incorporate these changes in their daily life.

Chapter 2 is a background chapter taking us back to the 1990s, and looking at the processes of privatization after regained independence in 1990 and at the early role of the EU in the process of preparing for the membership. By referencing the background of the outcome of privatization and the mechanisms behind the membership, I prepare the ground for the ethnographic analysis.

In Chapter 3 I look at the relationship between farmers and state representatives. Rather than assuming that information about the EU is passed on unchanged to the citizens, we should pay attention to the forms of communication between state representatives and citizens, the forums in which information is passed on and how local state representatives influence the implementation process.

Chapter 4 deals with how the perceived problem of aging farmers is intended to be solved through different measures. One of these is the Early Retirement Program for farmers above age 55; the other is the milk price policy in Lithuania, which pushes small-scale farmers with a few cows out of production. However, in the hands of local farmers, the aim to standardize production ends up as various strategies and incoherent practices, often working against the intended goals as set by the EU.

In Chapter 5 I look at the standardization and harmonization of production and their consequences for people selling products at the local marketplace in Marijampolė. Here, I work with two groups of people: the legal sellers (The Insiders) and the illegal sellers (The Outsiders), where the latter group, through a challenge of law and spatial borders, appears as a competitor to the EU market.

Chapter 6 discusses the unintended consequences of the coexistence of disintegration from the Soviet Union and integration into the EU, consequences that came about as an effect of an effect, yet still ended up having significant influence on people's lives. I suggest that the youth is often paying the higher price in periods of change, since the young people, on one hand, leave the villages to find work and, on the other hand, still have to meet their parents' expectations of work and care. Rather than opening up more liberal and individualized lifestyles, the outcomes of the integration into the EU are a reinforcement of kinship obligations as a way to cope with often insecure future prospects.

The book ends with Chapter 7's brief conclusion summing up the central points and arguments.

CHAPTER 2

Small-Scale Farmers at the Geopolitical Return to Europe, 1990–2004

My friend once received visitors from Germany. He showed them around in his village, he also showed [them] the ruins of the collective farm. They thought it was from the war, they thought [...] that the enemy had torn the buildings apart (laughing). My friend told them no, Lithuanians robbed the buildings and tore them apart. The Germans did not understand this. They said: "How can you tear apart what you yourself have built? How can you?" But Lithuanians could. You see the ruins of the collective farms everywhere [in the countryside].

—Farmer from Straigiai, July, 2004

If you can imagine, all this [land] used to be cultivated, we had big fields everywhere. Now, nobody uses it, nobody cultivates it, it does not pay off. You should have seen this place 25 years ago, you would not recognize it. The entire landscape has changed.

—Farmer from Bilvytis, April, 2007

Driving through Lithuania at the beginning of the new century, one could get a good sense of the reforms and events in the countryside since the declared independence; the landscape is characterized by many small land plots of uneven size, much land lays fallow and outside every bigger village there are ruins of a collective farm, robbed of building materials and everything else of value. Economic shock therapy and rapid privatization became the new agenda, driven by the political climate at the time, which advocated a rapid de-Sovietization. Medical care, work, housing and public canteens for the workers of the collective farms ceased to function, as the farms were closed. In the rural areas, it was about 1,200 collective farms the size of about 1,000 hectares each, and 200 state farms of about 4,000 hectares, which were to be privatized together with the property and livestock.[1]

---

1 Information from the Lithuanian Ministry of Agriculture, October 2003.

The privatization of former collective farms evoked confusion, insecurity and was characterized by a highly uneven distribution of property (Abrahams 1996; Pine 1996; Bridger and Pine 1998; Hann 2002; Verdery 2002b, 2003; Rausing 2004). It soon became evident that the rapid privatizations did not lead to improved living standards and socioeconomic benefits that had been expected and hoped for. With reference to the similar Romanian case, anthropologist Andrew Cartwright explains:

> [F]ar from there having been a transition to a "modern" agricultural sector, there appears to have been a return to a highly thinly disguised peasant mode of production. (Cartwright 2003, 172)

In this chapter, I will go into the Lithuanian case and outline the post-independence changes and the outcome of the initiated privatization and the early processes of preparations for EU membership. Rather than viewing it only from the perspective of de-Sovietization, I analyze the changes as coexisting processes of disintegrating from the Soviet system and integration into the EU, to underline the reasons for the hybrid political and socioeconomic constellations we still witness today in the new EU member states. In this regard I will take into consideration both "objective changes" in the realm of political economy and people's "subjective" experiences of these (Hann 2003).

Figure 2.1. Milkmaids at the collective farm in Straigiai in the 1970s. Private photo.

Collective Farming in Lithuania

Before going further into the political, economic and social changes that took place in the countryside after 1991, it is vital to take a brief look back to understand where this private farming emerged from – 50 years of collective farming.[2]

The collective farms had been established through forced acquisition of private property. Officially, it was said that people were free to not give their property to the collective farms, but in practice there was no such choice. If people did not give up their property voluntarily they would be harassed in different ways; they would be put to hard labor in the forest during the freezing Lithuanian winters or during the summers their crops would be destroyed at night. Another strategy was to deny their children access to school. Eventually, most people gave in, but in cases of the most "stubborn," the property would be taken by force and the owners sent away to the Gulag camps (work camps) in Siberia. If people from the onset were perceived as being too wealthy (e.g., if they had more land or cows than the average villager), they would also be sent to the Gulag camps. This was also the case for mentally handicapped people, for homosexuals, for the intelligentsia and for people who were overheard voicing critical statements or making jokes about the Soviet system. The deportees would have all their property confiscated and would be sent away without any personal belongings. Many deportees died in Siberia as a result of the often inhuman living and working conditions.[3] The years with the most deportations from Lithuania were 1941, 1948, 1949, and 1951. The deportations came to an end with Stalin's death in 1953 (Klumbytė 2006). This also opened up, for the first time, opportunities for people to return to their home countries.

The establishment of collective farming changed the landscape altogether. The private land plots were consolidated into large fields, and collective stables for cows, harvest and equipment were built in the villages together with collective canteens for the workers. Workers who lived a far distance from the collective farms were encouraged to leave their houses and move into the villages in order to keep the workforce closer to the collective farm. If outskirt houses were standing in the way for the expansion of the farms, they would be destroyed. In order to

---

2 This section is written on the basis of the material I gathered about the two collective farms in the villages where I conducted my fieldwork, both of which were representative of collective farming in Lithuania as such. It is built upon three interviews with former chairmen of collective farms, two interviews at the Lithuanian Ministry of Agriculture, and numerous interviews with previous workers on collective farms.

3 A 1993 archival study shows that a total of 1,053,829 people from the Soviet countries died in Gulag camps from 1934 to 1953. These numbers exclude people who died after their release, but whose death was caused by the harsh treatment in the camps (Getty, Rittersporn and Zemskov 1993).

house the newcomers from the outskirts, or workers who came from the cities, apartment blocks were built in the villages.

The hard rupture of forced acquisition of property marked the beginning of collective farming, which for decades meant a decrease in living standards for the Lithuanians. There was no experience with collective farming, people did not know how to cooperate on the large enterprises, they lacked expertise and there was far too little equipment for the farms. During the first few winters, the livestock starved to death in the stables. Salaries were not paid regularly to the workers and theft from the farms became a widespread problem. Only in the 1960s did people start to experience improvements in their daily lives as more machinery was bought for the collective farms and everybody started to get used to the new form of working. This did not necessarily mean that people worked harder; rather, according to a previous agronomist from Straigiai, they started to work less. A few hours here and there, and in between they had extensive breaks from work, during which the men often sat and drank. The alcohol was often acquired through their private networks, and the breaks with the bottle functioned as the main integrating social factor during the working days (see Firlit and Chlopecki 1992; Pawlik 1992). A former chairman recalled that the people who at this time had returned from the Siberian Gulag camps were those who worked the longest hours. They also did not cause any trouble or make any complaints the way their co-workers who had not been deported, did. From the chairman's point of view this was because the working hours and the everyday difficulties at the collective farms in Lithuania were easy to bear, in comparison with the life in the Gulags.

As the generations changed, the hard beginning faded in the light of the gradual but stable improvements in living standards, which in Lithuania culminated in a period of success in the 1980s. Indeed, the 1980s had been the best decade in the history of the collective farms, and this decade was remembered by my informants in Bilvytis and Straigiai as a period of security. The collective farm had become "a total social institution" (Humphrey 1995; Hann 2003) and instead of private property, the members received security for their work: housing, food, medical care and insurance. The chairmen of the farms also organized cultural excursions for their members to other places in the Soviet Union. It was precisely at this point that the Soviet Union disintegrated and the collective farms were divided and privatized again.

Independence and National Policy

The dominant political force that characterized the early 1990s was the idea of rapid de-Sovietization and the implementation of a market economy. This line of policy had a direct effect on the rural areas, as it provided the basis for the distribution of land and property among rural citizens. This political and economic line had been strongly promoted by the political group Sąjūdis,[4] a political foundation that is often linked directly to the declaration of independence. The original idea behind the establishment of Sąjūdis was to support President Gorbachev's program of glasnost, democratization and perestroika, which had been met with hesitation by the Lithuanian Communist leadership in the mid-1980s (Smith, Pabriks, Purs and Lane 2002). In October 1989 Sąjūdis held its founding conference in Vilnius where Vytautas Landsbergis, a professor from the Lithuanian Conservatory, was elected as the council's chairman.[5] In February 1990 elections were held for the newly authorized Congress of People's Deputies, and Sąjūdis won by a vast majority. The Communist Party only won two seats, one of them for Algirdas Brazauskas, the previous party secretary. As soon as the following month, on March 11, Sąjūdis declared the restoration of Lithuanian independence, being the first of the Soviet republics to do so. The authorities in Moscow did not accept the legality of the declared independence and undertook various countermeasures. The most significant of these were the economic blockade in 1990 and the unit of Soviet tanks that drove into the center of Vilnius in order to reestablish Soviet rule in January 1991. The events culminated on 13 January at the TV tower in Vilnius when civilians tried to prevent the Soviet troops from getting control over Lithuanian television and radio. Altogether, 15 people died at the TV tower event: 13 civilians were killed by the Soviet troops, one died from a heart attack in the cause of the events and one Soviet soldier died from a gunshot by a fellow soldier. Added to this, more than 1,000 civilians were injured by Soviet troops.[6] The following day around 50,000 Lithuanian demonstrators gathered around the Supreme Council building

---

4 "The Lithuanian Restructuring Movement."

5 "The Move Toward Independence 1987–91" – Lithuanian country brief. http://www.country-data.com/cgi-bin/query/r-8286.html (accessed 16 November 2011).

6 On 18 October 2010 Lithuania issued a European arrest order for the head of the operation at the TV tower, Michail Golovatov, and wanted him convicted as a terrorist. Following the arrest order, Golovatov paid eight visits to EU countries (Finland, Cyprus and the Czech Republic) without facing problems. On 15 July 2011 he was finally held back as he entered an Austrian airport. However, the same night he was released and sent back to Russia. Austrian foreign minister Michael Spindelegger defended the release by claiming that the Lithuanian arrest order was "too vague." Golovatov himself stated in an interview after his release that the Lithuanians' actual goal was to use him as an instrument to get preferential energy deals with Russia, such as lower oil and gas prices. In addition, he said that he could not be held responsible for his actions at the time, as he had acted under Gorbachev's orders. Gorbachev had likewise denied all responsibility for the attack. See http://lt.wikipedia.org/wiki/Michailas_Golovatovas; http://www.bbc.co.uk/news/world-europe-14202371 and http://en.rian.ru/analysis/20110722/165330536.html (both accessed 16 November 2011).

in Vilnius, causing the Soviet troops to retreat. Politically, the situation was still not settled until Gorbachev, in 1991, stated that due to health problems he could no longer act as president of the Soviet Union. Gorbachev was followed by Boris Yeltsin, who recognized Lithuanian independence on 6 September 1991 (Senn [1990] 2002; Senn 1994; Vebra 1994).[7]

In the first year of independence, key state institutions were established, such as a constitution, an army, borders, a national currency and embassies (Mincyte 2006). It was in this heated climate that some of the most important political decisions were made about the further development of the country with the aim of a rapid implementation of market policy, destruction of Soviet structures, closure of collective farms and quick transition to private farming. While significant political changes took place in the country, the former Communist Party still continued to exist. The party was now under the leadership of Algirdas Brazauskas and was renamed the Lithuanian Democratic Labor Party (Lietuvos Demokratinė Darbo Partija, from now on referred to as LDDP). Contrary to Sąjūdis, the LDDP represented a more moderate line and opposed the governmental politics on issues of property restoration in the agricultural sector. Still linked to the communist past, the LDDP had much to lose through a rapid "de-Sovietization." The LDDP warned the government that too hasty a privatization could undermine some of the economic advantages that big-scale farming had enjoyed. The coming years would show that this was not unfounded criticism (Smith, Pabriks, Purks and Lane 2002).

The government had introduced economic shock therapy based on the idea that the people were willing to suffer for a short while when better times were expected. The problem was, however, that for many Lithuanians these "better times" remained a distant hope. The people experienced a rapidly growing inflation, unemployment and a general decrease in living standards. For many, independence had turned into an economic disaster, as they lost their savings in rubles without being able to get compensation in the new currency, litas, which for a period coexisted with the inflated ruble before it was made the only valid currency in the country (Frohberg and Hartman 2000). In this very period, the leader of the LDDP, Algirdas Brazauskas, gained popularity, as he had a more conciliatory approach to Moscow than the radical Sąjūdis but still assured his voters that he would not adopt communist policies again.

---

7 Because of the specific history of Lithuanian independence, there are different references to when the country regained independence. Some will state that it was at the time of the declared independence (11 March 1990) from the Soviet Union (which is also the national day of independence in Lithuania); others refer to 1991, as it was only that year that the international community (Iceland being the first) recognized its independence and the same year Russia (no longer the Soviet Union) formally recognized the independence of the country. I refer to 1990 as the year of independence.

After the economic drawback under Sąjūdis, people were willing to give the former communist another chance. The result was that the LDDP regained power in the parliamentary election held in October 1992. The LDDP achieved 42.6 percent and was thus the strongest party in the Lithuanian parliament, the Seimas. In 1993, the first presidential election was held in Lithuania. Landsbergis, the politician who had pushed so hard for the restoration of independence, lost to the head of the LDDP, Brazauskas (Senn [1990] 2002; Senn 1994; Ališauskiene, Bajaruniene and Sersniova 1993; Vebra 1994).

The election of former communists was symptomatic of the period, when initial hopes gave way to disappointments and difficulties. Notably, urban workers and large parts of the rural population were disappointed with the outcome of independence and wanted legislation and reforms to go ahead at a slower pace. They found the solution to be the former Communist Party. However, it is important to pay attention to the fact that the election of the LDDP did not change the situation significantly, as it proved hard to make more than minor changes to the initial laws on privatization and shock economy introduced by Sąjūdis. This was also due to the fact that at this point the door had already been opened for a future EU membership, providing that Lithuania, together with other potential candidate countries, would keep a radical line of de-Sovietization and privatization as the foundation for the change to a sound system of liberal democracy as required by the EU.

Laws on Privatization

Looking at the former Soviet countries and satellite states at large, we witness two general outcomes of the privatization of the collective farms in the rural areas. (1) The collective farms were only cosmetically privatized, as former workers became shareholders of the farms. This meant that very few changes were implemented in daily life and the farms continued as large-scale farms with clear traces back to the former collective system. People continued to work as a collective unit of workers, not as individual peasants or farmers. This has been the case for countries such as Ukraine, Belarus and big parts of Russia (Spoor and Visser 2001; Kaneff and Yalcin-Heckmann 2003). (2) The farms were genuinely privatized and previous collective workers obtained private land plots and private property. However, in most cases they did not emerge as "economically viable" private farms, but as unspecialized semi-subsistence farms. This has been the case for countries such as Armenia, Azerbaijan, Bulgaria, Romania, Poland, parts of Eastern Germany, parts of Hungary and parts of the Baltic states (Spoor and Visser 2001; Eidson and Milligan 2003; Kaneff and Yalcin-Heckmann 2003; Cartwright 2003; Alanen 2004).

Privatization of the collective farms played a central role, as Lithuania was largely dependent on its agricultural sector and had counted as one of the

strongest agricultural producers during the Soviet occupation. The EU and the
World Bank were especially strong forces behind the creation of privately owned
enterprises, as it was believed that these would be more efficient than collectively
owned farms and that family farms could thus revive the agricultural sectors in
the previously socialist countries (Abrahams 1996; Alanen, Nikula, Põder and
Ruutsoo 2001; Alanen 2004). From the perspective of the liberalist movement,
property rights needed to be restored to the farmers in order to restitute a "normal
order" in Lithuania. Just as Lithuania had had the right to reclaim its territory
through independence, the farmers should have the right to reclaim their land
and act as stewards of the agricultural sector in an independent Lithuania. This
idea was interlinked with that of restoring order between man and nature, as the
giant agrarian enterprises were destructive to the natural surroundings and the
environment (Mincyte 2006, 2011).

In 1991 the Lithuanian government introduced two land reforms for the
privatization of collective farms and an additional reform for the privatization
of property. Although they were all different pieces of legislation, they were seen
by the public as parts of one single law. The first priority had been to enforce
restitution of property rights from before the Soviet period,[8] and thus give the land
back to those families who had lost it in the 1940s. It was stated that:

> The goal of [the] land reform is to implement the right of Lithuanian
> citizens to land ownership by returning the expropriated land in accordance
> with the procedures and terms established by law, and by buying land, as
> well as to create legal, organizational and economic preconditions for
> the development of agricultural production by freely chosen forms of
> farming.[9]

During an interview, an employee at the Lithuanian Ministry of Agriculture
expressed the initial idea behind the law for property restitution:

> The main purpose of the government was to re-establish social justice by
> returning the land to the former owners. [...] Nobody talked so much about
> economy in the countryside at that moment. [...] the main concern was to
> fulfill the wishes of those who felt nostalgic about their family farm.[10]

---

8 Government of Lithuania, *On the Procedure and Conditions of Restorations of Ownership
   to the Existing Rights*, 18 June 1991.
9 Government of Lithuania, *Law on Land Reform, Number 1-1607*, chapter 1, article 2:
   "The Goal of Land Reform," 25 July 1991, Lietuvos Respublikos Aukščiausioji Taryba,
   Atkuriamasis Seimas.
10 From an interview at the Agricultural Ministry, November 2005; interview held in English.

However, it soon turned out that the law for property restitution only benefitted a part of the population living in the rural areas. Indeed, many people living and working in the countryside 50 years later had no right to claim any land according to the law for property restitution. The reason was they had only moved to the rural areas in the meantime and thus, their parents or grandparents had been from the city. In order to solve this problem, a general land reform was introduced that was based on affiliation with the former workplace. This meant that every man and woman who had been working on collective farms was entitled to 3 hectares of land as compensation for the loss of the common property. The farms that were established on this premise were called *asmeniniai ūkiai* (private farms). The law was implemented in order to provide at least some social security to the former collective workers and was meant to prevent social and economic problems for the rural population.[11] The land granted by this reform was taken from the so-called "green areas." The green areas were chosen from the former collective farms or land designated as state property. Such land could only be obtained through this reform and could not be bought or acquired through other means.

The distribution of the granted 3 hectares turned out to be unfortunate for the farmers, as the land was seldom in one piece in just one place. On the contrary, many smaller parcels were often spread out in many different places. The idea behind this fragmented distribution was that everybody had the right to a land plot close to the farm. In order to give every family land close to their home, these close plots could not be of 3 hectares size and other plots of land further away from the village had to be added to reach the full size. It was not unusual to receive the three hectares in pieces in three or four different places. This hindered the effective cultivation of the land and turned out to be a severe obstacle to the modernization of the agricultural sector.

People who could claim land back according to the law of property restitution likewise faced difficulties. It was often impossible to identify the original plots, as the landscape had changed during Soviet times and/or the plot could not be given back because it had been encapsulated in one of the aforementioned "green areas". People often had to apply to get the same amount of land in a different place. However, as most people applied for land from the most fertile areas, the procedure was soon changed. Instead of on land quantity, the land distribution now depended on land quality. This meant that a farmer would get less land than he was entitled to if it was granted in a fertile area, whereas he would get more than he was entitled to if it was in a less fertile area. Another problem was that 50 years

---

11 Government of Lithuania, *Law on Land Reform, Number I-1607*, chapter 1, article 2: "The Goal of Land Reform," 25 July 1991, Lietuvos Respublikos Aukščiausioji Taryba, Atkuriamasis Seimas.

after the occupation, many of the former owners were no longer alive and the land was passed on to their children. It was not uncommon that three or four children had to divide a land plot between them.[12]

Livestock and machinery from the collective farms were also to be distributed among the former members. The Law on Privatization of the Assets of Agricultural Enterprises was adopted on 20 July 1991. According to this law, distribution of property from the collective farms was to be carried out through a system of green vouchers. Every previous member had the right to a part of the material from the collective farm. How much or how little each person was entitled to receive depended on age and/or the number of years he or she had worked for the collective farm (Klimašauskas and Kasnauskienė 1996). It was common that two or three people chose to use their green vouchers together. This way they could get more or bigger units from the farms. Other people only took what they were entitled to as a single person, and yet other people chose to sell their green voucher to others.

All of the three laws described above were often changed and adjusted according to the new circumstances. Therefore, there are several different references to the laws. I have even found different references to the dates of the laws, not to mention the additional changes and corrections to the laws, which continued well into years after independence. My summary of the laws for privatization and their impact is based on various interviews and official sources, some of which contradicted each other and required further investigation. If it was difficult for me to create a post facto overview, it was far more complicated for both administrative workers and rural citizens to stay up to date with the respective state of the laws during the time of implementation. This often led to internal disagreements and confusion. Disputes about which land belonged to whom lasted for several years in Lithuania, and many cases were taken to court. In addition, the land reforms created a highly segmented landscape, which has been causing problems and irritations for the farmers up to this very day. A woman from Straigiai remembered her shock when she got her land back:

> When I saw how they had split the land up... it was terrible. One small plot here, one small plot there, impossible to cultivate [...] I was angry at our agronomist, because it was him who had been in charge of it all. Still I knew that this was not his fault. In the end I did not know who I should be angry with.[13]

---

12 In an article about land privatization in Estonia after independence, Arvo Kuddo (1996) points out similar problems with the land distribution process, leading several people to claim the same piece of land.

13 Field notes 2006; my translation from Lithuanian.

The villagers often had to drive far to get from one field to the other. For the more ambitious farmers it hindered a specialized production and for people engaged in household production, the driving around from field to field was an obstacle in their everyday life they would rather have been without. Indeed, during an interview, a farmer referred to the privatization process as a "land murder" (*žemžudystė*),[14] as the former big fields had been divided into so many small and uneven plots.

Although the majority of the rural citizens reestablished household farming, others chose to reestablish the former collective farms as agricultural companies (*bendrovės*, sing. *bendrovė*). The *bendrovės* were typically created from what remained of a collective farm and were often run by the previous chairmen. In Straigiai, such a *bendrovė* had successfully been established in the aftermath of independence. The chairman had kept some land for himself and informed the villagers that those who did not wish to cultivate their land could lease it to the *bendrovė* for a share of the profits. It was mainly pensioners who agreed. Although the *bendrovės* cultivated on a far bigger scale than the small-scale farmers, the companies had some of the same problems: segmented land plots, lack of machinery or machinery that was too old. In Straigiai, the chairman explained how they had to drive hundreds of kilometers every day to reach all the members' land plots.

The destinies of farmers varied a great deal. Some farmers were lucky and got additional support from European countries. In Straigiai, such support had been granted from an agricultural group in the Netherlands to overcome initial problems and difficulties. Three young and promising farmers from Straigiai were selected to receive Dutch support in terms of knowledge transfer, money, and used agricultural equipment. Indeed, the three young farmers who received support at the time are today the wealthiest farmers in Straigiai. Another phenomenon was the creation of the "ad hoc" farmers, for example, people who had had positions related to the collective farm such as engineers or truck drivers, who had no special knowledge about or interest in farming. However, as it was difficult to find jobs in the aftermath of independence and as they had been given a plot of land and maybe a tractor anyway, they decided to try their luck as farmers. This has also been described by Nigel Swain (1996) with reference to the Czech Republic, Hungary, Poland and Slovakia. Others did not know what to do with their land as they were either too old to farm or did not have the necessary resources for it. These people would either chose to lease their land to the aforementioned *bendrovės*, or, as it often happened, the land would lie fallow.

---

14 Fieldnotes February 2004; my translation from Lithuanian. There is no such word as "land murder" in Lithuanian, but the man constructed it from the word for a murder on a human being (Lt: homicide – "man-murder" – *žmogžudystė*) and changed the beginning of the word "man" (*žmogus*) to "land" (*žemė*).

As argued by Kaneff and Yalcin-Heckmann (2003), the modes of privatizing land have a significant influence on the outcome. In countries where land was restored according to restitution of property rights, it is more likely that people start up private farming, whereas in countries where privatization primarily was based on affiliation with the collective farm, it is more likely that people establish agricultural companies and continue to work the land together. In Lithuania, they worked with a model based on *both/and*, which added difficulties to the privatization process. The result was the establishment of many small private farms and, as noted above, some new forms of cooperatives. This is comparable to the situation in Bulgaria and Hungary, where under socialism, more flexible models for farming and private ownership were tried and where the outcome of land reforms also resulted partly in small private farms, new cooperatives, and remaking of the old collective farms (Kaneff 1996; Hann 2003).

Theft and Administrative (Ab)Use of Property

One side of the story of privatization concerns the actual laws and legal procedures for distributing land and machinery. However, another and very important part of the story is how these laws and procedures were manipulated and abused. Despite that the idea behind privatization was to start all over on a clean sheet of paper, it soon turned out that Soviet models of owning and administrating property had a strong impact on the process of property restitution after independence.

The collectivization of land and livestock during Soviet times did not mean that everything had been collectively owned. Private property existed, but not in a capitalistic understanding of the word. In the Soviet constitution it was stated that property could be personal or socialist. Socialist property was furthermore divided into state property, the property of the whole nation, and cooperative/ *kolkhoz* property, the property of the collective farm and its members.[15] Personal property was people's own savings and their salaries; it could also be a house and equipment belonging to the household and a plot of land of at most 0.6 hectares for personal use, as it was forbidden to make profit from it.[16] Personal property was under strict control of the Soviet authorities in order to avoid any resemblance to capitalist ideologies.

Difficulties arose with the *kolkhoz* property, which belonged to all members of the collective farm. People in higher positions had easy access to property

---

15 *Sovietų Socialistinių Respublikų Sąjungos Konstitucija (pagrindinis įstatymas)* [*Constitution of the USSR (main law)*] (1936 [1940]), chapter I, article 5, 3–4.

16 *Tarybų Socialistinių Respublikų Sąjungos Konstitucija (pagrindinis įstatymas)* [*Constitution of the USSR (main law)*] (1977 [1983]), chapter I, section 2, article 13, 11.

and could make personal use of it without owning it (Verdery 1996). Hence, in order to understand the property system during the Soviet times, we should look not so much at the right to own, but at the ability to administer property. In this sense, even property that was collectively owned had private functions accessed through the right kind of administration and networks (see also Pawlik 1992; Firlit and Chlopecki 1992; Verdery 1996; Ledeneva 1998, 2006). Chairmen, agronomists and other people in higher positions had better access to goods and property and made use of it to obtain common goods through private connections. This was not so much related to the actual production of the collective farm as to goods in scarce supply, which they had to get from the cities. For this, certain exchange networks were put to use and often, produce from the farms was used to show gratitude to people in the respective networks. However, it was a requirement that such arrangements were only made with people in one's own network or with people who were related to one's network (Pawlik 1992). Another phenomenon was that produce from the farm frequently found its way into the chairmen's houses. Eventually, it became a question of definition as to what was theft and what was not. In her analysis of the Romanian case, Katherine Verdery (1996) explains the difference between (creative) administration of property and theft: it was only when goods circulated downwards in the system that it was classified as theft, whereas it was an "administrative matter" when they circulated upwards1996). We may find an additional explanation in a quote from an elderly woman who, during the 1980s, had been in charge of the workers at the collective farm in Straigiai:

When I got this job, the previous administrator made me understand that a part of my tasks was to bring goods and farm produce to the chairman and the secretary of the farm. Consequently, I had to steal much more than anybody else; first to give to the chairman, then to the secretary, and only then to myself and my family. Of course people noticed, like Mrs. Arlauskienė who never liked me. Even now she says that I was stealing too much during Soviet times, but she did not know the kind of job I had. I had to steal for both the chairman and the secretary. But she was also stealing. Once I met her with two bags of potatoes from the farm. When she saw me, she tried to hide them under her skirts. I did not say anything, I just walked by. Afterwards our relationship was strange, but she should not say anything about me, she was stealing too.[17]

We can compare the above statement with Firlit's and Chlopecki's article about workers in a Polish factory during Soviet times. The Polish workers did not see

---

17 From my field notes, 3 August 2007; my translation from Lithuanian.

it as theft as long as it was collective goods they took from the factory. Only if someone took something from another person or if someone took items from the factory that another worker had already set aside to take home would it be seen as theft (Firlit and Chlopecki 1992; see also Pawlik 1992). Contrary to this, my informants frequently used the word "stealing" when talking about taking collective goods. However, despite the difference in terminology, they also saw it as their right to steal. At my field sites, people had implied the logic that if everything belongs to all, then something also belongs to the individual person. Pawlik offers an accurate term for this logic: mutual stealing, which he defines as a zero-sum relationship between the individual and the state: "The State robs me, I rob the State, and it all comes out even" (Pawlik 1992, 89). In this sense, there was nothing wrong with stealing, unless, as in the example above, someone was stealing more than the others.

During the Soviet regime, property relations, administering property for personal gain, making use of networks, or taking goods or products from ones working place should not be seen as a parallel economy; rather, these practices were fundamental aspects of, and interrelated with, the Soviet economy and were, as such, necessary supplements to the daily economies of the households (Firlit and Chlopecki 1992). This system of economy, as it worked during the Soviet regime, continued to work after independence, albeit in a slightly different form. As Wedel (1992) emphasizes, it would be wrong to assume that people who were used to turning to their friends and acquaintances for support and goods were inclined to do otherwise, even when otherwise became possible. In this regard, Bridger and Pine (1998) argue that the people who used to hold powerful positions in formerly socialist countries during the Soviet regime were, in most cases, able to keep strong positions in the time afterward, since they were the ones who knew which strings to pull and how to implement the law according to their own interests, a pattern that is common in many countries as is shown by Kaneff (1996) with reference to Bulgaria, De Waal (1996) with reference to Albania, Verdery (2002a) with reference to Romania and Thelen (2003a) with reference to Hungary, to mention some examples. It was all about acting at the right moment and having the right connections and papers. Houses, land and collective property became registered in private names, and in some cases they were already registered as belonging to the people in charge before privatization had officially started. The villagers were quite eager to tell me such stories about unequal property distribution:

See the big house over there? It belongs to the vice mayor. He used to be in charge of the collective farm. At the time of the Russians he built this house for himself and his family with material from the collective farm. Officially, it was not his house, it was common property of the farm, but when he sensed that independence was coming, he ran off to visit important friends in high positions, and all of a sudden it was his house. This is how things worked here.[18]

An employee from the Ministry of Agriculture in Vilnius explained that there were many ways to acquire property, and it could often not be proven to be illegal when people held higher positions. She clarified:

The people with higher education, they were aware of the process [of privatization] and of course they had priorities when it came to the distribution of property. If they did it illegally they would be punished. So, they legalized it. They found ways to legalize it. They were very smart, I would say.[19]

A farmer explained:

Most land and property was given to the chairmen and their families, whereas other families were left with nothing at all.[20]

Clearly, even though the structural changes were limiting for some, they provided endless opportunities for others. Contrary to the actual ideas behind the reforms, Soviet systems and practices were the main force behind the administration of the laws that should ideally have implemented liberal democracy and sent anti-Soviet signals. In her article "Seeing like a Mayor," Katherine Verdery therefore urges us to look at the local level when analyzing property distribution. Indeed, with a specific hint to Scott (1998) she warns us that "Seeing like a State" may blur our understanding of how the processes of privatization really came about (Verdery 2002a, 2003). Verdery specifically argues against a theory which, in the case of Romania, is often used to explain the difficulties and delays in the privatization process, namely, that the Romanian state deliberately slowed the process down as the government had no particular interest in giving the land back to the citizens. Although Verdery recognizes the president's reluctance to enforce the restitution of property, she doubts that this alone would lead to the many flaws and difficulties that occurred in Romania. According to Verdery, this would be to grant the state too much power in a period in which it had a very weak position, and furthermore, focusing on the center would overlook the power that local officials had in the process of property distribution. Thus, in order to pursue their own interests, local officials could deliberately drag the process out

---

18 From my field notes, 2008; my translation from Lithuanian.
19 Interview, October 2003. The interview was held in English.
20 From my field notes, 2004; my translation from Lithuanian.

by demanding more papers and documents from the citizens, referring to diffuse laws unknown to the majority to the point where people gave up. The land was then mysteriously transferred to people in higher positions. Thus, rather than by a state agenda, the process was slowed down by agendas of the local level bureaucrats (Verdery 2002a).

If we compare the Romanian case with the situation in Lithuania in the same period, this will only confirm the idea that Verdery proposed about the determining role of local officials. Whereas in the case of Romania there was at least some evidence of the government's reluctance to enforce the restitution of property, the aggressive anti-Soviet politics introduced by Sąjūdis in Lithuania only bore witness of the desire to "return to Europe" as soon as possible, and thus to comply with the privatization suggestions given by European advisors, the World Bank and the IMF (Frohberg and Hartman 2000). Despite the eagerness to reintroduce private property, the process in Lithuania was also marked by flaws, confusion and difficulties, leading to a slow privatization process that resulted in uneven land distribution. Hence, in Lithuania as in Romania, the process of land privatization dragged out for many years, conflicts frequently arose over land rights, many engaged in illegal trade with land and many a villager was never granted the piece of land he or she was originally entitled to. The general situation of confusion and disorder resulted in former workers from the collective farm robbing the place at night for building materials and any other items of value. They often felt this was a way to fulfill a certain justice, since they had so many disadvantages during privatization.

Surviving the Transition

While the transition period was hard for the majority of the rural population, the difficulties varied, depending on the individual situation of the families and how well they were able to take advantage of the changing situation. The following case stories describe two very different outcomes of privatization for two families.

Case I

My landlord in Bilvytis, Kostas, is a cheerful man in his late 40s. He lives in a newly built three-story brick house together with his wife and their three teenage children. Next to the brick house stands an old big wooden house, where Kostas was brought up. In his late teens, he moved away from his parents' house to the regional capital, Alytus. Here he met Vida, who became his wife. Kostas had been working as a truck driver, and the younger Vida had not yet started to work as independence came. Kostas' mother was given the family's land back, 13 hectares, and gave all the land to Kostas. As a young man in his late 20s, Kostas moved back to his parents' old farm, where he took up farming. He was, he remembers, very optimistic and full of hope for the future in independent Lithuania. His wife Vida, however, was a city girl and was everything but excited. Moving to some remote village at the Polish border in order to milk cows and clean their dung away was not how she had imagined her future. She cried every day for the first couple of months, she conveyed to me. Kostas' optimism about his farm and the future in an independent Lithuania was also soon to fade. He had expected stable prices for products, regulated by the state, but he soon found out that this was not the case; prices were unstable, investments high and profits very low. In order to make ends meet, he started, as did many others in this region, to smuggle cigarettes from Russia. Soon he got an offer that seemed to solve his monetary problems: hiding illegal migrants from China, Kazakhstan and Afghanistan in his stables and helping them to cross the nearby border, which was situated less than a kilometer from his farm. The migrants passed through Lithuania and Poland in order to get to Germany. In a single night, Kostas thus made enough money to buy the family's first car, he told me. Soon after, he started to build new stables and then a new house next to the old one. His sudden wealth puzzled the neighbors, many of whom also had taken up farming after independence and could hardly make ends meet. How come that Kostas is so well off? they asked each other. And how come that he no longer receives any guests in his house? How come that he always buys so much food, more than the family can possibly eat? Eventually such suspicions resulted in calls to the police. Kostas was lucky; as the police arrived, the stables were empty. Just the night before, he had helped a group of migrants across the border. Still, the police found traces enough to arrest him. Although Kostas had to stand a long trial, he eventually got away with a fine, as there was not enough evidence to sentence him to prison. After the trial was over, Kostas returned to farming and was soon to face better times for agriculture. Today, Kostas runs a farm of 20 hectares, 13 of which he owns, 7 of which he leases. He has 23 dairy cows and lives entirely off milk sales. He has in recent years also benefitted from EU funding to buy more equipment for the farm.

Case II

About 15 minutes walk from Kostas' farm lives Daiva, a woman in her late 50s, in a small wooden cottage. Her house is in such a poor condition that it at first sight it is uncertain whether it is inhabited or simply abandoned. During Soviet times she lived in the same cottage with her mother, her husband and their six children. Both Daiva and her husband Kazys worked at the collective farm. The family had been offered a big brick house across the street by the chairman of the collective farm, who saw it as his responsibility to provide his workers with decent housing. This offer came in the early 1980s. Kazys, however, declined the offer, as he preferred to build a new house next to the old one with material provided by the collective farm. With help from friends and relatives they started the project of building a grand and new brick house. However, problems arose as Kazys went quite heavy on the bottle, which had an impact on his ability to work, both on the collective farm and also on the house. The building process therefore dragged out for many years. The new house was still not finished when independence was declared, and after 1990 the family could not afford to finish it and continued to live in the old house. Today, the half-built brick house still stands next to the wooden house, falling apart before it has been finished. Daiva and Kazys received two plots of 3 hectares after independence, according to the law granting land to the former workers, and they acquired a tractor from the collective farm with green vouchers. The only stable income they had was the grandmother's pension. For this family, independence meant a step into insecurity for many years to come. Most of their land lay fallow as they did not have equipment to cultivate it and, as had all other families, they had received their land plots in small pieces unevenly distributed within an area of 5 square kilometers. Both parents were unemployed and cultivated small quantities of different crops on the closest land plot, for the family's own consumption. In order to supplement her income, Daiva started to prepare food for weddings and funerals in Bilvytis and the surrounding villages. After the seventh child was born in 1992, two years after independence, the family's economic situation improved. The child, a son, was born with serious heart problems and the mother now received additional economic help from the state. Although it was only about 200 litas (approximately 58 euro), it was sufficient for the family to improve its daily living conditions. Today Daiva is the only one left in the house. Two of her sons died, the youngest from his heart condition and an older brother by a car accident; her husband Kazys has died and the rest of the children have moved away.

Kostas and Vida, still being a young couple in the early 1990s, had difficulties in the beginning, but in the end, managed the transition quite well. Today, they run a viable farm specializing in milk production. Kostas and Vida count as belonging to the exclusive group of wealthy farmers in Bilvytis – there are three of them – as their farm is mechanized, specialized, and Kostas in recent years has successfully applied for EU funds. However, had they not taken the risk of hiding migrants, they would never have gotten that far – or at least not that fast. Daiva and Kazys, by contrast, were older than Kostas and Vida, owned less land and only had experience in collective farming. They came out of the transition with a small family farm and had no choice but to engage in semi-subsistence farming. For small-scale farmers like them, which meant the majority, the privatization fostered what F. and K. von Benda-Beckmann ([1994] 2000) have referred to as a period of "no longer, not yet" in society in terms of provision of social security. On one hand, the collective farms no longer existed as units of social security; on the other hand, the Lithuanian state was not yet in a position to provide for the basic needs of the population.

The Reconceptualization of the Lithuanian Farmer

The situation for the small-scale family farms in Lithuania leads to related subjects of national identity and social history. In Lithuania, the reestablishment of the private farmer had at first represented a return to the "true" national values in the early post-Soviet years, as social history was rewritten in the light of the "reversibility of events" as described by Giordano and Kostova (2002). In this context, the return to the previously existing state of affairs meant a re-creation of the family farms. Lithuanians linked their national identity to the soil and the hard-working farmer as the fundament of the economy, and national and cultural values were closely linked to the agricultural sector. In this line of thinking, the newly established farmers had initially been seen as the "forerunners" of the changes after independence, and it had been expected that they would steer Lithuania into a better economic situation (Mincyte 2006). This was not only symptomatic for Lithuania, but also for the neighboring country Latvia, which likewise drew strongly on the revival of an identity based on agronationalism (Schwartz 2006), and for Bulgaria, where the "peasant myth" was likewise revived (Giordano and Kostova 2002).

However, as these early ideas and hopes attached to a privatized agricultural sector faded away, the Lithuanian family farmers found themselves between two developmental tendencies in the world's agrisystems, but without fitting in anywhere. The first tendency is an informal agri-food system based on small-scale farming, a trend that has been viewed as the solution to overindustrialization and intensification of agriculture in North America and Western Europe and seen as an answer to overproduction and a forerunner for sustainable development (Goodman 2003; Mincyte 2011). However, as Lithuanian farmers' productions were too diverse and since the vast majority did not produce organically, they failed to fit into the trend of small sustainable agrisystems. The second tendency is the further industrialization of the agricultural sectors, pushing for unification of production and large-scale, specialized and efficient enterprises, encapsulated in the idea of "Europe-building" (Bellier and Wilson 2000; Ong and Collier 2005; Dunn 2005; Mincyte 2011). This was not an option for the many aging small-scale farmers, as they did not have the needed resources, equipment, knowledge – let alone strength – to be a part of a large-scale industrialization. Thus, EU support was channeled to farmers who were capable of changing to an organic mode of production and to farmers who wished to expand and further industrialize their farms. The majority of Lithuanian family farms failed to fit into either of these modes of production. No special development programs were issued with focus on small-scale and diversified and nonorganic production as an answer to the general overproduction in the EU. The only apparent solution was to encourage small-scale farmers to retire and withdraw from any commercial production. Instead of the stewards of change, as promoted in the early 1990s, farmers had now become Lithuania's "national headache," as an employee at the Ministry of Economy told me during an interview.[21]

As Lithuania had had a leading position in the agricultural sector of the Soviet Union, the realization that the agricultural sector was weak by EU standards, especially after the destruction of the large-scale farms, was difficult to come to terms with for most Lithuanians. The turnaround in conceptualization affected the farmers' self-perceptions as well and was incorporated by rural citizens, creating what Diana Mincyte referred to as "non-farmers." By this she means people who work the land but no longer identify with the occupation of farmer, disregarding that all their work is centered on the farm, and most, if not all, incomes come from agriculture. This process of alienation both from the land and from the EU project had significant influence on the way the EU would later be perceived and integrated into the Lithuanian rural areas.

Reforms and Political Stands

If we again turn to the political development in Lithuania, it had become clear that the election of the former communists in 1992 did not bring about any real improvements for the rural population. The LDDP argued for more social welfare, employment for all and the establishment of minimum wages and agriculture subsidies. After the election, however, it turned out to be difficult to keep these promises, as Lithuania was bound to take a more liberal stand in the implementation of the market economy. It was hard to make anything more than minor adjustments in the policies that had been introduced by Sąjūdis.

---

21 Interview, Vilnius 2004; the interview was held in English.

After the election, the LDDP lost support among its traditional base, the rural population and urban workers, as the party failed to give them economic and social security. The Social Democratic Party (Lietuvos Darbo Partija, LDP) criticized the LDDP for betraying the interests of the rural population and urban working class, and the right wing accused the LDDP of being responsible for the economic failures in the period after the election. Only in 1995 did the national economy start to grow again, but not sufficiently for the LDDP to win the next election. More damaging than the economic situation was the party's reputation for being corrupt and untrustworthy. No less than 43 corruption scandals had been tied to the party since it came to power in 1992. The LDDP was also criticized for supporting former KGB agents in Lithuania and helping them regain power and money. Due to internal friction and rumors about corruption, Brazauskas decided not to run for a second term. Landsbergis, however, aimed for the presidential post once again, but to his great disappointment, he did not make it through the first electoral round. He then decided to give his support to the relatively unknown Valdas Adamkus. Adamkus did not belong to any political party and during the campaign had been supported mainly by the center and right-wing parties. Among his voters were many Lithuanians who had returned to the country after independence. Adamkus was himself a migrant and had spent most of his life in the United States, where he had been engaged in politics and supported the Republican Party. In 1997 Adamkus became the second president of independent Lithuania (Smith, Pabriks, Purs and Lane 2002). Although Landsbergis had not won the presidency, he kept his post as speaker of the parliament until 2000. Lithuanian critics referred to Adamkus as "the American" (*amerikietis*) and claimed that he was not a "true" Lithuanian (Klumbytė 2006). However, due to the long time he had spent abroad, Adamkus was not touched by corruption scandals or KGB associations, as was Brazauskas, nor was he associated with Sąjūdis' radical reforms that led the country into economic troubles, as was Landsbergis. Two years after this election, Adamkus had to deal with a severe economic crisis in Russia,[22] which had a negative impact on the recent economic growth in Lithuania (Komulainen and Taro 1999). Only in the beginning of the new century did the Lithuanian economy stabilize and improve.

---

22 The Russian financial crisis unfolded in 1998 as a result of the difficulties Russia had in changing to a market economy, political mismanagement and abortive reform efforts throughout the 1990s. Prior to the crisis, the country's GDP had decreased by 40 percent between 1989 and 1996 ("The Russian Crisis of 1998": http://www.twnside.org.sg/title/1998-cn.htm, accessed 16 November 2011). The crisis hit the previous socialist countries hard, as they still exported much of their produce to Russia. Among the farmers in my field sites, 1998 is remembered as the most difficult year in the 1990s.

Preparing for Enlargement

In 2004 the EU grew from 15 to 25 member states, and the population within the EU grew by almost 75 million people to about 450 million in total. The enlargement was an expensive and politically daring project: expensive because of the support paid to the application states in the years before the entrance, and daring because the EU would accept so many new member countries at once, which challenged the existing setup of the EU. However, accepting new members was also proof for the old member countries that they could act as a politically cooperative unit and make important geopolitical decisions. It furthermore gave them an option to formulate the actual values and foundation of the union, as they set the criteria the applicant states had to meet. Political scientist Heather Grabbe (2005) has divided the EU's transformative influence on the previous socialist countries into three arenas: (1) the post-1989 trade and aid programs; (2) pre-accession strategies 1993–1997; and (3) accession partnership and negotiation (tightened conditionality) 1998–2002.

In the first phase (post-1989), the EEC created the Phare aid program, intended to support economic transformation to capitalism, rather than political processes. Most countries only declared their independence from 1991 onward, so the EEC was well ahead of the development. In 1989 the European Commission was also given the task of coordinating aid from the G-24 (Intergovernmental Group of Twenty-Four) including the OECD, World Bank and the IMF. This was an unexpected extension of the EEC's mandate, which strengthened its political influence (Grabbe 2005; Sedelmeier and Wallace 1996).

In the second phase (1993–1997), the EEC itself had changed to the EU and formulated the Copenhagen Criteria, named after the Copenhagen summit in June 1993. The criteria had a double function. They should both secure economic and political stability in the prospective new member states, which was meant as a reduction of the risk of them becoming a burden to the EU, and, at the same time, the criteria were supposed to reassure the EU member states, which were more reluctant about an enlargement with former Soviet countries (Grabbe 2005). At the summit it was formulated as follows:

> The association countries in Eastern Europe that so desire shall become members of the Union. Accession will take place as soon as the country is able to assume the obligations of membership by satisfying the economic and political conditions. Membership requires: that the candidate country has achieved stability in institutions, guaranteeing democracy, the rule of law, human rights [...], the existence of a functioning market economy, as well as the capacity to cope with competitive pressure and market forces within the Union and the ability to take on the obligations of membership, including adherence to the aims of political, economic and monetary union. (Quoted in W. V. Wallace 2000, 10)

In order to prepare for EU membership, the candidate countries first had to sign the Europe Agreements.[23] These stated that the countries would work towards the adoption of EU policies and fulfill the criteria set by the Copenhagen summit. The EU would support the applicant countries in this process through a pre-accession strategy: each country would receive financial support in order to develop infrastructure, economies, and institutions. Lithuania signed the agreement in 1995, eight years before the actual referendum was held and nine years before the accession.[24] It soon became clear for the committees evaluating the countries' progress that the ten applicant countries were in very different stages in their preparations for membership. In 1997 the EU therefore announced that each of the applicant states could proceed at its own pace and that accession to the EU would be based on the individual country's preparedness.

This led to the third phase of membership preparation (1998–2002). While the Copenhagen Criteria had been very general and open to interpretation, they were now made much more explicit. It was the European Commission, rather than the member states that defined the requirements and shaped the conditions for membership (Grabbe 2005), which also led the developments at different speeds. Accession negotiations began with the six best-prepared countries in 1998, Cyprus, Estonia, Poland, Hungary, the Czech Republic and Slovenia. Six other countries, Bulgaria, Latvia, Lithuania, Malta, Romania and Slovakia, were not yet deemed ready for application.

In this period, the European Commission faced a specific problem with regard to the anticorruption criteria in the new member states. According to a report from Transparency International (TI),[25] the issue of corruption had largely been underestimated by the EU committees, and in addition, the EU itself did not have any comprehensive anticorruption policy. At the 1993 meeting when the Copenhagen Criteria were agreed upon, the achievement of European Standards was measured only with regard to democracy and rule of law, whereas no specific references were made to corruption. Corruption was only highlighted in Agenda 2000, and was as such an issue defined and made for the specific occasion.[26] Hence, old member countries had not undergone the same corruption evaluation as new member countries now had to undergo. Issues such as corrupt networks (involving politicians), and organized crime were identified as features of the political systems in the postsocialist countries. It was seen as a possible risk that the

---

23 See EUROPA, "The 2004 enlargement: The challenge of a 25 member EU." http://
   europa.eu/legislation_summaries/enlargement/2004_and_2007_enlargement/e50017_
   en.htm (accessed 24 November 2011).
24 Ibid.
25 Transparency International report on Lithuania. http://www.transparency.org/policy_
   research/nis/nis_reports_by_country (accessed 16 November 2011).
26 Ibid.

accession in itself would stimulate new forms of corruption as EU funds became available. Unforeseen problems like this put additional pressure on the candidate countries and forced them to work with strict anticorruption programs.

In 2002, all countries, except Bulgaria and Romania, were deemed ready for membership, as they had improved sufficiently in areas of economic development, political and administrative change and anticorruptions. As required, the candidate countries had now adopted the entire legislation from the *Acquis* and were legally compatible with the existing member countries, at least on paper. Although there had not been held any referendums yet, the actual membership was no longer a question to be decided upon. In the words of Grabbe (2005, 22), "[...] the rejection of one country's people would not have stopped the process; it would just have ruled out that country's participation in the 2004 enlargement."

Key Problems for the Agricultural Sector

Lithuania had not belonged to the first group of countries that entered into more serious membership negotiations with the EU; in the early 2000s the evaluating committees still recognized severe obstacles for Lithuania's membership. The problems were related to widespread corruption, high economic instability and Ignalina, the last nuclear power plant in Europe of the same type as Chernobyl still in operation. However, one of the most immanent obstacles for the evaluating committees was the unfortunate outcome of rural privatization. Lithuanian agriculture consisted of more than 300,000 family farms engaged in semi-subsistence production. These farms needed to undergo severe restructuring if they were to be able to compete within the EU, or alternatively, they would have to withdraw from agricultural production altogether. The paradox emerged that the path out of the Soviet system (privatization of land and the establishment of family farms) turned out to be a hindrance for obtaining membership of the EU. Added to this, the land reforms from the 1990s were still not completed by the time of the EU entrance in 2004, while the first laws from the *Acquis* were implemented in Lithuania in the mid-1990s.

Between 2000 and 2004 four major reports were issued in which the situation of Lithuanian agriculture was evaluated and goals set for further development. These were initiatives that should prepare the people working in the agricultural sector for actual membership by starting to implement new standards and EU legislation. The rural development plans did not resemble the interests of one specific group of people, but had come into being through broad cooperation between the Lithuanian parliament and the Ministry of Agriculture, the Rural Development Department and Agricultural Units at the district level. Furthermore, scholars of agrarian studies read and revised the plans. The EU likewise contributed with constant feedback and advice in order to assure that the planned development would take place in accordance with EU laws and would aim at the establishment of the kind of competitive agricultural sector advocated by the EU. The reports were furthermore based on two key legal documents governing agriculture and rural development. The first of these is the Agricultural and Rural Development Strategy, which was approved by the Lithuanian parliament 13 June 2000 and set forth agricultural and rural development plans for 2000–2006. The second is the Law on Agriculture and Rural Development, which was adopted by parliament 25 June 2002. The legal documents are in line with the EU Common Agricultural Policy (CAP) and EU regulations on rural development (Lithuanian Ministry of Agriculture 2004, 103–4). Taking into consideration the many actors who were involved in drafting the rural development plans, it is remarkable that everybody reached the agreement that the small-scale farmer was the most serious obstacle for future development (Mincyte 2006). Indeed, the central problems in the agricultural sector were first and foremost seen in the size of and the sheer number of family farms. The many small and divided land plots hindered an efficient use of natural resources. The 2004–2006 rural development plan explained:

The most serious weakness in terms of economic development [...] is the small size of agricultural holdings. The small farm size creates serious obstacles for improvements in farms due to lack of investments needed to comply with quality requirements. (Lithuanian Ministry of Agriculture 2004, 90)

Another problem was that the soil was cultivated inefficiently and that many people lacked machinery. Indeed, much of the land was not cultivated at all. This was rightly seen as a direct result of the process of privatization throughout the 1990s and the adoption of an open market policy (Lithuanian Ministry of Agriculture 2004, 28). It was suggested that land consolidation programs would be a sensible solution. However, this was problematic, as the privatization process was not yet finished. At the time of publication of the 2004–2006 rural development plan, 21 percent of agricultural land in Lithuania had still not been privatized. Therefore, the government first had to finish the reforms started in the early 1990s, and thus keep on dividing the land into small plots before it could be consolidated again.

   A related aspect was that the majority of farmers were close to or above retirement age. Put in numbers, it looked as follows: 21 percent of the farmers were 50–59 years old, while 49 percent were 60 or above. Only 14 percent of the farmers were below 40 (Lithuanian Ministry of Agriculture 2004, 32). Twenty-nine percent of the farmers were engaged in milk production. By 1 January 2002 there were 224,582 dairy cow owners in the Animal Register, more than 95 percent of whom owned fewer than five cows (Lithuanian Ministry of Agriculture 2004, 32). Regarding technology in the dairy sector, it was common that no machines were used at all, as such small production meant that it made no sense for the farmers to invest in milking machines or cooling equipment for the milk. For this reason, the majority of Lithuanian dairies could only sell dairy products to Russia, where the regulations were less strict than in the EU. Another issue mentioned in the 2004–2006 rural development plan is the lack of employment possibilities in the rural areas. This led to a situation defined as "overdependence of agriculture." At the time, 33 percent of the population was living in rural areas, 16 percent of whom were registered as being engaged in agriculture (Lithuanian Minisry of Agriculture 2004, 93–4). However, it would have been more realistic to state that about one-third of the Lithuanian population was engaged in agriculture, as basically all citizens in the countryside are, to a greater or lesser extent, involved in some kind of farm production.

The abovementioned issues were the most serious obstacles for the agricultural sector according to the evaluations from the Ministry of Agriculture and the EU evaluating committees. The reports and the analyses of the situation constituted the backbone for the restructuring and development of the agricultural sector. To finance the restructuring of the agricultural sector, 608 million euro was accorded, 489.5 million of which was financed by the EU and the remaining part by Lithuania. The new initiatives were now based on a number of pre-accession programs for which the EU offered monetary support to applicant states and support also came from European advisory boards in order to achieve the European models and standards. For the rural sector, the policy now advocated by the EU was in opposition to the laissez faire governing that had marked the first period of rural privatization. There had to be more central control in the agricultural sector, a policy that hitherto had been avoided in order not to resemble the Soviet past. The new programs were also to support young farmers and offer the older generation an opportunity to leave the farming sector. The farms were to be bigger and focus on specialized production. Such initiatives were meant to prepare the people working in the agricultural sector for EU membership, little by little implementing the new EU standards and legislation. According the EU advisory boards, the situation in Lithuania on these grounds changed sufficiently to let the country become part of the first round of the enlargement together with nine other countries in 2004.

The Maxima Referendum

I remember this shot on the TV. You saw a man walking down the street and suddenly money was pouring down from above, and all he should do was to bend down and pick it up (laughing). This was the way the politicians advocated the EU before the referendum: [the] EU was money. But I thought to myself: people must be informed that [the] money has to come from somewhere, there is also a cost for Lithuania if we enter the EU. People got fooled to think that [the] EU is an endless supply of money, and if there is a shortage, then they can print more money in Brussels. But the truth is that Lithuania has to contribute to the overall economy in Europe. [...] I did consider voting "no" at the referendum because the campaigns were so one-sided. I wanted to show them that there exists another opinion. But I voted yes, I mean, I am for the union, but I was against the campaigns.[27]

This statement came from Povilas, a 35-year-old employee at the municipal administration in Marijampolė. Povilas had studied in London, was fluent in English and was now employed in the municipality in an administrative post. Although Povilas was fully supportive of EU membership, he expressed concern about the campaigns that ran prior to the EU referendum. He found that they conveyed a simplistic image of the EU as a cradle of wealth and a road to quick money. Povilas, however, did not belong to the target group of such campaigns, as he, a young, educated man with international experience, was, a priori, assumed to be an active voter in favor of the membership. The target group for such campaigns was, instead, the part of the population whose enthusiasm for capitalism had decreased throughout the 1990s. It was these people who could be tempted to show their dissatisfaction and doubt at the EU referendum. Rural citizens from my two field sites did not doubt that the eager agitation for the EU among politicians would mean better times and more welfare for the very same politicians only, and surely not for the average citizen. Consequently, the wider political and economical implications were not the cards played in the campaigns; rather, they appealed to what the population seemed to need the most – money. The political leaders who had been involved in the process of gaining EU membership ever since the early 1990s were convinced that too much work, preparation and money had been involved to let the project fail because of a referendum.

The preparations and campaigns for EU accession were leading up to the actual referendum about membership in 2003. Political actors regarded the referendum with excitement, but also with a concern for the outcome. The concern was not whether people would vote yes, as most of the politically active were also assumed to favor pro-European cooperation. The question was rather whether people would vote at all. The voter turnout would be highly relevant; if less than 50 percent of eligible voters participated, the referendum would not be valid. In order to give people more time, the referendum was held on a weekend, 10 and 11 May 2003. This was a practice implemented in all countries voting on the European referendum in that period, and it gave the governments an overnight chance to secure the necessary votes.

Opinion polls taken before the referendum indicated that Lithuania still was the most EU-friendly country of the three Baltic states. It was therefore a political

---

27 Interview, Marijampolė's municipality, November 2007. The interview was held in English.

strategy to hold the referendum first in Lithuania. It was very unlikely to result in a "no" to the EU, and if Lithuania first said yes, none of the other Baltic states would want to stay out of the European community. Lithuania's chief EU negotiator, Petras Auštrevičius, said before the referendum:

> I would say that this referendum is historic in the sense that it will consolidate all the achievements Lithuania has made during the last 15 years. It will give them meaning, will legalize them very clearly, and will confirm the fact that our people accept the [accession] treaty, [...] it will be one more confirmation that people approve of all the work and the efforts made, which was all done very quickly, I think it is an important – and without any doubt – historic event. [...] now many people feel in control of their destiny and the fate of their country.[28]

Auštrevičius may have referred to young English-speaking people, who already felt secure and "home" in Europe, able to travel, able to work abroad and able to benefit from the membership. There were, however, many older rural and urban citizens, who felt that Europe was a fuzzy political creation of the future, whereas they saw themselves as primarily having their knowledge and social capital in the past (De Munck 2007, 2008). However, many had been convinced that there was no other way and were decisive to vote for the EU, if not for themselves, then for the sake of their children and grandchildren. A retired woman expressed it:

> We are not dreamers, and we do not indulge in fantasies about a life in ease. Life has never been easy, and the EU can do nothing to change that. That does not mean I am against the EU; the EU is probably a good thing, but not for people my age. The EU is for the young people. I voted yes [at the EU referendum], not for my own sake, but for the sake of my grandchild. When he grows us, he can go abroad, work hard, save money and get himself a decent life when he returns to Lithuania.[29]

While the "yes side" was very well organized and ran numerous campaigns, the "no side" was fragmented into smaller groups that had different reasons to oppose the EU. The best, if any, chance the no-voters had was not to vote. If they voted, they would only contribute to the overall percentage of voter turnout; if they did not, they had a chance to keep the number below 50 percent. In that case, they would have won anyway, as the referendum would be declared invalid. The

---

28 Quoted from "Voters Likely To Approve EU Membership in Weekend Referendum": http://www.globalsecurity.org/military/library/news/2003/05/mil-030509-rfel-171853. htm (accessed 16 November 2011).

29 From my field notes, January 2007; my translation from Lithuanian.

turnout of the first day of the referendum was 23 percent, by 10 a.m. Sunday it had jumped to 27.8 percent. This result was followed by a public statement of Adamkus saying that "measures had to be taken" if the voter turnout did not reach the required 50 percent. However, measures had already been taken, as the shopping chain Maxima decided to get involved. If you went to vote, the chain advertised, you would get a small green sticker saying "*aš balsavau*" (I voted). You could then go to the nearest Maxima shop with your sticker and buy the cheaper brands of chocolate, beer or washing powder for only one cent. Four hours later, another 17.8 percent had voted.[30] The distribution of chocolate, beer and washing powder would normally have been subject to condemnation by Western European institutions, as the manipulation of voters opposed democratic ideals, but this time they remained quiet.

In the referendum, 63.4 percent of eligible voters cast their ballots. The result was 91.1 percent in favor of the EU.[31] Although it was promoted internationally that it had been more than 90 percent in favor, it was not taken into consideration that about 36 percent of the Lithuanian population had not voted, and 8.9 percent had voted against the EU. Approximately 45 percent of eligible voters were thus either against, indifferent to, or had ambiguous feelings about the EU. Auštrevičius' very positive comments about the population's approval of the 15 years of work, therefore, did not reflect the whole truth. Although many indeed appreciated the political work for the membership, others did not, or they were uncertain about the fast accession to a new union. This uncertain atmosphere was also reflected in other previous socialist countries with low voter turnouts; in Slovakia 52 percent of eligible voters went to the referendum, in the Czech Republic 55 percent voted, while 59 percent of Poles and 60 percent of Slovenians voted. The Baltic states had the highest voter turnouts; 63 percent of Lithuanian voters came to cast their ballots together with 64 percent of Estonians, while Latvians hit the record with a voter turnout of 73 percent (Grabbe 2005, 22).

My landlord from Bilvytis, Kostas, had, like many others, decided not to vote in the 2003 referendum. He had been annoyed by the heavy promotion of the EU and found that he, a grown-up man, had been treated like a child during the campaign. This feeling only grew stronger as Maxima got involved in the referendum. Kostas

---

30 I was in Lithuania during the 2003 referendum, went with friends to the ballots, and saw the distribution of goods in Maxima to voters with the voting sticker. However, it has since been difficult to find sources that write about these aspects of the referendum, as it was a sensitive issue for the government and for the EU and was silenced in the media. The one article I found is on the Propaganda Matrix website: "The Lights are going out over Europe" by John Laughland. http://www.propagandamatrix.com/the_lights_are_going_out_over_europe.html (accessed 16 November 2011).

31 See http://www.electoralgeography.com/new/en/countries/l/lithuania/lithuania-eu-member ship-referendum-2003.html (accessed 16 November 2011).

had very ambiguous feelings towards the EU, and he did not like Maxima playing a role in the referendum. It was simply not "correct" to go outside your domain as a shopping chain and interfere in politics. Kostas explained:

> It was like giving candies to kids when they have been good. Go to vote and you will get candy at Maxima. This was not my style. I felt they were looking down on me, the politicians and this Maxima chain, like I was a kid they could tempt with sweets. I did not vote. I was with my friends instead, and we got drunk.[32]

Indeed, in the light of the political turnarounds, corruption scandals and unfulfilled promises, the question remains whether the many people who chose not to vote did so in response to the EU or, as I would suggest, as a response to the national political climate. This also relates to the fact that the continuously unstable situation marked by unfulfilled promises in the 1990s has reinforced a general feeling of insecurity and distrust in the system, leading people to approach political agitation and promises for a better future with skepticism.

The Way to EUrope

The actual accession to the EU in May 2004 was in the end not such a big step for Lithuania. Many big steps had already been taken prior to the entrance, as strict adjustment to EU legislation had been a requirement in order to apply for membership at all. Ever since the mid-1990s the EU had taken a central position in the political and socioeconomic development of Lithuania, meaning that the actual integration took place at a much earlier stage than otherwise is stated in public. Although the pre-accession EU programs designed for the countryside had been framed in apolitical terms of development, modernization, help and support, it was part of a highly politicized agenda that was to redirect the applicant countries to capitalism and a functioning market economy. Membership became a way to redefine the perception of the country as belonging to a market-oriented and progressive Europe. However, the strongly politicized promotion of past and future was nevertheless far more blurred for the older population who had lived most of their lives under the Soviet Union. The "New Lithuania" was not constructed in an embracement of the farmer; rather, the small-scale farmers were the contradefinition to the new national image.

---

32 From my field notes, June 2009; my translation from Lithuanian.

CHAPTER 3

Paradoxes of Aging: On Aging
Farmers and Aging
Politicians

In the light of the entrance into the EU, implementation of uniform practices according to the *Acquis* grew in importance in the new member countries.[1] On the agricultural front, this meant securing comparability of production between the various member countries (Barry 2001; Dunn 2004, 2005). The EU, achieving the status of a "suprastate," worked through the premises of legitimizing power through vertical encompassment (Gupta and Ferguson 2005), especially for new member countries that first had to fulfill requirements in areas of law, economy and democracy in order to geopolitically return to Europe. In the early phase of membership, reaching out to the rural population and informing them about EU requirements, standards and options for funding was required of the state, and via the state, of all municipal administrations. The goals were to further the restructurings of the agricultural sector and encourage people working the land to become EU-minded farmers. In this way, Lithuania was to become competitive on the agricultural front and eventually match the production of the old EU member countries. This process of creating EUrope inside the expanded territory of the union was referred to as "Europe-building" (Bellier and Wilson 2000). If the EU was thus successfully being built in every corner of the union, every region and every village would ideally become a metonym of the EU. Hence, the EU would be recognizable everywhere inside its own territory.

The process of Europe-building still remained a question of local capacity, as local bureaucrats became the closest link the rural population had to the wider decision-making institutions, just like the local state representatives had gained central positions during the privatization of land after 1990.[2] Their task was now to reach the rural population and make them aware of the greater unity they were

---

1 Although many laws had been introduced already in the mid-1990s, and although several pre-accession programs had been launched in the early 2000s, the actual membership meant new forms of support and more control of the agricultural production.
2 See Chapter 2.

a part of now. This should be done through meetings and seminars about EU regulations, brochures and booklets about requirements and options for funding, and consultation for farmers to support their further restructuring. Although centrally controlled, Europe-building was performed locally.

The problem emerges that there is no guarantee that the local forces themselves are EU-minded and unbiased when building the EU. Since municipal administrations are all subject to the local environment, norms, and past and present practices, the communication of the EU is carried out differently in different regions. We thus have, on one level, Europe-building as the (ideal) idea of evoking small EUs in all member countries through umbrella models and on another level, the "filtration" of the EU through municipal administrations' local orders, where the umbrella models are (re)adjusted. This is not only a matter of the local environment but, more importantly, of the persisting Soviet influences and the way these throughout the 1990s and up to the present day had merged with political constellations and external (EU) requirements, resulting in apparently EU-friendly practices, yet modified by personal calculations and new emerging options that came about with the EU. Thus, instead of producing a recognizable EU in member countries, uniform models were likely to be processed to a number of various and unlike "local EUs."

Expanding on the thought about how local forces communicate the EU to the wider public, I employ Norman Long's (1989) concept of "interface encounters." Long stresses the critical point of intersection when two parts with incongruent interests meet. The interface shows us areas of structural discontinuity, which can be found in life in general but are more visible in intervention situations. Even though interface encounters put a specific angle on communication between state representatives and rural citizens, they also, if not seen in a broader context, tell but a partial truth; because, as has been pointed out by F. and K. von Benda-Beckmann (2007), state representatives have multiple and ambiguous statuses and roles. In order to evoke a closer understanding of the complex role of the state representatives, I wish to emphasize here the notion of their ability to work "On- and Off-State" (F. and K. von Benda-Beckmann 2007). Whereas On-State refers to the formal work and duties state representatives carry out in the name of the state, Off-State refers to the possibility of advancing deals and personal affairs due to the position On-State. Both On- and Off-State activities are ways of communicating the state, or as in this case, the EU policies, laws and regulations for new member states, to the citizens, as there is no sphere in this regard that can be labeled "private" (ibid.). As these interfaces would rank from official meetings and paperwork to the making of deals and informal gatherings, I therefore find it useful to speak about "multiple faces on the encounter," as this term better covers the variety and complexity of such interactions, entailing both On- and Off-State activities. Such different kinds of interactions highlight the multitudes of rules and strategies used by state representatives and citizens alike, as both parts have to adjust their behavior according to the given frame. This blurred mixture of state and non-state activities should not be miscomprehended as a random or coincidental choice of behavior, but rather as a different set of rules applied in appropriate situations.

Paradoxes of Aging

With regard to the Lithuanian case, I will suggest that two factors play a central role regarding the "localization" of the EU. These are best understood as "paradoxes of aging": despite the focus on the youth and its role in leading Lithuania into a new era, it was still the old people who controlled the majority of the land and resources as they had been the ones entitled to land and equipment after the breakup of the collective farms. The other, less publicly vocalized problem is that while the farmers are encouraged to retire due to their age, local politicians from the same generation are reviving their image in the EU era, based on their long-standing experience in politics.

The first paradox I was alerted to, I frame as "targeting the wrong audience." Older farmers are formally encouraged to retire, as they are perceived as an obstacle to progress.[3] As many of them have no interest in doing so,[4] the state representatives (knowing that many older farmers are neither going to retire nor going to implement the required changes, thus are not seen as useful in developing the EU) are put in a position where they have to communicate development and modernization to people who, from the outset, are perceived as the wrong audience. The farmers agree on this point, as the majority of them have no interest, resources or abilities to implement changes according to EU legislation. The paradox remains that while all parts agree that older farmers do not lead the way to the agricultural models promoted by the EU, they are still very determining for further development.[5]

The second paradox regards aging state representatives. I refer to this as "overcoming the past." This refers to the fact that many of the present-day political and economic elites in Lithuania as a rule had high positions during Soviet times. Consequently, they now have to combat their own past in order to appear trustworthy and have to show that they, despite their increasing age, are still capable of adjusting to the geopolitical and socioeconomic changes. The paradoxical aspect of the second paradox is that many politicians and bureaucrats have only succeeded in keeping the political power by use of their "Soviet ways,"

---

3 See Lithuanian Ministry of Agriculture, *Agriculture and Rural Development Plan 2000–2006*; *Rural Development Plan 2004–2006 Lithuania*; and *Lithuanian Rural Development Program 2007–2013*.
4 This will be discussed further in Chapter 4.
5 In Romania, they have a similar situation with aging landowners (see Cartwright 2003; Thelen 2003).

such as extensive networking and secret deals, practices that they rhetorically both dismiss and despise. Merging the two paradoxes, it appears that while one of the groups (the farmers) is recommended to withdraw *because* of age, the other group (the state representatives) experiences its political prime *despite* age.

By loosely comparing my two field sites, in this chapter I look at the interaction between farmers and state representatives.[6] I cover two main areas: the first is official meetings held for farmers in order to convey information about EU laws. The second is constituted by a case study of a political party, illustrating the methods present-day politicians use to cover up their own pasts and gain popularity in a challenging political period. All case studies point to the concept of EUropeanization, the gap between the ideal Europe-building as led by the EU and the actual changes and outcomes.

Meeting in Graižiūnai

In late autumn of 2006, a meeting was arranged to inform about the basic legal changes after EU entrance. The idea was to present important information and answer the farmers' specific questions about laws and regulations. It mainly addressed topics that were to ensure the legalization of work on the farms through registration, contracts, insurances and sale of products. The lecturer was a young lawyer from Kaunas who had specialized in EU law with regard to the agricultural sector. The meeting was taken "on tour" to various Lithuanian cities in order to provide the same basic information in as many cities as possible. One of the meetings was held in my field site, Graižiūnai, in Dzūkija.

> The meeting room in the municipality of Graižiūnai is furnished in dark wood, which makes it seem smaller than it really is. The lawyer has a place close to the audience. He has prepared a PowerPoint presentation for the meeting. Sixteen people have shown up at the meeting, mainly older men dressed in working coats or leather jackets; a few older women are also present, dressed in dark colors and all with scarves that cover their hair. No younger farmers are attending the meeting. Some of the people sit on the chairs, whereas many stand leaning against the sidewall, seemingly undecided whether they should stay or leave.
>
> The lawyer starts his presentation with the subject of farm registration in the national register for agricultural production: "It is important that the farm is registered. If the farm is not registered, you are nothing. There is no farm and no farmer, you have no legal rights and cannot receive any funding. What

---

6 With the term "state representatives," I refer to civil servants and politicians working in local municipal administrations. I apply this restricted use, as these are the people who, in the context of my research, inform about laws and legal changes locally.

is worse," he continues, "is that you risk to get fined if you cultivate the land, sell products or if people work on your farm. This is all illegal if the farm is not registered and the farmer risks to pay a fine of 10,000 litas [2,896 euros]." People mumble uneasily in the room. "We have to follow the guidelines from the EU," the lawyer says in an attempt to calm the audience down. "You have to do the paperwork." The lawyer goes on with the next topic, the making of contracts. "You all have to make contracts from now on; if a man comes and reaps hay at your farm, then it is work, and there should be a contract for it. You have to have such agreements on paper." The lawyer continues, "Your name has to be written with readable letters on the contract and there has to be a signature. The signature has to be yours, otherwise it has no value. When you lease your land, there has to be such a contract. Even if you only get 1 litas as rent, there has to be a contract." People laugh. "But," a man in the audience asks, "you cannot truly mean that I should make a contract with my mother-in-law if I cultivate her land?" The lawyer confirms that this is the case: "We are in the EU now, we have to tidy things up. I can only repeat; you have to do the paperwork." People mumble again among each other, some voice disapproving outbursts: "This cannot be true." "Should we make contracts with our own family?"

A man comes in, leans towards a table, and rocks impatiently from one leg to the other while looking at the PowerPoint presentation. After a few minutes, he leaves the room. Several people follow him, among them an old man. As he passes me, he touches my arm and whispers, "[T]his is only for you young people." He pats my arm a few times before he sets direction toward the exit again. After an hour, seven people are left in the room and the lawyer ends the meeting. "Today we made it short," he says, "but all information is available at the agricultural university in Kaunas. Or alternatively, you can write me an email if you have any questions." "We do not use email," a man shouts from the back. Another contributes, "Do you see people like us at your university?!"

After the meeting, I approach one of the organizers and ask if contracts are a big problem for the farmers. She replies that it depends on the region. "In some regions almost all questions are about the contracts; in others not. It depends on how educated people are. In Kaunas,[7] there are many farmers with a longer education from the department for agrarian studies at the university, but here it is different." She looks at the lawyer: "As you said to me earlier, we could compare it with pupils in the third and the twelfth grade. How to teach depends on the level. So when we teach in Kaunas, we are in twelfth grade, and here... this is third grade."[8]

---

7 Lithuania's second largest city. The Lithuanian University of Agriculture is located in Kaunas.
8 Description based on my field notes; 29 November 2006.

City Expert Meets Rural Citizens

The meeting in Graižiūnai was situated within the municipal administration, and the lawyer upheld all characteristics of what the participants saw as a "city expert" far removed from the lived reality at the farms. He had arrived in a big car, dressed in an expensive suit, kept physical distance from the audience while speaking and had addressed the audience in a very official manner, making frequent references to the EU as a body of the new system. He was from the city and he was young, educated and EU-minded. In other words, to the farmers he represented the future within the EU, a future that they did not consider themselves part of. As the elderly man who passed by me on the way out remarked, these rules were for "young people," meaning the new generation of farmers who produced within the new legal framework. He did not see the new legislation as applicable for people like him who had lived most of their lives under the Soviet regime, people who had already retired and only kept up a small production to support the household economy.

The miscommunication that marked the interface was driven by different forms of both knowledge and practices, some of which were incompatible with each other. Added to this, there were no intentions to create common understandings, neither from the lawyer's side nor from the participants' side. The lawyer was paid to give the same meeting in a certain number of regions and this was the last stop before he went to Brussels. From the outset, he had presented the information with the idea in mind that people here belonged in the third grade. The farmers, due to their reluctant participation, lack of engagement in the meeting and early departure, only confirmed this prejudice. However, he had likewise confirmed the expectations they had had from the very beginning; a distant city bureaucrat with no understanding for the local environment and their daily realities. And, as was obvious to the farmers, the lawyer talked down to them. Although there were no open conflicts on display at this encounter, there was no common understanding either, as opposing sides – bureaucrats versus farmers – were actively reinforced during the meeting.

Contracts and Circumvention of Trust

One example of the miscommunications between the farmers and the lawyer was seen in the question about contracts. The contract embedded several important features: it had a pragmatic function (to create legal and documented work relationships) and related to this, it had a legal function (to follow the EU law), and it had a geopolitical function in enforcing Europe-building (to create uniform practices in all EU member countries). Added to this, we also find a symbolic function of the contract as a tool to embed Lithuanian farms in the EU framework, which was promoted as "order," contrasting Lithuanian "disorder" (according to the lawyer's statement of the farmers having to "tidy things up").

Studying Turkish sugar beet farmers, Catherine Alexander (2002) showed how the contracts are sources of security, as an agreement with the state entitles the farmers to social and economic security based on their production. She found that the making of the contract is a social act in itself, provided that people understand and agree upon the specific use of the contract. A similar argument is made by Monica Heintz (2006) in a study of urban Romania. Heintz noticed how the contract with a working place becomes a guarantee for social security, as people at the age of retirement need to show that they have worked a number of years, and that they thus are entitled to receive state pensions. In both studies, the contracts serve a clear function as a means to obtain social security and guaranties from the state. Indeed, in this light, Alexander specifically denies the idea that contracts are impersonal and a sign of distrust. In the case of Lithuania, most people would make sure that they had papers for employment outside the agricultural sphere and/or that they had papers for leasing or renting agreements with the state. With institutions or people who per se were seen as distant and impersonal, the papers provided a guarantee, just as argued by Alexander and Heintz. The problem that emerged at the meeting was that the lawyer advocated the importance of having contracts with "each other." In other words, he wanted contracts to enter the personal sphere. It was under such circumstances that the people attending the meeting found it difficult to envision the use of contracts.

As I noticed during my fieldwork, exchanges and cooperation and acquaintances were important for the household economy of the small farms. These normative networks, which sustain the families, are closely linked with resources, both material and immaterial. Resources and social capital within the family have a strong impact on the specific economic and social strategies employed in everyday life and how and to what extent other households are included as an extra resource. If a household has many internal resources, the surrounding society loses its value as a contributor to the farm economy, whereas the logic is the opposite if the household has few internal resources, which is the case for many, if not most, of the small-scale farms run by aging people. In the latter case, it means that the surrounding society contributes to the household through a range of favors and exchanges. However, the economic function of these reciprocal relationships is not to be talked about. Indeed, as Bourdieu argues in his theory about an all-embracing economic model, the hidden aspect of such economy exchanges is an important part of their function. Such favors function through a noneconomic discourse, as they necessarily have to be understood as favors and social obligations, and not in terms of their economic value. By pointing to community exchange, the economic aspect is repressed and, thus, "misrecognized." Thereby, the economy, without being understood as an economy, becomes a part of the social and economic relations and obliges all people involved (Bourdieu [1977] 2000, 171). During Soviet times, people made use of such bonds to cope with shortages and supply special goods (see Wedel 1991; Ledeneva 1998; Haukanes and Pine 2005). However, in light of the unstable years after independence, the importance of such networks was reinforced in order to cope with new forms of shortages of machinery, workforce and money and an abrupt change in institutional provisions. Due to repeated disappointments in the years after independence, people had more trust in personal networks than in institutional support, since they felt more in control of arrangements, which they themselves had evoked through their know-how and habitual understanding of the local environment (for comparison, see Brandtstädter 2003). As the lawyer suggested that such models of mutual assistance should be legalized with a contract, it would be clear that the economic aspect of the exchanges would be made visible and thus work against the necessity of the misrecognition of favors. In this context, the contracts for rent or lease of land are not perceived as a social guarantee, as it would cut into kinship or friendship relations. Rather, evoking a contract would arouse distrust, not only in relation to your neighbors, but also to your family.

At the meeting in Graižiūnai, the contract thus became a point of conflict and misunderstandings, as the lawyer applied a set of reasons that made the use of contracts sensible and logical. The farmers, on their side, applying their practical reality to contracts, found it to be illogical and possibly even offensive towards friends and neighbors. In this sense, the disagreement about contracts illustrates the general problem of the meeting, namely, that the lawyer and the farmers reasoned and talked from different perspectives and worldviews, which were incompatible with each other (see also Long [1977] 1982).

Meeting in Marijampolė

The second case study is from my other field site in Marijampolė, where monthly meetings are held for farmers at the municipal administration. At these meetings, the latest update about agriculture and directions from the EU are conveyed to the farmers. It is the local agricultural advisor who leads these meetings, supplemented by spokespeople from various companies and organizations who had offers, suggestions or advice to give to the farmers. Such a meeting was held in December 2006. It had been announced in the newspapers that this meeting would contribute information about laws that would take effect in January 2007. The subjects to be addressed were new regulations for milk and the registration of sales of farm products.

The meeting room is filled with people on this cold December day. The meeting has been advertised in the newspapers as important information will be given before the New Year. People are sneezing and blowing their noses because of the cold weather and a slight smell of stables hangs over the room. I sit next to a woman from Straigiai, a woman in her early 50s, named Vilma. She pulls my sleeve and whispers to me, "Look around and see, all the people here are old; here you have your Lithuanian farmers."

A man in his late 50s from the agricultural department of the municipality starts the meeting with an introduction of the new rules for milk quotas. He barely gets to speak for more than a couple of minutes before Vilma raises her voice and shouts out loudly, "Why do we need a new system, why do we need new papers? Nothing is going to change anyway!" People around her mumble supportively. "That is right, nothing is going to change!" "What good does it do us with more paperwork?" "Yeah, nothing will be better anyway!"

The speaker raises his voice and repeats that the papers have to be filled according to EU legislation. There can be no discussion about it. "It is the same with corn," he continues. "Corn has to be registered before it can be sold. It has to be marked with your name, address and registration number. It will be controlled, so you cannot get around it." A man shouts from one of the back seats, "Then we just sell it from the farm." Again people start to mumble. A woman takes a counterpoint to the one raised by the man. "But that is the problem; people sell from their homes, or in front of the market.[9] Why should we register and pay, when others sell illegally in front of the market hall? People do not buy from the one who has the papers; they buy from the one who sells cheaply. What kind of order is that?" Voices are raised again. The speaker chooses to shout in the microphone to be heard. People fall silent. "You have to address that to the administration of the market hall. They have to handle it. I am not saying that what is happening is good, but you must declare and register your products anyway."

The speaker gets back to the milk quotas and says that the quota system is to be changed, as the old system functioned too poorly. They need to renew their quotas and new papers are to be filled before the New Year. The payment and registration will differ. People mumble and talk with dissatisfaction. "According to the EU," the speaker says in a defensive manner, but he is barely heard. Some shout, others laugh as if it was a joke, "The EU, always the EU!" "Of course, the EU again." Vilma is actively taking part, shouting or loudly discussing with the people around us.

---

9 As described in Chapter 5, there are divisions of the marketplace: inside the market hall where people whose products have been approved by the authorities are located, and outside the territory of the market where people sell their uncontrolled products illegally.

The speaker ends his talk and makes room for a woman who will inform about the rules for the registration of animals. She quickly mentions the procedure and the costs for it. People constantly talk with each other or voice frustrated outbursts. "They give with one hand and take with the other!" "Do you think we can afford to pay more?" "It is much too expensive!" Every comment is followed by applause and supportive mumbling from the rest of the audience. "I am only here to tell you how things have to be," the woman says. "I am only here to inform you about the rules." Her voice drowns in noise again. A few people leave the room.

The first speaker now gets back up, as one of the managing directors from ARVI Fertis – a branch of the ARVI company, specializing in pesticide production – shows up with a few employees. He is dressed in a suit and a long dark coat, and is standing against the wall with his people, listening without interrupting. When the speaker notices the managing director, he nods in his direction. He then interrupts his talk for a moment, and looks directly at the managing director. "It is a shame the prices for pesticides are so high," he says and continues, "this makes the production costs high, but still the Lithuanian farmers have to sell cheaply." The managing director replies, "ARVI always sells cheaply." The speaker chuckles and shakes his head in disagreement, supported by applauding comments from the audience in the room. "You should stick to the agenda of the meeting, instead of discussing ARVI's business," the managing director says loudly. He decides to leave the room together with his employees. People mumble and concentrate on the speaker up front again. It is almost noon, and the speaker cuts the meeting short, knowing that people have cows to attend to.

Situational Alliances and Interface Encounters

Vilma was normally not interested in leaving her farmhouse, nor did she fancy attending meetings or discussions. It was not because she did not care about agricultural issues, but these topics were always discussed with her sister over a cup of hot coffee in her small and cozy kitchen. This time, however, the issue of the milk quotas had been so relevant for her that she had decided to go to the city to hear more about it. She was one of two people from Straigiai who had attended the meeting; the other was the chairman of the local agricultural cooperative in the village. Vilma did not know most of the other farmers who were present, but the situation in itself created a bond between them, a bond Vilma used well. Not only was she shouting her dissatisfaction out loudly, knowing that she would be applauded by others, she also quickly engaged in small talk with the women around us in order to share her frustration and complaints with them. I do not recall ever having seen her so upset, or having seen her so engaged. The following day, I decided to visit her, eager to discuss the events of the previous day and to hear her opinion about it all. Vilma, however, had already lost interest in the meeting and would rather talk about her daughter's problems in school and my prospects of getting married to a local. Why had her interest evaporated so quickly?

At the meeting in Marijampolė, the farmers had all been in the same boat, as they were all subject to the same external regulations. Hence, they created a certain kind of rhetoric, which reflected a specific angle of their points of view; they agreed to disagree with the speaker up front, applying a "kill-the-messenger" logic. Extra paperwork is never good news, a reason why the farmers responded with negative outburst. In this way, the audience shaped its position in opposition to the speaker (the system) and created internal solidarity. This did not mean that they generally agreed with each other, which became obvious as the subject of illegal sale was raised; rather, the solidarity was situational and dismantled quickly after the meeting.

Although people attending the meeting likewise acknowledged the unspecified body of EU decisions makers as being responsible in this matter, as was shown by their outbursts, they still took their anger out on the local state representatives, as they embodied the closest link to the decision-making institution. The position as expressed in this interface was formed from the very beginning of the meeting, as the speaker hardly had started to talk before Vilma interrupted him, forming a counter position through the generalized statement that "nothing is going to change." She did not clarify what should change, nor in which ways it should change. Still, the rather simple rhetoric was effective in the larger setting as it was a statement everybody in the room could agree on due to its lack of context and, one could say, even content.

How quickly interfaces can be created and then dismantled became clear when the managing director from ARVI arrived. Both the speaker and the audience created a short alliance against him as a representative of the world of business and commerce, making him responsible for the high prices of the pesticides. As the managing director lived with his family in Straigiai and was one of my informants, I knew very well – as did the speaker who confronted him – that he was not the person responsible for the pesticide prices. What was intriguing about the short disruption of the meeting was that the speaker had put the managing director in the same position as he himself had been put in by the farmers: a (responsible) representative for another entity whose actions he was to account for. In this, he had a common cause with the participants and a short break from the farmers' attacks, as they agreed to be in opposition to ARVI. When the managing director left the room, the brief interface of opposition against the world of commerce was dismantled and people got back to the previous division of the room: farmers opposing state representatives.

As I went to visit Vilma the next day, I had hoped to engage in an interesting talk about the meeting, experiencing the same level of interest and engagement from her side as during the meeting. This, however, did not happen. She shrugged and said that she had better get the new papers for the quota, since there apparently was no way around it, and then she turned to other topics. I believe she already knew during the meeting that she needed to fill the new papers if she wanted to keep her quota, but the meeting still served as an opportunity to express her dissatisfaction with the system.

Multiple Faces on the Encounter

Although I apply the notion of interface encounters as a tool to comprehend the dynamics enacted at the meetings in Graižiūnai and Marijampolė, I want to stress that we do not speak about people meeting face to face on an even level. From the outset, the state representatives have the juridical power behind them and are backed up by the law and the EU governing institutions, while the farmers have no such power behind them at the meetings (although they might change the rules when applying them to their farm business). This does not mean that the state representatives have an easy task during the meetings, as they have no choice but to act the part of the institutional authority.

Here we must take into consideration the notion of multiple faces on the encounter. People who form alliances may have contradicting views, and state representatives can be pushed to play a role they might be uncomfortable with. Indeed, the obligation from the official side, such as conveying the latest information, might force people to take a position that contrasts their personal points of view. The farmers might well know that their mode of production is incompatible with EU requirements, and in this sense they might understand very well the difficult position of the state representatives, as they have to convey information the addressees almost certainly dislike and even disregard. However, at the very encounter, such mutual understandings are not applied.

As I frequently participated in such meetings and paid attention to the many tensions between farmers and state representatives, I noticed that there were yet other underlying conflicting points in the meetings that were visible and apparent, yet never addressed directly in public. I referred to these as "paradoxes of aging." The first paradox was expressed in how the older farmers attended meetings meant for another target group. In both meetings, the majority of the farmers had been close to or above the age of retirement. This had also been explicitly pointed out to me in both meetings, first by the man who passed me in Graižiūnai, stressing that this information was for the young people only, and by Vilma in Marijampolė, who had asked me to pay attention to the fact that all the participants were old. "Here you have your Lithuanian farmers," she said to me. The question remains why it was always the older farmers who attended the meetings even though older people were not seen as the target group for modernization programs? Part of the answer was that they had been entitled to the land. At the time of independence, these people were in their 30s, 40s, 50s and even 60s. At the time of my fieldwork, about seventeen years had passed and those who were in their 30s at the time of independence were now in their 50s and the other age groups in their 60s, 70s or 80s, if they had not died in the meantime. This brings local state representatives a specific dilemma; to address legal changes to the "wrong" target group.

This dilemma is not only recognized by the decision makers and local state representatives, it is also seen as an obstacle for the aging farmers, who find that their way of farming does not correspond with the EU regulations and most likely never will. Some of the aging farmers still reluctantly go to the meetings to keep themselves informed on the situation, especially if issues are addressed that have direct relevance for their farms. The young farmers in the two regions of my research, however, hardly ever attend such meetings, despite the fact that they constitute the target group. As I asked around among younger farmers why they did not attend such meetings, the answer I got was that the information conveyed at such meetings is of no importance to them. They need more specific advice than is given in such general meetings. Larger-scale farmers, and thus often younger farmers, tend to solve their problems through individual consultations with the agricultural advisors where they would get better advice on how to run their farms. The result is that meetings arranged for people who want to and have the resources to implement EU rules and regulations are dominated by aging people who have neither the intention nor the capability of doing so.

The second paradox of aging comes about because the bureaucrats and politicians in charge of implementing EU rules and regulations are the same age group as the farmers who are encouraged to retire. This poses two interrelated problems. First, contrary to the aging farmers who are viewed as "too old" for modernization, the aging politicians have to show that they are still capable of responding to the changes. They now fight for their political prime, promoting their age not as an obstacle but as an advantage (experience). While one could argue that politics and farming are incompatible businesses and that this comparison is therefore inapplicable, the crucial point lies in the argumentation behind the opposing age-logics. This leads me to the second problem: Retiring the older farmers is, again, a way to combat Soviet practices and thinking. Thus, for the politicians it becomes a question of "overcoming the past." By this I mean that they have to downplay their previous political attachment to the communist party and reinvent their image as devoted EUropeans.

I was alerted to this complex situation of state representatives and politicians renewing their political life while still relying on Soviet administrative patterns as I conducted fieldwork among people from the Farmers' Party, Valstiečių

Sąjunga, in Graižiūnai. In the case of the *valstiečiai*,[10] the past is rejected through an embracement of a nostalgic recreation of the pre-Soviet peasant, within their own perception of modernity, where the EU is fit into already existing structures of governance. In this way, they aim partly at communicating a more conservative equilibrium while still showing that they are capable of responding to the present circumstances. This is all done in a combination of private goals through public means, which in itself is a continuation of their work strategies from the previous regime (see Bridger and Pine 1998; Ledeneva 1998; Vonderau 2007). It is exactly in the interplay between past and present, between formal law and local interpretations, that we are able to see how uniform regulations are molded by local environments and thus turn into site-specific entities.

Politics and Populism

Valstiečių Sąjunga celebrated their annual meeting in late Summer 2007. All regional branches had met and the day had been spent with music, dancing and drinking. I had participated as a guest of the branch of Graižiūnai. We were now on the way home in the bus, people were still singing and drinking, and comments about sex and women were loudly passed around by the men. An older man who had been singing along with the folk songs suddenly rose from his seat and shouted to the head of the Valstiečių Sąjunga that he was unhappy about the party's political achievements lately. He said that they needed to work harder and be more focused. No one responded to his outburst, except with laughter. His wife sitting next to him tried to pull him back into his seat and to silence him, but he was not so easily deterred and kept on talking. The wife, now clearly embarrassed, started to pull him by his ear. The man kept talking while pushing his wife away. Finally his wife pulled him back in the seat, pressed her hand over his mouth while beating him hard and firm with an umbrella. The scenario made everyone laugh. The man, now fully occupied by his wife's attacks, was finally silenced and the music and drinking continued as before. As we got off the bus, the man's wife approached the wife of the head of the party, deeply apologetic on behalf of her husband. She hoped that no offense was taken and that this episode would not be remembered in the future. The other woman responded that there would be no further talk about the little incident.[11]

---

10 People from Valstiečių Sąjunga referred to themselves as such due to their political belonging. It is an emic concept. *Valstietis* (sing.)/*valstiečiai* (pl.) means farmer/farmers, a person/persons working the land.
11 Based on my field notes; 14 July 2007.

It appeared strange to me that it had been perceived as embarrassing that the man had questioned the political achievements of the party. It appeared strange that it was necessary to apologize when a man spoke about politics in the aftermath of a political meeting. As a matter of fact, the only words said about politics the entire day came from him. I would say that what had been embarrassing that day was the middle-aged men slapping the younger women on their behinds at every given opportunity. Clearly, I was wrong.

This incident provides some hints as to how the local politicians of the Valstiečių Sąjunga do politics in a rural town in the outskirts of Lithuania. In an era when most Lithuanians are disappointed with politicians and state institutions, the *valstiečiai* in my field site have chosen to promote their party through populism and the establishment of a feel-good environment for the voters. In order to strengthen the official political power, the politicians continuously work informally in a constant shift between different legal systems. This is in itself not remarkable, as it does not differ from the making of any other political party or system. However, in the case of the Valstiečių Sąjunga, the populist approach is used to cover up a problematic and repressed (Soviet) past, which helped them get their present positions, while they seek rescue in two, for them, "safe" time periods: a romanticized "authentic" pre-Soviet peasant past, and the modern era of EU membership.

The Valstiečių Sąjunga – History and Conceptualization

The Valstiečių Sąjunga was founded with this name in 1905, sponsored by the Lithuanian Democratic Party. In 1920 it became an independent party, and two years later the name was changed to Lietuvos Valstiečių Liaudininkų Sąjunga (Lithuanian Peasant Popular Union). During the Soviet occupation of Lithuania, the party was banned, but continued to exist in exile and was finally revived in 1990, this time as a purely agrarian party.

The Valstiečių Sąjunga is particularly devoted to the rural population and favors the less privileged groups in society as opposed to the elites. On the official website, it is explained that concerning economic policy, it is a central party, but it does at the same time favor many conservative values in terms of family and Christian morality.[12] The party remains strongly represented in municipalities in Lithuania, mainly in the poorer rural regions, a feature that bears witness to effective local policies. The trademark of the party remains the focus on the countryside and the development of the rural areas, though details about how this development should be achieved are not to be found in the official and available party information.[13]

---

12 The homepage of Lietuvos Valstiečių Liaudininkų Sąjunga: http://www.lvls.lt/lt/index. php?option=com_xmap&Itemid=36 (accessed 18 March 2012).
13 See the leaflet "Lietuvos Valstiečių Sąjunga – Lietuvos Ateičiai," LVLS, Vilnius, 2007.

The vague political agenda responds well to the current times, when many Lithuanians claim that it is hard to tell the difference between the political parties in Lithuania. As is shown by Klumbytė in her work about postsocialist Lithuania, it is a common understanding among people that politicians by definition are corrupt and untrustworthy, just as their way to power has been based on their connections and ability to make use of resources and opportunities (Klumbytė 2010). Throughout the 1990s, Lithuania had a very unstable voting climate, as Lithuanian voters showed their disapproval with the pace of development by consistently changing the parliament. Many finally came to terms with their disappointments by not voting at all, as a way to show their dissatisfaction with the state institutions and the politicians. Furthermore, it was a way to express the lack of hope for a better future. If people voted, they preferred not to vote for specific parties, but to vote for individuals whom they trusted or knew outside their political position.

Political Front Figures

Alvydas is such a front person for the Valstiečių Sąjunga in Graižiūnai. Alvydas is an easygoing man who likes to dress sloppily in big sweaters and old pants and always claims that he feels much better in rubber boots than any other footwear. He is a tall and big man in his early 50s, with a strong voice and an impressive vocabulary including many words that I, during my time in Lithuania, had been instructed never to say in public. He told me that he spoke "*liaudiškai.*"[14] However, a friend of mine from Vilnius who came to visit me during my fieldwork, pointed out to me that Alvydas actually spoke Russian, as almost all swearwords in Lithuanian have Russian origin. Because of his father's high position in the previous system, Alvydas was granted a high position at a young age, and many aging people know him today as their former chairman at a collective farm.

During Soviet times, he got his education as an agronomist and later on worked as chairman of one of the collective farms in the region. He has been working as an agricultural advisor in the years after independence and is also the local head of the Lithuanian Farmers' Union, (Lietuvos Ūkininkų Sąjunga, LŪS). It is mainly through this position that he remained known in the area, because he always was central when it came to individual farms (through his position as agricultural advisor) and activities and meetings organized for farmers (through his position as the head of LŪS.) One of his close friends is Gytis, a man in his mid-60s who also worked as the chairman of a collective farm during Soviet times and after independence became the front figure of the regional branch of the party. He was

---

14 To speak *liaudiškai* is in this context to speak like the "common man," with no censorship or modification of the language.

once mayor of the town but then lost an election, and his post was later taken over by Alvydas. Gytis is now merely taking care of practical and organizational matters for the party. Other prominent figures in the local branch are the director of the technical school in the neighboring town, the local forester who was also head of the local riding club, several prominent farmers and one of the local businessmen. Except the head of the riding club, a man in his late 30s, all other core members are in their 50s or 60s, and all of them have had higher positions in Soviet times and are known to have benefited from such positions and through their network at the time of independence. Their current practice is to downplay their past and thus, "change their political shirts," as one farmer explained it to me.

During my research, I became aware of how past practices were mobilized in order to satisfy the current needs of their voters. The immediate benefits of staying close to politicians from this party thereby overshadowed their past. At the time I got to know Alvydas, he and the other *valstiečiai* were running the campaigns for the local elections, which would take place later that year. Alvydas and his crowd were out in public advertising for the party, not so much through political speeches but through feasts, performances, parties and heavy drinking with their possible voters. They had a successful election that made Alvydas the new vice mayor. This was done in cooperation with Tėvynės Sąjunga, whose front figure became the new mayor.

Working Off-State to Achieve Goals On-State

The work carried out in the name of the Valstiečių Sąjunga required constantly being among people. It was what I, with reference to F. and K. von Benda-Beckmann (2007), call Off-State activities, where they use their official position within the municipal administration (On-State) to achieve goals outside the municipal administration, which they again use to strengthen their position within the municipality (Off-State). Advice, latest news and developments help in moving swiftly through the system, not to mention possibilities for employment; these were all achievable if you stayed close to the *valstiečiai*. It was the basic line for the party members that bureaucratic work will not get you anywhere. Things had to be done in a friendly manner, as they say (*draugiškai*). They worked hard to personalize official connections in order to be able to refrain from formality (Ledeneva 1998). The *valstiečiai* were working on fulfilling expectations of their immediate surroundings with interpersonal pleasing of the voters, and thus submitted to norms outside the state. These norms were just as crucial and important for the continued existence of the Valstiečių Sąjunga as the official rules were. The network did not only include villagers, it also comprised more prominent political figures in Vilnius and through their access to higher national political figures they obtained personal privileges or privileges for their work.

The brand new car for the local branch of the Lithuanian Farmer's Union, with the mark Lietuvos Ūkininkų Sąjunga is but one example of this. During my second visit to Graižiūnai I learned that they had been without an official car for the Farmers' Union for a long time and they found this to be a representational problem. Finally, Alvydas decided to leave for the capital Vilnius with a large number of bottles of homemade vodka (*samagonas*). He laughed heartily as he said that it had not taken much time after the trip before the branch of the Farmers' Union had been granted this new car to represent them. Alvydas, however, seemed to use it as much for his personal needs as for his official needs, so whose car it actually was remained an unanswered question. This hardly differed from the past, when someone with a good understanding of the Soviet economical system channeled public goods to private use, either for their own gain or by giving it to people in their network, who again could then contribute back with other favors, a phenomenon known as "blat" (Lt. *blatas*) (Ledeneva 1998). Just as they previously channeled resources from the Soviet system (due to their central positions), they now channel resources (funds) from the EU in the same spirit.

People from the surrounding villages often remarked to me that Valstiečių Sąjunga "does something for the farmers," even though they could not respond to any questions about the actual political line of the party. As it appeared there were official political strategies, aging or known manipulation of property rights after the regained independence, unimportant in comparison to the fact that the politicians were reachable, easygoing and able to connect to their voters. That the party worked in favor of their interests was thus not based on a specific political program, but on personal experiences with the *valstiečiai*. Since most voters were farmers, many knew Alvydas through his position as agricultural advisor, where he helped people out with matters related to their farms. It was mostly large-scale farmers who were in touch with him, but he was not formal in his relations with people or with his willingness to give advice. Either people would come to his office or they would call him directly on his phone. In the context of friendly favors, the EU was more than welcome. The EU meant extra resources and funds for the farmers. It was also perceived as being modern and Western European and, most importantly, a contrast to the Soviet past they so strongly rejected in their daily talk.

The idea of advancing deals by using a network and connections became a strong card in relation to the voters. The *valstiečiai* incorporated new funds and possibilities into their world, and they also willingly helped the farmers to gain more information about access to different funds from the EU. It was no secret that having close relationships with Alvydas was an advantage when applying for EU funds, which were regionally distributed and locally administrated. The possibilities coming from the EU were incorporated into the already existing framework and used according to existing structures and relations. While this functioned well in principle, it contradicted the party members' strong rejection of the Soviet system and their embracement of the EU, as this was incompatible with their consistently Soviet ways of doing politics. In the aftermath of the election, for example, I once mentioned to Alvydas that I heard people talk about the fact that the son of the director of the Technical School suddenly had moved to a central post in the municipal administration, and that this had happened despite the fact that he was only in his 20s with basically no political experience. I asked, maybe a bit too bluntly, if this had anything to do with the friendship between Alvydas and the director of the Technical School, the father of the young man. Alvydas raised his voice so loud that my ears almost started whining and he said:

> This young man has solely been chosen due to his outstanding career and his political beliefs. If this would have anything to do with his father, he would have been employed at the Technical School, not at the municipal administration![15]

Romanticized Images of Peasant life

The *valstiečiai* were visible in the public space of the town. They held many activities for their members and took part in every town festival or arrangement for the town's denizens. Their personal battle against their past had systematically been embedded in such festivities, as they referred back to – for them – a safe time period. The *valstiečiai* re-created a romanticized picture of the pre-Soviet peasant past and inserted it into a modern society by use of easily recognizable symbols such as folk songs, traditional regional food and folk clothes. The horse plays an important role for the *valstiečiai* as a symbol of traditional agriculture. In any celebration, they will arrive with horses, both riding horses and working horses that are used partly as a show, partly to entertain the members with riding tours or tours in horse wagons. The *valstiečiai* arrange annual plowing competitions in order to show that they have not lost the old ways of working the land. Furthermore, risky performances on horseback are part of their repertoire, performances that always attract a lot of attention from the audience and communicate an image of the *valstiečiai* as daring cowboys. Other attributes are clothes – often folk clothes or cowboy-look-alike clothes – that underline tradition-rooted Lithuanianness vis-à-vis a fun, daring and very masculine image.

In the aftermath of a celebration, the inner core of the Valstiečių Sąjunga will gather and drive away, preferably in horse wagons. Then the second part of the event follows, which normally takes place in a remote forest, where the party members engage in another set of rules: male-bond and "let go." The second

---

15 From my field notes, March 2007; my translation from Lithuanian.

part is a creation of a feel-good environment where alcohol, music, dancing and sexual interaction take place. Often they do not bring their wives along; instead they cherish female company, usually 15–20 years younger than themselves. Certain people in the core group are known for having multiple such young female relations from all over the region. Even though some of the members had relations with prostitutes, the women who attended the parties were often plain girls from the region, women the *valstiečiai* met during festivals and celebrations and efficiently impressed on horseback and charmed with their fun and easygoing behavior. One of my informants from a village close to Graižiūnai, with insider knowledge about the Lithuanian mafia, made me aware of the fact that the pattern with women worked in identical ways in political circles and in the circles of organized crime; local women (not prostitutes) were attracted to the seemingly easy and fun life of the group of men, their power positions and the men's generosity (big parties, vodka, cigarettes, good food and fancy cars). Thus, in both cases, identical items and symbols were made use of in order to attract female company.

Despite the celebrations in the forests being seemingly carefree, they are not devoid of politics. On the contrary, it is in the forest that more informal political agreements are made and bonding between the core members is reinforced. While I often had difficulties finding Alvydas in his office or at formal meetings, I consistently found him engaged in political debates and agreements while in the forest. If any political meetings were held, the doors were closed and no one allowed entrance except from the core members of the party.

Bridging between the Pre-Soviet Past and the EU-Present

If we recall Giordano's and Kostova's analysis of the "actualized history," they underlined that after the Soviet breakup, new history-making was characterized by a "reversibility of events." Thereby, the Soviet past was done away with, while the future was built upon the re-creation of the pre-Soviet past. As is seen through the case study of the Valstiečių Sąjunga, this not only relates to the re-creation of the country's history, but likewise to personal life stories. Thus, through the exercise of "overcoming the past," the politicians do away with their previous Soviet attachments and "reinvent" themselves both as "traditional" Lithuanians attached to the soil of the fatherland and as "new European citizens." Thus, just as new history is written, new identities are created. In this context, we can furthermore recall Zinoviev's descriptions of the Soviet man, the *Homosos*, who masters to perfection the ability of changing opinion and belief in order to suit the given circumstances (Zinoviev [1982] 1985). Thus, through the rejection of the Soviet system, we witness continuous traces of it.

The central position of Alvydas and his crowd gave them space for more independent actions, actions that most likely would not have been tolerated if the *valstiečiai* had had a less significant position. Being in the center of the network and with access to political privileges, they created their own laws for behavior. The local forester, a core member of the party, kept a wild boar as a "pet," although it was against the laws for public safety. The boar escaped one day and injured an innocent man and it was put down by a local farmer. Although charges were pressed against the forester, and although the story attracted much attention in the newspapers, the case was shortly after dropped for reasons no one could explain. This was only one example out of several where the *valstiečiai* were directly breaking the law or stretching the bounds for "moral" behavior. Going to the forest with women was another public secret that was tolerated more or less by the community (though most likely not by the their wives, if they knew about it). The *valstiečiai* could also eat in the local restaurant and leave without paying by giving the impression that the payment would return at a later time. But, as I was told, it seldom did. That they were drinking at work and driving drunk was another public secret. Due to their strong position in the area and their good relations with people, they managed to maintain such space for negotiation.

Figure 3.1. Horses having a short break at a celebration for the Valstiečių Sąjunga. Lithuania 2007. © Harboe Knudsen.

However, it should be mentioned that there were limits. In 2010 I learned that the local forester (the one who had kept a wild boar as a pet) had been dismissed from his work after he three times had caused car accidents with the official car owned by the municipality. In all three incidents he had been drunk. Added to this, there had been drunk-riding accidents, when he went horse riding under the influence and put other people in danger.

The attempt to unite people in a feeling of comradeship and through male bonding is a strong way to promote the party. The populist agenda, which favors the common man and the deprived part of the population, is advanced through the activities, all embedded in a frame of good (Soviet) comradeship – a feature that was underlined by Alvydas' persistent way of addressing people as "comrade" (*draugas* when addressing a man, *draugė* when addressing a woman). Clearly, it also has advantages for the farmers; however, these advantages may not necessarily be reached through formal bureaucratic work but through informal work. The politicians reach many people and embrace them in their wide and rich network. To be "in" is therefore a matter of protection, benefits and networking, but it is also a matter of leading a fun life in which it is accepted to undo the structures of everyday life and let loose, both with the bottle and with women. Thus, the more pragmatic rules of the party flourish through what is effective, which in this respect, may very well be throwing a big party for the voters and disregarding certain "moral" standards.

Their capability of making use of the local rural community worked well in their favor, as Alvydas was elected the new vice mayor and the party moved into a more central political position. In present-day Lithuania, where many people are reluctant to vote because of a general disappointment with politicians, the *valstiečiai* have, stemming from a "gut feeling" about the situation, aim first and foremost at creating an atmosphere of comradeship. In this way they respond to the recent voting climate in Lithuania, where personalities and not politics attract votes. More important than the apparent misfit between their own age and the ideas of generational change is their ability to create a secure and familiar environment for people who vote for them.

It is in the creation of the feel-good environment that we find the reason for the reactions to the old man's outburst in the bus. Most laughed at him, others ignored him, and the wife was deeply embarrassed. By questioning actual political achievements, he went against the light atmosphere that characterizes the *valstiečiai*'s celebrations. Not only did he speak about politics, he was also critical toward the actual political agenda. Thus, he touched a taboo, which made his wife apologize on his behalf afterward. This is not to argue that the politicians do not work to achieve certain goals, but these goals are never addressed directly in public. Rather, political deals are made under more informal circumstances. By appearing young, masculine and virile, the aging politicians wish to show that despite their age and despite their past in the Soviet Union, they are still capable of responding to the present EU environment.

Entering New Dilemmas On-State

Intriguing in the case of the Valstiečių Sąjunga is that the tactics that made the party achieve power in the first place were a hindrance for the politicians when they got into power. When Alvydas was elected vice mayor, his new position came with a number of new duties. He had to keep office hours and represent the municipality on various occasions. The new position increased his formal activities and limited the time he had for bonding with the members. More than that, his overall appearance needed to be changed. He was expected to dress formally in suits and ties and he got his own private driver. This worked against the image he wished to present, namely being "one of the people."

However, it is to be assumed that many informal activities continued to function after the election. In April 2009 Alvydas came into the media's spotlight in a case about misuse of EU funding for agriculture. The normal procedure for controlling the regions' exact use of EU funding is to check the budgets every third year. However, in 2009 they made an exception and controlled the use of money for the second year in a row. It was discovered that the use of around 100,000 litas (28,962 euros) given to agricultural development in the region of Graižiūnai could not be accounted for. Part of this money had been given to farmers and agricultural companies who had not used the money for the purposes they had originally applied for. A part of the money had been given to the local horse-riding club, whose chairman was one of the important members in Valstiečių Sąjunga. Other parts of the money had been given to the organization of LŪS for various projects. It was revealed that LŪS and the riding school had set the prices for various projects much higher than they actually were, and thus had received more money than they had been entitled to. In the online version of the newspaper *Lietuvos Rytas* (Lithuania's Morning), the journalist reporting from Graižiūnai called it a public secret that much of this money had been used for festivities, food, and drinks, and in part had been channeled to individuals. Alvydas was called upon to make a statement and he admitted that part of the money had not been used according to the regulations, but when confronted with the camera, he would not name any responsible persons in the case.[16] Afterward, the case was transferred to the regional capital of Alytus in order to conduct further investigations.

---

16 The exact references to the newspaper articles and the internet video about this case cannot be given, as it would then be clear which region I had been doing research in and which people I had been in touch with during the fieldwork.

The Local EUs

The different interfaces discussed in this chapter mirror the often contradictory ways in which Euro-building is communicated to the rural citizens. One can only imagine how these forms of communicating the EU may be perceived by the farmer who one day attends a meeting where the strict EU rules are emphasized and the next day drinks and participates in extramarital activities in the forest in the company of politicians doing the same, acknowledging that the party is financed by EU money. Behind these gaps in procedure lies my argument that it becomes necessary to point to the multiple faces that such encounters between state representatives and farmers can entail. And I could add that all of the ways in which new regulations are communicated, implemented, changed or channeled influence perceptions of the EU among rural citizens. The EU is not only deriving from remote decision-making institutions in Brussels or Strasbourg, but actively reproduced on an everyday level in even the smallest communities. In daily situations, state representatives have to perform the authority of the EU for the citizens. However, more than acting "on behalf" of the EU, state representatives are often subjected at the same time to norms and expectations deriving from the previous socialist system, in which bureaucracy had coexisted and overlapped with personal networks in an "economy of favors," to paraphrase Ledeneva (1998). This dual aspect affecting legitimacy and personal positions brings in more complex aspects of communicating the EU as new member countries are still driven by premises from their (past) socialist systems (see also Wedel 1992; Bridger and Pine 1998; Ledeneva 1998, 2006; Verdery 2002a, 2003). The prevailing interplay between past and present means that the initial aim of submitting new member states to Europe-building, the idea that the same laws, standards and bureaucratic procedures should be alike in all EU states is thus most likely to end up as a plurality of locally negotiated EUs.

CHAPTER 4

Effects of and Responses to the EU Programs in the Countryside

In the late summer of 2007 I got a lift to town with Gytis, the right hand of the vice mayor of Graižiūnai. He was also the previous chairman of the collective farm in Bilvytis and known as a sensible man. As Gytis and I drove out of the village of Bilvytis, we passed an older woman. She was wrapped in layers of clothes on the chilly morning, bandages on her legs and a scarf around her grey hair. She was busy almost dragging a lazy cow to a new grazing place on a field next to the road. Gytis pulled the car over and stopped. "Look at her," he said to me. "This woman is in her 70s and she is probably a widow. She has this one cow, some hectares of land she can't cultivate, and maybe a kitchen garden. She is working many hours a day, milking the cow twice a day, feeding it, giving it water, moving it to a new spot. She also has to look after her vegetables and take care of her household. She cannot imagine her life differently; she cannot imagine selling the cow or leasing her land to a neighbor. She would never buy vegetables in the store. She has to have the cow and the land. She thinks the cow is an economic contribution, whereas in reality it eats up her pension. There are thousands like her in Lithuania, and they give us problems because they cannot change."[1]

Gytis did not actually know the specific situation of the woman, but he was most likely right. Her dragging a cow along was the typical picture of an older woman from the countryside living in the situation he had described. Whereas Gytis argued that the cow was an economic loss and the woman therefore acted unreasonable by not selling it, I wondered if the social and economic instability of the 1990s had caused distrust in money and reinforced the importance of the cow as a reliable contribution to the household economy. Although it may very well have been a loss, the feeling of insecurity that had haunted the rural population since the 1990s was not easy to dispense with. Gytis, however, was giving voice to the current official discourse, which pinpointed the main problem for the agricultural sector to

---

1 Based on my field notes, 9 July 2007; my translation from Lithuanian.

be the semi-subsistence farms with small-scale and unspecialized production run by older people, resulting in low-quality products, as people were unable to fulfill EU requirements due to their lack of education and lack of technology at their farms. These problems were primarily related to the dairy sector, which in 2004 had been dominated by pensioners with one or two cows. This group was one of the main targets, as the EU, in cooperation with the Lithuanian government, started the restructuring of the agricultural sector in the country.[2] The EU initiatives were to break what was seen as the vicious circle of inefficient agriculture. One of the most important steps was the introduction of the Early Retirement Program. This program supported farmers above 55 if they withdrew from agriculture, stopped commercial farming, leased or sold their land, leaving 1 hectare, and sold or butchered all cows except for one. If successful, this would release thousands of hectares of land that, together with the released milk quotas, should be transferred to young farmers. By supporting the young in enlarging their farms and paying the older to withdraw, the road to a restructuring of the agricultural sector was paved, rearranging land, cows and milk quotas among the rural citizens.

In the aftermath of the EU entrance, I noticed that although many changes had taken place as a result of EU programs and EU legislation, seemingly little had changed in the everyday life of the villages. It puzzled me. Why was everything so different and yet, just like before? As Gytis pointed out, there are still thousands of older people with a couple of cows farming a few hectares of land. But when people keep small plots of land and a single cow, is that a reluctance to change, as Gytis argued, or is it the exact result of the development plans for the countryside? It could very well be both, and this duality of the development was intriguing. I suggest two interlinked explanations for this. First, the EU supported a great number of people in decreasing the size of their farms and withdrawing from commercial production. Therefore, bigger farms increased in size, but many other farms decreased in size, leaving the rural areas still dominated by small semi-subsistence or subsistence farms. Second, even when facing all-encompassing changes, the rural denizens kept their everyday lives as unchanged as possible under the premises of the new circumstances, as formal law was adjusted to the routines and practicalities in their everyday lives. These dynamics between external influences and local incorporation reflect what I frame as "practical negotiations of the situation": EU legislation influences local life in the village, but will necessarily be adjusted to rural life and local practice and changed in the process, as people only can respond to change within the scope of options they have at hand. The farmers must consider the legal requirements against what is practically possible for them. In this way, the interaction between the external law and the local framework creates a new form of practice, a re-localized practice

---

2 Lithuanian Ministry of Agriculture, *Rural Development Plan 2004–2006 Lithuania*, 2004, 93–4.

influenced by the external system (Long 1996). This plays out in the ways various programs are used and interpreted and in the outcomes of the programs, which may be a far cry from what originally was aimed for.

The Armchair Farmers

In the months before the official entrance to the EU, Lithuanian farmers could apply for Direct Payments (DP) from the EU. DPs were part of the reform of the Common Agricultural Policy (CAP) in 2003. The World Trade Organization (WTO) had pointed out that the EU paid too much direct support to farmers, which was inconsistent with WTO regulations, to which the EU is subject. In order keep supporting the farmers and prevent further criticism from the WTO, the EU decoupled the payments in 2003. While EU farmers had received payments for land and crops in one package before, they would now receive a separate payment for land and separate payment for crops. By the end of the day, the direct support had not been decreased; it had only been channeled differently. The purpose of the law was to keep supporting European farmers and especially to give the farmers in new member countries a stable income for land and thereby strengthen their economies. Another important function of the decoupling was to invest in the preservation of land in the EU. It was made a special requirement that people only could receive the direct funding for the land they owned if they kept it in good agricultural condition.[3] Furthermore, it was a condition of the DP application that the farm was registered in the Farmers' Farm Register (Ūkininkų Ūkio Registras). By requiring registration of the farm, two goals were achieved at the same time: people gained access to EU support, and the government reached a better overview of farms and farm sizes in Lithuania. The size of the land plot of each applicant was measured with the help of a geographic database, which had been specially designed for the agricultural-based subsidies in the EU member states. The program, a land-parcel identification system (LPIS), made use of orthophotographic maps of the territory in order to calculate the surface area (for comparison with Romania, see Fox 2009). In order to receive DP, each applicant had to go to the nearest Office of Agricultural Affairs with their application form and the papers for his land. In the office, the applicant identified his land plot(s) on an aerial photo of the area. The officials could then cross out specific land plots in the database and ensure that the same land plot was not subsidized twice.

The biggest problem linked with DP was, ironically, that it became too popular in Lithuania. As DP were not attached to other EU programs, they could be obtained by basically anybody as long as they owned a piece of land. The decoupled direct support boomed after EU membership was obtained: in 2004

---

3   Information given from COPA/COGECA, Brussels, November 2007.

the registrations increased by 470 percent, and again by 130 percent in 2005.[4] Also, urban residents who owned a piece of land in the countryside had the opportunity to sign up as farmers. They would register as farmers and label their countryside plot "grassland" and thus receive a DP on equal basis with the rural citizens. The main reason for the urban residents to register was not the DP, but building permissions. Better-off urban residents who wished to build a summerhouse in the countryside often had difficulties obtaining building permissions due to strict regulations on nature preservation. They could only obtain the permission if they registered as farmers. Instead of oversight of farms and farming activities, the farm register became highly blurred and included almost every landowner in the country. The new generation of farmers was popularly referred to as "armchair farmers" (*fotelio ūkininkai*). By January 2007, 240,000 farms had been registered.[5] I overheard jokes and remarks such as "Today everybody is either a basketball player or a farmer," referring first to Lithuania's national sport and second, to the high frequency of "farmers." Or "Soon we will have 3.5 million farmers in Lithuania," which was the entire population.[6] The armchair farmers became a great concern for the Ministry of Agriculture and for the Lithuanian Farmers' Union (LŪS), not only because they blurred the registration, but also because they frequently broke the law by burning the grassland. This was their way of keeping the land "in good agricultural condition." Although the ministry was aware of the situation, there were insufficient resources for controlling every possible armchair farmer.

In 2007 the situation had gotten out of control, and the Lithuanian Farmers' Union and the Lithuanian government demanded new regulations for the registration of farms. It was no longer enough to own a piece of land; people were also to prove that they actively cultivated it and were residing in the rural areas all year round and not just in the summer. The case of farm registration exemplifies the adjustment to and the circumvention of the law. First, by how land measurements affected leasing agreements and created a new understanding of the land plots and their boundaries and second, by how the popularity of the DP caused an over-registration of farms, which urban citizens used as a shortcut to building permissions in the countryside.

The Return to the Mini-Mansholt

While the Farmers' Farm Register initially served to obtain an overview of Lithuanian farms, other programs were aimed at restructuring the agricultural sector. One of the main initiatives for restructuring was the Early Retirement

---

4 Lithuanian Institute for Agrarian Economics (2005).

5 Source: "Žinios apie tikruosius ūkininkus – miglotos." http://verslas.delfi.lt/archive/article.php?id=11734086 (accessed 17 March 2012).

6 From my field notes, November 2006; my translation from Lithuanian.

Program (henceforth, Early Retirement), which was specially designed for the older generations of landowners. The EU defined the problem in Lithuania as being related to the many aging farmers. In 2004 the numbers were as follows: 21 percent of the farmers were 50–59 years old, whereas 49 percent were 60 years or older. Only 14 percent were below 40, while 16 percent were 40–49 years old. The goal of Early Retirement was to reduce the current over-55 farmers from 60 percent to 45 percent. Thereby, 30,000 farms were planned to join the program for Early Retirement.[7] Support would be granted to farmers over 55 years of age who decided definitely to stop all commercial farming activity after having practiced farming for at least 10 years. According to official statements from the EU, the goal was to ensure that older farmers would have enough income to stop farming and could be replaced by younger farmers, that is, by assigning the land to the children or by reassigning land to nonagricultural uses (e.g., forestry).[8]

In reality, Early Retirement was an echo of an earlier EEC initiative, the Mansholt Plan.[9] This program had been introduced in 1967 by agricultural commissioner Sicco Mansholt as a way to solve the overproduction of milk in the EEC. The ideas of Mansholt were to introduce:

[1] Co-financed monetary incentives to encourage half of the farming population to leave the sector [...] by taking Early Retirement [...]and [2] Much of the land thereby released to be added to farms with approved development plans for expansion [...]. (Quoted from David R. Stead 2007, 41)

This meant a slaughter of three million dairy cows and an additional transfer of five million hectares of land from small farms to bigger farms. The program resulted in passionate protests of farmers in the EEC and Mansholt was nicknamed "The Peasant Killer" (in my opinion, "The Cow Killer" would have been more to the point). The program was eventually modified and took on a more moderate form called the "Mini-Mansholt" (Stead 2007). One of the surviving initiatives was Early Retirement, still promoted as a way to overcome demographic problems by removing small-scale dairy producers and by supporting economically viable farms. The approach to copy the Mini-Mansholt and implement ideas from the 1960s in the present-day restructuring of the agricultural sector in Eastern and Central Europe is pointing to the core of the EU policy for the enlargement: new member states have to integrate on the premises of existing policies based on

---

7 Lithuanian Ministry of Agriculture, *Rural Development Plan 2004–2006 Lithuania*, 2004, 126.
8 Source: "Lithuania's Rural Development Plan." http://europa.eu/rapid/pressReleases Action.do?reference=MEMO/07/369&format=HTML&aged=0&language=EN&guiLa nguage=en (accessed 17 March 2012).
9 European Economic Community, the forerunner of the EU.

Western European production. In the former EEC, the Mini-Mansholt had been an approach to solve overproduction; now it was used to cope with inefficiency in the agricultural sector caused by small-scale production.

The hope was that Early Retirement would help reduce the number of older farmers who had a milk quota for two to four cows. This group represented the majority of the Lithuanian dairy producers. Farmers who took part in the Early Retirement Program would be compensated for their milk quotas, which would be recirculated to younger farmers. The farmer who retired would have three months to butcher or sell his or her cows except one, which he was permitted to keep for household consumption. Furthermore, s/he was not to cultivate more than 1 hectare of land. Concerning the remaining land, s/he could either sell or lease it. S/he was to resign from the Farmers' Farm Register and stop all commercial farm activities. In other words, farmers were paid by the EU to take up subsistence farming. Farmers who applied in 2005 would receive compensation until they turned 75. Farmers who applied in 2006 only received compensation until they turned 70. The idea was to pay the full compensation of the milk quota the first year, and then slowly decrease the payments in the years up to 70 or 75. From 2004 to 2007, 21,500 farmers applied for and were granted Early Retirement[10] – 8,500 less than initially planned. The last call for applications was issued in 2007. Early Retirement compensation was paid in addition to the basic pension, since it – despite the wording – functioned as a compensation for milk quotas and not a pension in itself. Hence, farmers could receive Early Retirement (compensation for quota) and a basic pension at the same time. When they reached the age limit for receiving Early Retirement money, they would be left with the state pension, which varied depending on the years people had been employed. The problem of the many small-scale dairy producers had had a high priority. Early Retirement was, however, not the most efficient tool to solve it. As I learned from small-scale farmers in the two field sites, the national regulation of milk prices was a more efficient way to deal with the many milk producers. To give an example: a farmer with three cows could get about 45 centai (0.13 euro) for one liter of milk, whereas a farmer with 20 cows would get about 80 centai (0.23 euro).[11] In other words, production was regulated through prices, as it did not pay off to have only a few cows, due to the low price for a liter of milk, although prices were not set specifically depending on the number of cows, but according to other criteria pertaining to the quality of the milk. The bigger farms had invested in milking machines, adequate equipment for storing and refrigerating the milk, numerous quality tests of their

---

10 Information obtained from a Lithuanian Farmers' Union representative in Brussels, June 2008. See also the Lithuanian national paying agency www.nma.lt (accessed 16 November 2011).

11 Based on numbers from 2005.

products and in veterinarians and special fodder for the cows. Farmers with only three cows usually had a bucket and a stool to sit on. Consequently, farmers with many cows were paid a higher price, and the many small-scale farmers who could not comply with the quality regulations were paid a lower price. Furthermore, they could not afford to invest in the required quality improvements. The government only set the requirements for the milk quality,[12] while the actual price was based on agreements between buyers and sellers according to the criteria of milk quality. While this price policy did not directly aim at reducing the number of small-scale farmers as such, the consequence of the price differential was that small-scale farmers were more easily pushed out of the market.[13]

Attempts and Direct Effects

With the implementation of programs and the attempts to restructure the agricultural sector, the EU changed the central characteristics of rural life, which in turn led to new social differentiations. With a loose comparative analysis based on a household survey conducted in my two field sites, I suggest that the EU regulations, rather than creating uniform models and practices, resulted in a production of local EUs. My objective with the survey was to ascertain if there had been any significant changes in the households in recent years. I emphasized the decrease or increase of land and animals belonging to the farms, whether people had or had not applied for EU programs and how many landowning households had applied for DP. Therefore, a comparison held the possibility to find out if one village was more "EU-targeted" than another. I compared the situations before and after EU entrance. I chose 2002 as the year prior to entrance, because this was the year before the EU referendum was held and a period in which households had stabilized after the hectic 1990s. I compared these findings with numbers from 2007, three years after the accession. In order to highlight differences between households, I grouped them into categories depending on the number of people living in the house, from a one-person household to families with more than six members. Concerning the land categories, I distinguished between subsistence farms (1–3 hectares), semi-subsistence farms (4–10 hectares), small farms (11–20 hectares), medium farms (21–50 hectares), big farms (51–100 hectares), large farms (101–200 hectares), and finally, farms with more than 200 hectares. The first table below pertains to land use in both villages in the year 2007, whereas the increase or decrease since 2002 is indicated in a parenthesis. Since much of the

---

12 See Government of Lithuania [Lietuvos Respublikos Vyriausybė], *Nutarimas dėl Tipinių Pieno Pirkimo-Pardavimo Sutarties Sąlygų Patvirtinimo*, 4 June 2003, Vilnius.
13 The section about milk prices is also based on an email communication with Lilja Tepelienė from the Lithuanian Ministry of Agriculture, May 2009.

Table 4.1. Changes in land under cultivation, 2007 (compared to 2002).

	Bilvytis 2007 25 households					Straigiai 2007 70 households				
Persons per household	1	2–4	5–6	6<		1	2–4	5–6	6<	
Hectares					Households					Households
0		3			3	5 (+2)	9 (+1)	3 (-2)	1	18 (+1)
1–3	2	7	3	1	13	2 (-1)	8 (-2)	5 (+2)	1	16 (-1)
4–10		2	2		4	(-1)	20 (+4)	3		23 (+3)
11–20		1	1		2		3 (-2)	3 (-1)		6 (-3)
21–50			3		3		3 (-1)	(-1)	1	4 (-2)
51–100								2 (+2)		2 (+2)
101–200								(-1)		(-1)
200 <								1 (+1)		1 (+1)
Households	2	13	9	1	25	7	43	17	3	70

land in the villages was leased, I chose to attribute the land to the household that cultivated it and not to the one that owned it.

The number of households without land is significantly higher in Straigiai than in Bilvytis. Yet, not owning land is not necessarily a sign of poverty in Straigiai, since employment possibilities are better in this area and people may have other occupations than agriculture. To give one example, the richest businessman in the village owns no land. The situation differs in Bilvytis. Here, agriculture is one of few possible occupations, other than retirement or social support for physical disabilities. In Bilvytis, not owning land can very well be equated with poverty.

When comparing the numbers from 2002 with the numbers from 2007 in Straigiai, we see a change regarding both bigger and smaller farms. The biggest landowner expanded his farm to more than 200 hectares after the EU entrance. Other households expanded from 11–20 or 21–50 hectares to 51–100 hectares. However, only families with 5 or 6 persons expanded, since they obviously also had the workforce in the family to take on the extra workload. For the biggest landowner, this does not hold true, he hired people to work his land. All other families in Straigiai decreased the size of their land. Most of the land in Straigiai changed hands not through buys and sales, but through lease agreements. Farmers who had previously concluded oral lease agreements were now obliged to draw up formal contracts. By contrast, in Bilvytis, no changes occurred regarding land lease. The two biggest milk producers leased part of their land before EU accession and continued to do so after. Nothing changed, as it had been a formalized contract from the beginning. Some of the small-scale farmers also leased land, but they continued to do so as they always had done it, through oral agreements. Concerning land, there were no "direct effects" in the isolated village of Bilvytis, whereas there had been an impact in the more centrally located Straigiai.

The Lonely Cows

At the beginning of August 2007 my PhD supervisors drove through Lithuania in order to pay me a visit during my fieldwork. On their way, they noticed the many single cows standing outside the farms and upon their arrival they asked me, "Why are there so many lonely cows in Lithuania?" It was a valid question, as many of the problems defined by the EU had been directly linked to the dairy sector, where combined efforts of pushing people on the prize and offering them money for withdrawing had resulted in the "lonely-cow phenomenon," as I have referred to it ever since. To illustrate the lonely-cow phenomenon, the next table shows the changes in the number of cows in the individual households in Straigiai and Bilvytis. Compared to the land issue, the cows are a greater indicator of changes when we speak about small-scale household productions, for the following reasons: (1) one may register land as grassland and be a "passive farmer," but no one owns a cow without milking it; (2) one may own land and not own cows, but no one owns cows without owning land and (3) one may lease land, a reason why the numbers in the previous table indicate other shifts than actual ownership changes, but no one leases cows. The table below show actual ownership of and transactions with cows. The household survey showed that there was a general tendency to own

Table 4.2. Changes in cattle stocks, 2007.

	Bilvytis 2007 25 households					Straigiai 2007 70 households				
Persons per household	1	2–4	5–6	6<		1	2–4	5–6	6<	
Cows					**Households**					**Households**
0	1	5 (+2)	1(+1)		**7 (+3)**	7 (+2)	24 (+11)	9 (+4)	2 (+1)	**42 (+18)**
1–2	1	6 (-2)	4		**11 (-2)**		11 (-2)	5 (-1)		**16 (-3)**
3–4		1 (-1)	1 (-1)	1	**3 (-2)**	(-2)	(-9)	(-2)		**(-13)**
5–10		1 (+1)	1		**2 (+1)**		8	3 (-1)	1 (-1)	**12 (-2)**
11–20			(-2)		**(-2)**					
21–30			2 (+2)		**(+2)**					
Households	2	13	9	1	**25**	7	43	17	3	**70**

fewer cows after 2004. One of my informants from Straigiai told me, "Our cow is the last one in the street,"[14] indicating that all the neighbors had already sold theirs. I counted the amount of productive dairy cows, excluding the number of calves. The table is designed to compare smaller households with bigger ones. The single cow is relevant for small-scale production units, whereas one cow makes no difference for bigger production units, so that only bigger changes in the number of cows can be considered significant for them.

In Bilvytis, there were a few changes in the number of cows. There was some downsizing among a number of farmers, while two big milk producers greatly expanded their cattle stock. The two biggest milk producers had benefited from the rising prices for (bigger scale) milk production and had been able to expand their farms with more cows. They went from the category of 11–20 cows to 21–30 cows.

In Straigiai, the situation differed and overall, showed a great tendency toward downsizing and no increase in the number of cows. Most people decided either to keep a single cow or to sell all the cows they had. Several households that had 2–4 or 5–10 cows before now had zero or 1–2 cows. Four households received Early Retirement payments and were thus allowed to keep one cow for the household, whereas one of them had decided to sell all cows. As the main objective of the EU had been to decrease the number of production units with more than four cows, the program appeared rather successful, but was Early Retirement really the driving force? The low prices paid to small-scale dairy farmers actually seemed the most efficient tool in pushing the reduction of cows. As milk prices went down for households with only few cows while production costs rose, it did not make sense for small-scale farmers to maintain production. As can be seen in both villages, keeping 2–4 cows is quite disadvantageous in present day Lithuania. It was thus not forbidden to have a milk quota for three cows, but it was very difficult to profit from it. The low price for milk based on the state quality regulations was an indirect way of controlling the number of cows. I noticed that this indirect "cow control" appeared similar to measures that had been taken during Soviet times. At that time, practically no one had more than a single cow for their household. It was not forbidden to have more cows, but it was forbidden to own more than 0.6 hectares of land. No one could feed more than one cow from 0.6 hectares of land and thus, the number of cows was indirectly controlled through the direct control of land. Today, the number of cows is indirectly controlled through the direct control of the milk prices. The ideological reasoning behind the cow control obviously differs. Whereas the Soviet regime kept strict control over personal property in order not to foster any resemblance with capitalism, the EU measures keep small-scale farmers under

---

14 From my field notes, August 2007; my translation from Lithuanian.

control in order not to block the development of capitalism. Fostered through different ideologies, the result remained the same: one cow in each household and big-scale production centered on the big production units: collective farms before, economically viable private farms today. In this sense it was only in the period of independence it made sense for the villagers to have 2–4 cows.

"It is of no use for us"

After having made a general overview of the changes in land and cattle stock from 2002 to 2007, I will now focus on another question of importance: whether the respondents in the survey had or had not applied for one or more of the EU programs for support, which had been advertised in the year of the accession. Here, I was particularly interested in programs other than the DP.

Very few respondents had applied for programs other than the DP. Two households in Bilvytis and five households in Straigiai had applied. In Bilvytis, the two big milk producers had both applied for a program supporting milk production, whereas one of them had applied for an additional program supporting the modernization of farm buildings. In Straigiai, four of the respondents had applied for Early Retirement and one family for support for cattle farming. As 3 households in Bilvytis and 18 in Straigiai did not own land, they could not apply for any programs. Therefore, out of 25, there remained 22 possible applicants in Bilvytis, of which two had applied. In Straigiai out of 70, there remained 52 possible applicants, out of which five had applied. Consequently, I asked the 20 households in Bilvytis and the 47 in Straigiai why they had not applied. I listed the answers exactly as they were given, even if an answer only represented one household.

Table 4.3. Reasons for not applying for funds.

Why did your family not apply for EU funding? **Straigiai and Bilvytis (67 out of 74)**	
No use for us	35
We do not trust the EU institutions	3
We do not want to apply	1
We lack information about how to apply	1
We find the application process too difficult	4
We are too old to apply	8
We do not have time to apply	4
We were too late with the application	3
We plan to apply later	7
We do not know	1

In both villages, the most common answer was "it is of no use for us" (*mums tai nenaudinga*). Many people expressed the hope that their children or grandchildren would benefit from the EU membership, whereas they saw themselves belonging to another generation and thus, their time had passed. Other answers reflected some of the same issues either due to lack of knowledge or help or due to old age. People would shake their heads or shrug their shoulders and give me answers such as "We are not real farmers, it is of no use to apply" or "That is something for the younger people, I already get my pension" or "What should we apply for anyway?" or the often-repeated counter-question, "Don't we have to pay it back some day?"[15]

The answers gave voice to two phenomena, one being the problem of age and the alienation of the EU project, which I have emphasized earlier, and the second being an expression of insecurity about the EU and the funding. The risk of applying was often considered too high and many respondents considered it safer to own little but own it with certainty than to own much and have debts or get involved in incomprehensible programs. People were not altogether wrong when they saw themselves as the "wrong" target group for the EU programs. Except for Early Retirement, most of the other funding programs were for younger people who could restructure their farms, improve the facilities, specialize production and meet required standards. This limited many of the respondents' options to only one: applying for Early Retirement. The situation differed, however, when it came to DP. People considered this program as different from the other EU programs, as it had been advertised and promoted in a different way. While most other programs aimed at a specific target group, DP was open for all people who owned land. In Bilvytis, 18 out of a possible 22 had applied for DP, whereas the numbers were 38 out of a possible 52 in Straigiai.

According to a regional development report, the district of Graižiūnai, where Bilvytis is located, benefited the least from EU support up to 2005. This was, curiously enough, followed by the neighboring region of Marijampolė, where Straigiai is located, a region that gained the second lowest benefits from EU support, the report concluded. Graižiūnai had received approximately 2 million litas (580,000 euro) for authorized applications, whereas Marijampolė had received approximately 3.8 million litas (1.1 million euro). In comparison, the Utena district in eastern Lithuania had received the most funding, about 19.5 million litas (5.6 million euro), followed by the district of Vilnius, which had received about 17.5 million litas (5 million euro).[16] The report concluded that the low efficiency of agricultural production in Graižiūnai was caused by the inability to utilize EU support, as the typical farm was too small to receive funds

---

15 From my field notes, September 2007; my translation from Lithuanian.
16 Dzūkija Rural Development Association of Partners (Dzūkija LAG) (2006), 51.

for restructuring.[17] While I will not argue against this, I still find it important to take one additional point into consideration. The report fails to take into account that Graižiūnai is sparsely populated, with only 24,528 citizens, compared to the 181,219 citizens living in the district of Marijampolė. Even if we do not count the 50,000 living in the city of Marijampolė, the number of citizens in this district is still much higher than in Graižiūnai. Thus, the application results for the entire district (which obviously differs from the number in my small survey) do not look quite as pessimistic as is suggested by the regional experts. That Utena is the top receiver in spite of it having close to the same number of citizens as the district of Marijampolė, namely, 172,580, is partly due to its categorization as a "less favored area," where people can apply for more funding, an option which is not available to citizens from the Marijampolė district.

The latest rural development program covering the next period of EU support, 2007–2013, entails an evaluation of the previous period. The options for the export of agricultural products and EU support and investments in the rural areas were seen as positive outcomes so far, but the basic problems remained the same: small average farm sizes, milk production of still too small scale in comparison with the old member states and many older people keeping up production.[18] The average size of farms was slowly increasing, from 9.3 hectares in 2003 to 12.4 hectares in 2007. The average dairy farm size had grown from 2.3 hectares in 2003 to 3 hectares in 2007. The improvements, according to the goals set by the EU, were brought underway; however, the same measures and objectives remained important for the following period of 2007–2013. This time, however, there was a greater emphasis on land consolidation projects, as the small farm sizes were still seen as the biggest weakness of Lithuanian agriculture.[19]

The Early Retirement Program

The majority of my informants were close to or above the retirement age and fit the national image of small-scale farming and diversified production. They were typically the kind of farms benefiting from the first measure of the 2004–2006 rural development plan – Early Retirement. Early Retirement had been advertised in the years after 2004 in newspapers and radio and TV commercials. The newspaper for farmers, Ūkininkų Patarėjas (The Farmers' Advisor), published a special edition in autumn 2006 giving detailed instructions and information about the application procedure. People engaged in the local

17 Ibid.
18 Lithuanian Ministry of Agriculture, Lithuanian Rural Development Program 2007–2013, 9.
19 Lithuanian Ministry of Agriculture, Lithuanian Rural Development Program 2007–2013.

Figure 4.1. Lithuanian farmer, 2007. © Harboe Knudsen.

governing of the agricultural sector saw Early Retirement as the best solution for small-scale farmers, since they were paid for not working. Most of them were, frankly speaking, irritated by my many questions about whether there were other options for these farmers than to retire. Early Retirement was mainly a compensation for milk quotas; it was not intended to replace the actual pension people were paid. The basic pension was 266 litas (77 euro); added to that was an additional pension depending on the years one had been working. Most pensioners in the countryside had worked at the collective farms and had thus earned both basic and additional pensions, but the majority had not added active years since independence, as working on one's own farm was considered private business and did not count. Most of my informants received a pension between 400 and 800 litas a month (116–231euro).

Although Early Retirement had been popular in Lithuania, at 8,500 below the set goal it had still not fulfilled the expected quota of applications. Why had people been reluctant to "take money for not working?" In the municipality of Graižiūnai, the woman responsible for distributing program information explained the late success as a general feature of the Lithuanian character: "Lithuanians are always like that. Nobody wants to be first, but if people see that the neighbor gets this money and that it works for him, well, then they want it too."[20] Agricultural advisors from both Kaunas and Graižiūnai explained the lack of applications based on the same reasoning as Gytis, whom I quoted in the beginning of the chapter. Having cows was "a habit," and it was difficult for older people to imagine their lives without cows, even if having cows did not pay off.

I would suggest that the initial hesitation was based on more fundamental considerations, and that keeping cows is thus much more than "a habit": it is linked to the past instability of and lack of trust in the institutions. When social systems undergo administrative and legal changes, it has a direct impact on peoples' (backup) resources and property. Through Early Retirement, people were encouraged to give up one form of property (cows) and replace it with another (money). This is more than a simple exchange of money for cows; it also challenges the people's perception of values, as the cow hitherto represented reliable property, whereas money and institutional promises have proven little reliable in the past. An older woman from Straigiai told me that she had not applied for the Early Retirement Program, although she easily could have. Her husband scorned her daily because of the meager surplus she made from the milk. But she could not let go of the cows, she explained. She felt safer with the cows than without. The initial reluctance to dispose of the cows should therefore be seen in the light of the economic instability people had experienced throughout the 1990s. Many had first lost their savings in rubles, then the economic shock therapy caused a steady decrease in living standards, and then the Russian economic crisis struck in 1998. As F. and K. von Benda-Beckmann ([1994] 2000, 17) have pointed out, the understanding and perception of social security is "based on a combination of past experiences, on promises encapsulated in existing mechanisms, in entitlements and the continuing availability of resources, and on some estimations on future developments." Radical changes and corrupt procedures during the time of privatization had eroded trust in money as having a stable value and in state institutions as the provider of social needs. In comparison, cows had been reliable sources of dairy products for the households. However, the value of cows was challenged, as milk prices went down while production costs rose, which meant that cows generated little or no surplus for the household. Still, the perception of the cow as a stable resource was hard to do away with, especially in exchange for what was perceived as vague institutional promises. Only after a number of years, when more and more people had dared to apply and had had success with Early Retirement, did the interest in the countryside grow as people saw that the program provided a "real value."

Early Retirement did not mean economic surplus. It was a choice that decreased the workload at the farm and compensated for part of the loss incurred through

---

20 Interview, May 2007; my translation from Lithuanian.

the withdrawal from milk production. The first year, the people who retired were paid full compensation; afterward, it decreased year by year. One farmer gave the following example: his quota had been 10,000 tons of milk annually. The first year he would be compensated with 6,000 litas for the entire ten tons (1,737.75 euros). The following year, he would receive 5,000 litas (1,448.13 euro) and the year after that it would be less than 4,000 litas (less than 1,158 euro), and then less and less until it finally stopped when he reached age 75. It was only in the first year that one could keep up the same income level as before Early Retirement. In Straigiai, all in all, six families had applied, all of them either in 2006, two years after accession, or in 2007, when the last call for the program had been issued. It took time to consider all things involved: whether it was a reliable solution, whether it would be enough for the family, whether the EU would really pay the money and whether the family was comfortable with living on institutional support.

The Family Jankauskas

The family Jankauskas lives at the very edge of Straigiai in a two-story house that they built during Soviet times, partly with help from the collective farm and partly with profits from homegrown vegetables the family had sold illegally in town. The Jankauskas is a three-generations-under-one-roof family. They comprise father and mother who are in their mid-60s, one of their daughters and her husband who are in their early 30s, and their two children of 8 and 2.

During Soviet times, the father worked as an agronomist at the collective farm in Straigiai, whereas the mother had stayed home raising their children, two daughters and a son. After the privatization of the collective farm in Straigiai in 1991, the family received 5 hectares of land from the collective farm (3 hectares for the father, 2 for one of the daughters) and an additional 6 hectares due to property restitution. They had two cows, two pigs, and a few chickens. The farm was not big, but the soil was fertile and with the father's agronomic background, they successfully optimized the resources. They always had a new crop or vegetable ready for sale at any time of the season. Their most important crops were wheat and cabbage. The mother, Jankauskienė,[21] was responsible for cultivating carrots

---

21 In Lithuania the ending of the female surname changes according to the woman's status as married or unmarried. Endings for unmarried women are –ytė, –aitė or –iūtė/–utė after their fathers surname, whereas married women get their husbands surname with the ending –ienė. Hence, Jankauskaitė is the daughter of Jankauskas, whereas Petrauskienė is the wife of Petrauskas. Men keep their surnames (ending –as, –ys/–is, –(i)us or in rare instances –a) all their lives, independent of their status as sons and independent of their marital status. Even though the daughter of Jankauskas in reality is married and thus has a surname with the ending -ienė, it is, in the context of my report, the relationship

and flowers for sale at the market, whereas the youngest daughter, Jankauskaitė, was responsible for making cheese and sour cream (*grietinė*) from the milk. Every Saturday, Jankauskaitė went to the market in town with the products and thus made an extra contribution to the household economy.

The family managed with multiple incomes. The father had reached retirement age and received his monthly pension. His pension was above average as he got compensated for his deportation to Siberia during Soviet times. The mother had chosen not to receive her state pension and worked on the farm. The reason for her choice was that she had had so few years of employment that the pension would be minimal and hardly contribute to the household, anyway. The daughter worked full time as a teacher at the local school. Her husband worked at the farm, but once a month he drove to Germany to buy used cars, which he then sold at a higher price in Lithuania. The family Jankauskas' son at 19 still went to high school in 2004, but helped out with the work at the farm after school. The oldest daughter lived in the city of Marijampolė with her husband and their children, but she came to Straigiai as often as possible to help with the farm work. In Straigiai, the family was known for being "better off." They dressed nicely, bought much of their food in the supermarket, had nice cars and the house was well renovated. Although the family Jankauskas was respected in the village, people mockingly nicknamed the family members as Mrs. (*ponia*) or Mr. (*ponas*) as a way to indicate that they led a better life than most others.

In 2005 the situation of the family started to change. The son had no intention of becoming a farmer and left for Ireland to work in a factory. He only came home to visit during holidays. The son-in-law started to drive to Germany more often in order to become economically independent of his wife's parents. The father, who had had severe problems with blood circulation for a number of years, finally had to have his leg amputated as a last resort. After the father got sick, extra pressure was put on the son-in-law, as he was the only male family member working on the farm now. He, however, was unhappy with the extra burden, as it was contrary to his plans of spending more time in Germany. It was an unstable situation, and there were many family meetings dedicated to solving the problem of the farm's future. I was not aware until after the fact that they finally had applied for Early Retirement. One day in the kitchen, I understood this from a comment the mother made:

"Soon our daughter will not go to the market anymore, and we only keep one cow." I was astonished and asked: "One cow?! Why do you want to keep only one cow?" "The milk quotas, you know. The milk quotas have to go to

---

with her father and mother that is stressed as being important. This is also the way her own family and other citizens from Straigiai relate to her (she is always referred to as "daughter of" and not "wife of").

the young people now. This is how they want it. We are too old now." Only at
that moment did it occur to me that they were applying for Early Retirement.
"In other words, you are withdrawing?" I asked. "Yes, we are withdrawing. It
is because of health issues; otherwise we would work as always. But I have
heart problems, my daughter's back hurts, and my husband only has one leg.
What kind of farmers are we? I mean, it is not that we do not want to work.
We do, we always worked, and you know that. It is just getting very hard now.
So we thought that in this way we would get our quota compensated until my
husband turns 70."[22]

At first, it seemed strange to me that no one had told me before, since they all knew
that I had an interest in EU programs. It seemed like the mother had been ashamed
of telling me. She kept stressing the health problems as the reason, reminding me of
their work ethics. Indeed, this family had always taken pride in being independent
and self-sustaining. When others had stripped the collective farm of all possible
value after independence, the Jankauskas family had left the collective farm with
no property at all, although they had been entitled to it. The mother, especially,
did not want the family to be accused of having misused her husband's position
and network. Similarly, she had chosen not to apply for a state pension, as she did
not want to stand in line in the municipal administration together with the poor.
Receiving Early Retirement money seemed shameful to her, as it did not fit her or
her family's idea of staying as independent as possible.

The Family Petrauskas

The Petrauskas family lives in a two-story house at the very edge of the village,
but on the exact opposite side from the Jankauskas. The Petrauskas family never
worked at the collective farm during Soviet times. The husband had worked as a
tailor, and the wife had worked as a secretary in town. They had married when
she was 20 and he was 28. They first lived in a smaller house in the village, but
in the late 1970s they built the house they lived in now. They kept 0.6 hectares of
land and a cow, as was permitted for everyone. They used the land for growing
vegetables and potatoes and for feeding their cow.

   After independence, the husband received 10 hectares of land due to property
restitution of land his father had once owned. The Petrauskas family then bought
three cows and started to cultivate the land. They had grassland and grew beets
and potatoes and some vegetables. They almost had the same amount of land as the
Jankauskas, but the farm was still merely seen as a side occupation. The land was
never optimized or used as intensively as did the other family; it only provided
fodder for the cows and vegetables and potatoes for them. Although they did

---

22 Field notes, January, 2007; my translation from Lithuanian.

not perceive themselves as farmers, they still registered their farm and obtained permission to sell their dairy products in the market hall in town. The wife had calculated that she would earn more if she sold homemade dairy products at the market. In 2007 Petrauskienė had turned 67 and Petrauskas had turned 75. They had both retired and received a state pension of approximately 1,300 litas (376.51 euro) for both of them. They were still going to the market on Saturdays in order to make extra income for the household. After 2004 the situation became harder. More requirements, more control, more expenses. The Petrauskas still managed to stay on the market, but it was not easy. At one point, a bacteriological test of cheese came out bad, and the wife lost her market license for some time, until she again could provide good-quality cheese. In the meantime, she had sold cheese from the car before dawn in the urban yards.[23]

The last call for the Early Retirement Program went out in 2007 and the Petrauskas were interested now. Their son was a grown man in his early 30s, but he was working in the city and had no interest in farming. As the husband already had turned 75, he was above the age limit and could not receive the compensation. However, as the wife was only 67, she still had the option. The farm had hitherto been in the husband's name, but she now applied for partnership. She received the partnership and then applied for Early Retirement, which she received in the spring of 2007. The Petrauskas were both very satisfied with the convenient solution. Petrauskienė explained:

> Farming does not pay off. The European Union has introduced many sanitary restrictions, and our farm is not specialized [...] the stables and everything are not specialized. Now, so they say, there has to be a certain blanket under the cows in the stable, things like that. [...] We are not big farmers, no, and we are getting old, there is no purpose, no purpose for us anymore. What we get is enough to live on, but for the person who does not get this compensation, I do not know. What does that person do? I do not know. He still has to pay for the quotas, for the tests, for the veterinarian, for the improvements... But that is no longer our business.[24]

Two Perspectives

Contrary to the wife in the Jankauskas family, the wife in the Petrauskas family took much pride in the fact that she had been able to make use of the new possibilities provided by the EU. Their different opinions were based on different views on the meaning of support, which also reflected a general attitude: whether institutional support was acceptable for hard working people. It was not only a question of

---

23 The sale of dairy products will be elaborated more closely in the following chapter.
24 Interview, June 2007; my translation from Lithuanian.

state support, but it also reflected the primary identity of the two families. The Jankauskas family worked hard on the land that was their main source of income. Although the farm was small, they were still proud of their achievements, which also were due to the husband's agronomic knowledge. The Petrauskas, however, had almost as much land as the Jankauskas family. That they had been able to engage in some farming was an extra bonus, but they did not have the same sentiments for land and livestock, nor the same pride in the work as the Jankauskas family. Their employment in the city was their primary identity in terms of work. Thus, the emotional sacrifice that the Jankauskas family made by officially withdrawing from a lifelong occupation was by no means perceived as a sacrifice or loss of status in the Petrauskas family.

The Jankauskas were not at ease with receiving state support for "doing nothing" as it was in contrast to their work ethics. It was not only this family who held this opinion. I noticed a general tendency of disrespect for people who did not work, people who did not work hard enough or people who lived off state unemployment compensation. Work and money were tied together in an inseparable relationship. Michal Buchowski (2003, 16) reflected upon similar tendencies in a Polish village and concluded that hard work was a way for people to express identity. He writes, "Real farmers [...] never pay by credit in the shops and are opposed to the generous policies from the state towards 'lousy people.' Farmers rely on their own hard work and believe that everything they have they owe to their own sweat." Living "off the state" or any other institution was not regarded as something to be proud of; rather, it revealed a person to be a "lazybones" (*tinginys*) or "irresponsible" (*neatsakingas*) or in some obvious cases a "drunkard" (*pijokas*). Thus, accepting Early Retirement was in contradiction to the work ethic within the family and possibly a reason why the mother of the Jankauskas family decisively repeated the health issues as the cause of their decision.

This view towards people living off the state was shared by the Petrauskas family, who likewise did not respect "lazybones." However, for this family, Early Retirement was embedded in a different framework. It was an achievement obtained because they were educated enough to apply to the EU. Here it was not seen as a matter of living off an institution, but as a matter of being up to date with the latest developments. During an interview, Petrauskienė took her time to mention all the women in the village who could have applied for Early Retirement, but had not done so. Cows no longer pay off, she argued, which she convincingly proved by making calculations for several of the other farms, guessing their current milk quota and how much they could have been paid in support had they only applied for Early Retirement. Keeping cows was now perceived as old-fashioned, whereas benefiting from the EU was keeping up with the modern times.

Thus, the exact same program came to play different roles in the two families and was consequently perceived in different ways, either as a "shame," as it meant giving up a farming identity and receiving money for "doing nothing," or as a "pride," as it was a way to replace a secondary identity as farmers with a more beneficial one of modernity and ability to keep up with development. Out of the six families in Straigiai who had obtained Early Retirement, three did so with hesitation and three with joy. The people who hesitated did so partly because of the calculations they made for the years to come and partly because some of them were uncertain if they would really get the money from the EU. Furthermore, the idea of getting paid for "doing nothing" made them uneasy. The three families that gladly applied had only referred to themselves as farmers with a certain irony and said that the market was for the young now, not for the old. Early Retirement money would decrease the burden of daily work and instead of losing all, they would get compensation.

After the Jankauskas and Petrauskas had accepted Early Retirement, I was curious how things would change at the farm as a consequence of their participation in the EU program. According to official regulations, it would actually cause several changes and restructurings. In the Jankauskas family, the parents would have to retire completely and leave the farm and farming, and all decisions would be up to their daughter and her husband, who now officially ran the farm. The idea would thus be that the young people would bring some changes into the farming system, would ideally invest more in restructurings and be more open to changes and modernization. In the case of the Petrauskas family, the program would not have such drastic effects, since they had not transferred the land to their son. They would simply have to lease their land to others and stop selling milk and dairy products. Over the following months, however, I did notice that very few things actually changed at either of the farms.

In the Jankauskas family, the daughter had decided to stop selling milk at the marketplace in town. Since she had permission to farm, she could, in principle, have continued to sell her dairy products there, but she thought it too much work for too little money. Therefore, she had decided not to take over the parents' milk quotas. Together with her husband, she kept on cultivating the fields. Production of wheat was kept as usual, but they changed the hard and time-demanding cultivation of cabbage to the easier and less-demanding cultivation of lettuce. These were the main changes I saw at the farm, while some activities, like the sale of milk, were carried on as before, just in a slightly different form.

The mother kept working as before, in the vegetable garden, the green houses and with the flowers, while the father, for obvious reasons, worked little. He was, however, still the one in charge of the farm, the one who was consulted for all questions regarding the farm and the one who made the final decisions. According to the regulations for Early Retirement, neither he nor the mother should have had anything to do with the farm anymore, but in reality, it had always been a family farm and it remained a family farm. The mother found the mere thought of leaving the work tasks to her daughter and son-in-law repulsive. "Should I sit and be lazy in my chair while my daughter is sweating in the fields? Could you imagine that?"[25] Some internal changes of work division were made due to the father's health. He started to take care of some of the areas that had formerly belonged to the mother. He baby-sat the youngest grandchild during the day and although he did not cook, he made sure to heat the food and keep it ready for the others when they returned from the fields. After a few months of paying close attention to possible changes in the family, I forgot, little by little, that they were in the program, since the daily life mostly carried on as before. Indeed, the more time I spent in rural Lithuania, the more it became clear that dividing the family into nonworking parents and working youth was an idea which would never fit the general organization of the family farms, where parents and children run things together.

For the Petrauskas family, the situation differed. They had no children to transfer the farm to. They considered leasing the majority of their land, as they no longer had permission to cultivate more than 1 hectare. Agriculture had not played a major role in their life before Early Retirement, nor did it play a major role after. They had sold a cow, and had lost their official status as farmers, but it was a status they had never cherished anyway. They also had, just like the Jankauskas family, a surplus of milk by the end of the week, which they did not want to waste. So they continued to sell milk as before, but the wife now had to stand in the row of illegal sales people outside the marketplace. Previously, they had, like the Jankauskas family, talked badly about illegal sales, but the practicality of the situation had long overpowered former moral stands. One should always be able to renegotiate according to the situation.

Supporting Subsistence Farming?

In the beginning of this chapter, I grappled with the two intertwined phenomena of continuity and change. With reference to the older woman, Gytis had explained that many aging people were unwilling to change their lives, as the habit of work was deeply integrated into their understanding of how things ought to be. However, I still saw how one family after another sold cows and pigs, annulled oral leasing agreements, substituted them with formal contracts or stopped the leasing agreements altogether. If we in this light take another glance at the older woman with the cow Gytis had pointed out to me that morning we drove to town, it is actually impossible to know if she had the one cow because she was unable to change her life, as he had stressed, or if she had the one cow exactly because she had changed her circumstances according to the regulations of small-scale farming. Indeed, by paying people to withdraw to subsistence farming and/or by

---

25 From my field notes, September 2007; my translation from Lithuanian.

pressing them on the prices for milk, the policies resulted in a downsizing of farming and an increase of small-scale farmers, who made extra money by selling their surplus illegally.

I wish to broaden Gytis' explanation and stress that multiple factors influence people's persistency to keep their everyday lives relatively unchanged under changed circumstances. It is not unwillingness to change, and it is not only habit. People *did* react to the new circumstances, but they also tried to hold on to as much of their established everyday lives as possible. Thus, many would keep a cow if possible, and a few pigs and chickens, some hectares for grass and beets for the animals, a potato field and a big kitchen garden with vegetables. If people produced more than they could consume, they would freely sell the surplus, even if they knew it to be against the law. Semi-subsistence farmers were engaged in circumventing the EU, as they did not have the resources, knowledge or options to comply fully with the rules and regulations.

During the first years of Lithuania's membership, the EU had reduced the number of productive older farmers, transferred milk quotas from older to younger farmers, and many a cow had been slaughtered in order to regulate the milk production. As was evaluated in the development report of 2007, the size of (commercial) farms and dairy farms slowly increased. Still, reducing the number of small farms with diversified production remained the main goal for the next period of development, 2007–2013, and it will probably be a central goal after 2013. Although the size of commercial farms was increasing, the duality of development prevailed: the process of restructuring and modernization came along with a reinforcement of subsistence farming. Going back to a more unspecialized, nontechnical form of agriculture had been an option not only possible, but even intended by the development programs. Important was that the commercial production went in the right direction, that is, towards more specialization and standardization. The real problem arose as most people did not stay away from commercial production, although they were paid to do so. While neither rejecting the EU, nor being capable of complying fully with its demands, the farmers found intermediate solutions between what was required and what was possible. People incapable of keeping up with the recent developments necessarily adapted the regulations in order to make them applicable to their everyday situation. These were not acts of resistance against EU regulations or the national government, nor did people try to make any explicit or implicit statement by bending the rules. It was, I argue, a matter of practical negotiations, a way to find a solution between regulatory requirements and realistic options, a way to adjust the law to the local environment and thereby to "keep going." People long ago developed skills of manipulating rules and using their network to further their interests, and they apply this logic to the new circumstances in a negotiation of options and restrictions.

CHAPTER 5

The Insiders and the Outsiders: EUropeanization of Products and People in the Marketplace

It was seven o'clock Saturday morning and the market hall was already getting crowded. The women behind the dairy stalls had arranged their products neatly and were now waiting for customers. They wore white aprons and had white scarves around their heads. One of the women took a bottle of vodka out of her basket, filled a shot glass and passed it to her neighbor. "In order to keep warm," she said. Although the winter had been unusually mild, it was still cold in the morning hours and it could very well be a long day before they sold out their dairy products, if that would happen at all.

"Could you run outside and count?" one of the women asked me. I left the market hall, passed through the outdoor non-food market and gazed on the other side of the market territory. There were 11 today; 11 women who sold their dairy products illegally outside the area of the market. I went back and reported the number. As expected, the information caused frustrated outbursts inside. "Then we'll have to stay long today," the oldest of the women said, as she emptied a shot of vodka. "We will have to stay long..."[1]

The old woman spoke from experience. She had been selling her dairy products in the market hall for years and the competition from outside had always been a problem, but in recent years it had gotten worse. As Lithuania entered the EU, the requirements for dairy products became stricter. Many of the women, who previously had enjoyed the privilege of selling inside the hall among other certified farmers, lost their right to sell their milk and cheese, as they could not fulfill the EU regulations for dairy products. Because they could not afford to lose income from the sale of dairy products, rather than withdrawing from commercial production as demanded, they instead started selling illegally outside the bounds of the market. I referred to the two groups of salespeople at the marketplace in Marijampolė as the

---

1 Based on my field notes, January 2007; my translation from Lithuanian.

"Insiders" and the "Outsiders." The Insiders were factually inside, that is, within the market hall, operating in compliance with the EU legal orders. In contrast, the Outsiders were situated outside the market bounds, selling their products in defiance of EU legal orders. It intrigued me that this was not a case about homemade products versus products from the store, but a case of commercialization of and competition between essentially similar products that ended up on opposite sides of the law. However, with the new discourse about food safety and standardization of production, people were soon to learn that these were no longer the same kind of products: there were the "safe to eat" EU-certified products inside, and the potentially dangerous products without certification outside.

The manipulation of space as vividly displayed by the Outsiders thus posed several problems at the marketplace. Not only was it unwanted competition for the Insiders, it also ridiculed the authorities and displayed the shortcomings of EU law at the local level, as a change of place seemingly was enough to outdo the requirements from Brussels. It appeared that although all production now was subjected to the new EU regulations, the actual enforcement of law was practiced only at certain places that could be controlled and against producers who, from the outset, had an interest in being controlled. Contrary to the intentions, the number of people illegally selling grew after the EU entrance.

In her study of raw milk production in Lithuania, sociologist Diana Mincyte (2009) has noticed that despite the introduction of EU standards and the zero-tolerance policy towards uncertified dairy products by the Lithuanian Health Agency, the raw milk market in Lithuania has not been weakened since the EU entrance. The new discourse about food safety has, as such, not combated ideas about nutritious products straight from the farm (or more precisely, straight from the cow) but rather, reinforced them: the Outsiders now gained ground for legitimization of their products as traditional (see also Roberts 2007; Caldwell 2009; Mincyte 2009). Thus, and here I draw on ideas proposed by Simon Roberts (2007) in his discussion about commercialization of products and invention of heritance, the invention of tradition was both a counter-discourse to food safety talk and it emerged from that very discourse. The situation at the food market in Marijampolė bears witness to the intriguing situation when law becomes subject to local circumventions and interpretations; in this instance, it becomes a spatial challenge to the law. Furthermore, the Lithuanian case shows how standard making triggers new ideas about products and consumption, which bear wider connotations to perceptions of the changing society through a reinvention of Lithuanian products.

Setting Standards – Making Persons

Elizabeth Dunn (2005), in a case about Polish meatpacking companies, has given an analysis of the logic behind the EU standard making and its local consequences and outcomes. Dunn poses two interrelated arguments: the first regards the making of certain *standards* within the EU, the second and interconnected point is how the making of standards turns into a making of certain *persons.*

Dunn's first argument is that the standardization of production within the EU serves to further a political construction of a single geographical area. This zone is named by the EU the "techno-zone," referring to a modern and competitive zone of capitalistic industry. The requirements are part of the central process of "harmonization" of products within the EU. Harmonization means that products and the manufacturing of products should be subject to the same legislation in all member countries, a "one fits all" model (Dunn 2005). As this commensurable standard shows us, the EU can only include products that from the outset are similar to those in Western Europe or have the potential of becoming similar to them. This does not mean that the production necessarily becomes "the same" everywhere, but that production and products are made so much alike that they can be measured according to the same criteria. This is, thereby, just as much a question of being able to measure as enforcing a certain quality (Dunn 2005). The integration of new member states into the EU is thereby necessarily based on hierarchy and exclusion as a premise for their promised modernization as a part of the market economy.

The other argument Dunn proposes is that such standard making results in what she names "person-making." Hence, in order for people to apply the logic of standards, they need to internalize the values attached to such measurements. The ability to do so thereby not only reflects their understanding of the measurement as part of production within the EU, it also mirrors them as people and as producers, as integration in the EU market is exclusively for the "right" kind of farmers. Thus, producers need to incorporate notions of food safety and, we could add, adhere to self-control, as they take on the interest of improving their production according to the external scheme of measurements. Thus, by adhering to the laws and internalizing the values and scaling of products as decided by the EU, the farmers turn into certain kinds of persons – persons who fulfill certain standards set by the EU, persons who thereby operate with certain standards and quality, persons who are engaged in the modern EU market – thus, persons who differ from neighbors and villagers who are excluded from the market due to their methods of production that are not in line with the EU requirements.

I suggest that the shortcomings of law in the Lithuanian marketplace are closely connected with what I – with reference to Elizabeth Dunn – refer to as "failed" person-making. Thereby, it is understood that the "making" of such producers is challenged by the local actors' understanding and negotiations of the rules, as normative constellations and socioeconomic and shifting laws continue to influence people's decisions. This balance between structure and action should be seen in relation to my conceptualization of law: law is not limited to formal laws such as state law or EU law, but applies to different constellations of normative orders in society. In this sense, law becomes an umbrella term for different orders and regulations (F. von Benda-Beckmann 1997; F. and K. von Benda-Beckmann, 2006). Since people already have their own social settings, their own daily practices and their own (unwritten) norms and codes of behavior, any incoming law has to find a place in this constellation and may be hybridized or creolized in interaction with the local surroundings, resulting in various different outcomes. Rather than adapting to a certain measurement of EU standards, they seek to optimize their possibilities either within or outside the boundaries of the law. This is closely connected with a "failed" making of the customer: as long as the Lithuanians favor the "authentic" Lithuanian product, the EU-standard regime and its measurement for product quality will face intense competition by small-scale (illegal) producers.

Trading in Marijampolė

The market where the women from Straigiai went to sell their products was located in Marijampolė, which is a lively and commercialized city due to its location close to the international highway Via Baltica and its many trading activities. The most attractive market is the big car market placed just outside the city bounds, an internationalized market for car imports and exports. Lithuanians drive to Germany to buy used cars, which they repair and sell for a higher price to other Lithuanians or to foreigners from further east. Besides the car market, there are other marketplaces in the city, for example, the outdoor Belarusian market in the city center, where people go to buy cheap and fancy clothes. The competitor is the bigger Lithuanian clothes market, located inside a big hall at the western end of the city. On both sides of the city's main street you will find additional and numerous small wooden houses (kiosks and small stores) selling water, soda, coffee, bus tickets, cigarettes, top-ups for prepaid cell phones, various magazines, shoes, clothes and flowers.

In Marijampolė you also find numerous shopping malls: two Lithuanian Maxima malls, one RIMI shop that is a part of a Swedish and Finnish chain, and then there are a number of smaller Belgian-established IKI shops around in the city. Two of the malls, a Maxima and the RIMI, are located next to each other on the main street and in fierce competition with each other. However, despite the number of malls and options for shopping, many Lithuanians still prefer to buy dairy products from the marketplace or from uncertified sellers, meaning that a big part of potential customers still avoid the chains' processed products. The market where I conducted research was distinguished from the others, as it was the only official marketplace selling homegrown and homemade food products.

The market hall is made of metallic plates, grey and hangar-shaped. It is located in the center of the city, just off the main road and not far from the two biggest and competing malls, Maxima and RIMI. Looking at the market hall from the outside, nothing tells you that this is one of the liveliest markets in Marijampolė. Starting at 7 a.m., sellers are ready in their stalls with a variety of food products. People circle in and out among one another; regular customers normally buy from the same person every time, others prefer to go through all the products and visit every stall in order to be sure that they always get the best quality at the best price.

Seen from the main entrance, the section on the right is mostly for various meat products, such as a wide variety of sausages and smoked or salted pork. The people engaged in meat sales are all men. The left side is partly for fish sales and partly for processed food of the kind you would also find in a supermarket. The stalls in the center are occupied by farmers selling dairy and honey products. Two women, a man and his son are selling their honey, covering all nuances from light green to deep yellow depending on the flowers on which the bees fed. They also sell candles made of beeswax, and a concentrated, thick, honey purée, which is taken as an extra supplement of vitamins to boost the immune system. Behind the honey people, the stall facing the other direction is Elvira's, the cookie lady. Elvira sells all kinds of sweets and goodies for the everyday coffee table and large and decorative cakes for holidays and celebrations. The rest of the stalls in the middle are occupied by women selling homemade dairy products. The most popular product in this section is *grietinė*, a product similar to sour cream, only much thicker and sweeter. The women keep it in big buckets, and when customers come, the women put in a big spoon, lift it up and let the *grietinė* run down into the bucket again. In this way, the customers can see how thick it is. The Lithuanian white, compressed egg-shaped cheese (*baltas sūris*) is also a valued product, as is *varškė*, curd packed in small plastic bags. A few of the women also sell raw milk in two-liter bottles. All products are kept in an open cooling box in front of the women, assuring that they are kept at the right temperature. Whereas other salespeople come to the market hall every day to sell their products, the farmers with dairy and honey products only show up on Saturdays, which is the day with the most customers in the marketplace.

The open-air market outside only comes alive on Saturdays and is characterized by random sale of non-food and food products in what appears a messy mixture. Here you will see everything you desire and do not desire, from home-knitted woolen socks to shoes, old books and journals, imported Belarusian clothes laid out on the ground, vegetables, fruits and berries, technical equipment, big spoons and forks made of wood, cheap cosmetics and perfumes, small prayer books, painted pictures with romantic or religious motifs, used plastic bags from Western European stores, blankets, flower and vegetable seeds and many other goods. Often, you see people wandering around offering illegally imported vodka from Belarus and Ukraine and old women packed in layers of clothes, scarves around their heads, standing on random corners with a piece of pork in the one hand and a box of eggs in the other, hoping to supplement their pensions with a few litas.

Just on the other side of the almost invisible sign that marks the market boundary is a row of elderly women. This is the third sales space located outside the open-air market. On the ground, in front of the women, are baskets with white cheese and *varškė*, and big milk bottles and buckets with *grietinė*, the very same products that are sold inside. The location is cleverly chosen, being just outside the market bounds; the authorities of the marketplace can claim no control over the products and no fees for the sale. Still, every customer who wishes to enter the market from the main street will pass the row of Outsiders first, giving everybody an opportunity to buy dairy products at a cheaper price.

Trading Inside

The women inside the market hall mostly come from relatively small households with a few cows. Their families are wealthier than the average rural citizens; maybe they have a few more hectares, maybe a little savings in the bank. Importantly, the Insiders view themselves as decent, law-abiding citizens. Due to the milk price policy, as described in a previous chapter, they have calculated that delivering unprocessed milk to the dairy does not pay off. Instead, they can make money by selling homemade dairy products at the market. In order to fulfill the criteria within the market hall, they must have better knowledge of milk production and hygiene and be able to invest in facilities that are in line with the requirements.

It was at this market, safely placed inside the market hall, that Jankauskaitė and Petrauskienė sold their products prior to the engagement in the Early Retirement Program.[2] The thick and sweet *grietinė* Jankauskaitė sold was by far the most popular in the market hall. At seven o'clock in the morning, when the market opened, a row of customers would already be lined up in front of her place. Her secret was that she carefully separated milk and cream in a special machine, which meant that all the fat was used for the *grietinė*. This meant that the remaining milk that she used for cheese was very light. As Petrauskienė did not separate milk from cream so carefully, the milk she used for cheese had more fat. Consequently, customers valued the cheese Petrauskienė made higher than the cheese Jankauskaitė produced. Sometimes Petrauskienė also made an extra specialty, a sweet white cheese with eggs, sugar, and raisins. The two kinds of fat cheese she sold were very popular among the customers. Milk products had to be fat, I was told. If a cheese is not fat, the women told me, it does not have any substance, and you have to sell it for less money. The women laughed and shook their heads when I told them that in my country, people pay more for low-fat dairy products because they want to stay slim.

---

2 See Chapter 4.

The Jankauskas and Petrauskas families had, along with the other Insiders, official permission to sell their dairy products. Their animals had been thoroughly checked by veterinarians, their products were tested and controlled, their production facilities were carefully checked and the women all paid 6 litas (1.74 euro) to the administration of the market hall every Saturday when they came with their product baskets. Within the hall, products were also controlled by a system of random testing. At the marketplace, a woman with two cows could make about 480 litas (139 euro) a month in the winter and up to 580 litas (168 euro) in the summer, when the cows give more milk. A normal state pension was about 500–600 litas (145–174 euro),[3] thus, the sale at the marketplace was a necessary extra income.

As costs for production grew with the EU, it became a costly affair to sell products at the market. Consequently, the women had to sell their products at a higher price. As prices rose, the costumers grew unsatisfied. People went to the marketplace expecting to get a good deal, that is, to buy fresh products at a low price. The customers now realized that the price level in the market hall came dangerously close to the price level in the grocery stores. A cheese that prior to the EU entrance had cost 3 litas (0.87 euro), cost 5 litas (1.45 euro) at the time of my fieldwork; *varškė* was now sold for 3.5 litas (1 euro) a bag in comparison to the previous 2.5 litas (0.72 euro). The same price example is valid for half a liter of *grietinė*. Sometimes there was no longer a difference between prices at the market and in the grocery stores. Hence, half of the point of going to the marketplace was lost, especially for the pensioners who had to count every litas they had, and hitherto had saved a great deal of money by buying market products. Many an unsatisfied customer now turned away from the women inside with the remark, "it is the same as in the stores" (*tas pats parduotuvėse*), meaning there was no longer money to save by purchasing products in the market hall. Sometimes the Insiders would have to return home with several cheeses and liters of milk that did not sell. The customers they lost were those who could no longer afford to buy inside the market hall. However, those who stayed despite the rising prices were those who valued the fact that the products had been controlled. It was not unusual that the customers who bought inside asked about the dairy product, how it was made and if it was safe to eat.

Trading Outside

Whereas it would be the same people trading inside the market hall every week, the group of Outsiders was not as consistent. Some women were regulars, others only came from time to time. Sometimes there would be few traders outside, other times many it ranged from 5 to 13 (in comparison, there were 6 Insiders). Trading outside

---

3 Figures from 2007.

was tough. Most of the women were above retirement age and it was challenging to stand outside for many hours. If it rained, they had to protect their products from the weather; if it was freezing, there was the danger that the cheese and *grietinė* would also freeze, which would make the products less attractive to customers. In the summer, however, it was best to sell the products as early in the morning as possible, as they could not keep the dairy products outside in the hot sun for a long time. The weather was the main challenge the Outsiders faced; indeed, this was much worse than the rare confrontation by a police officer, who would come and send them away. Consequently, the number of Outsiders on a given Saturday would depend on the weather conditions; the worse the weather, the fewer the Outsiders.

While the weather often turned out to be an obstacle for them, the Outsiders benefited from their location in front of the market and from their low prices. The Outsiders did not have the necessary money to improve their facilities at home, send tests products to bacteriological controls or pay for a stall inside. Consequently, they could not move inside. However, because they therefore had no fees to pay, they could cut prices and sell their products for anywhere between 1 and 3 litas cheaper than inside. A woman who sold outside explained:

> We make cheese the way we always have done. There is nothing wrong with our cheese, it is fat and tasty. But we are not rich people, no, we cannot afford to go through all the tests, no, not simple folks like us. It is too expensive [...] and they demand too much. We do not have that kind of money. If we did have such money, we would not stand out here at all (laughing). We would be in our warm beds. But we sell tasty products at a low price. [...] Why would people pay twice the price inside?[4]

Two of the women had only joined the Outsiders in 2004 after they lost their permission to sell inside the market. There were others who had lost their permission, too, they said, but they had instead chosen to sell to friends and neighbors instead of standing outside of the market hall. "Maybe they were ashamed to stand out here with us," one of the women pondered.[5] Other women had never sold inside. However, none of the Outsiders strived to get a place inside the hall, either because they felt that battle was already lost, their having been removed, or because they had never had that option or the desire for it. "Our milk is also white," one of them explained, as a way to underline the, for her, ridiculous division of what appeared to be the very same products.[6] Although the Outsiders were excluded from official production, they often had

---

4 Interview, March 2007; my translation from Lithuanian.
5 From my field notes, January 2007; my translation from Lithuanian.
6 From my field notes, January 2007; my translation from Lithuanian.

Figure 5.1. Cow. Lithuania 2007. © Harboe Knudsen.

better sales than the Insiders. This led to legal and spatial conflicts between the two groups of salespeople, to which I will now turn my attention.

Changing Spaces – Challenging Laws

In studies about marketplaces in postsocialist countries, it has been noted how officially approved markets and dubious semi-legal markets are separated from each other through spatial distinctions. What is interesting in this regard is that such distance appears to be significant. Hence, we have the approved market in the city, and the contested market several kilometers outside the city (Smigielska 1992; Hohnen 2002; Dunn 2005; Humphrey and Skvirskaja 2009). In Marijampolė, this space of "outside" is created *inside* the city. The intriguing thing about the marketplace is thus not the illegal sale in itself, as it takes place in various locations in Lithuania (and in other postsocialist countries), but that the legally approved and legally disapproved markets are next to one another. The Outsiders use location and space to circumvent rules, as they benefit from the flow of customers who have to pass them in order to enter the market inside.

This use of space both demonstrates the strength of EU law (strict enforcement inside) and proves the limitations of EU law (the lack of enforcement of law outside the official territory). The competition from outside distressed the Insiders, especially on the days they had to return home with unsold dairy products because the customers had bought outside. This led to an ambiguous relationship with the Outsiders, as they were partly looked down upon, partly cursed, partly envied for their go-around-the-rules strategies. The feeling of being in line with EU regulations and therefore superior to the outside competitors was challenged by a feeling of unjustness, as effort was not rightly awarded, neither by the legal system nor by the customers. The irritation was hard to overcome. Petrauskienė told me:

> The question [of illegal sales] was raised many times. I always asked: "are we a bad kind of people, since we are treated worse than [the Outsiders]?" We had to meet all requirements, do all the tests, pay for everything, and pay for selling at the market. We stood there smiling to the customers and still we had to wait until the women outside finished their sale, and then, only then, the customers would come to us. [...] We also raised the questions at meetings but no one was interested. We called the police. The officers came and told the women to go home. As soon as the officers left, the old močiutės [7] came back. [...] It was very difficult; we raised the question many times.[8]

The question of the Outsiders came down to a matter of space and interpretation of space. "Inside" and "outside" were clearly bounded and discrete physical spaces, but they were embedded with different meanings and were subjects for different interpretations of law. The law was negotiated through a clever play with space, which in the end outdid the actual legislation. As K. von Benda-Beckmann and Griffith (2009, 5) argue, "Spatial constructions as embodied in legal categories and regulation provide sets of resources that become part of 'spatial idiom-shopping.'" What the Outsiders did was to use the options they had by way of the limitations the law posed for them. The notions of physical, social and legal space can be seen as interacting phenomena, such that the bounded space governed by law influences interaction. Likewise, the law and its (spatial) limitations provide resources for people, making them capable of pursuing their own (economical, political) interests within the given space (ibid.) I saw this as a practical negotiation of the situation: people find themselves in situations where they, on the one hand, are unable to do what was required of them and on the other hand, still need to maintain daily life and make a living for the family.

The Outsiders turned their exclusion from the market into a benefit by creating a "non-EU space." The non-EU space was a normative construction, a circumvention of rules as a response to their exclusion from the market, and was mobilized against the inside market as a way for the Outsiders to meet their

---

7 Grandmothers. In the countryside, all elderly women are addressed as such, no matter if they actually are grandmothers or not.
8 Interview, May 2007; my translation from Lithuanian.

economic goals. The fact that the women stood outside the market did not legalize their sale, it only meant that the market administration could not interfere. It was a matter of 50 centimeters that separated the Outsiders from the official market. The only thing the administration could do was to put up notes and posters inside the market hall emphasizing that they had no responsibility for food products sold outside the market. Alternatively, the problem was passed on to the police, who had a legal right to move the women from their spots.

At the local level, however, the laws against illegal sales worked poorly. Despite the intensification of control inside the market hall, the responsibility for the concrete situation of illegal sales is submitted to a local scale of crimes. The police officers in Marijampolė are already occupied with the local mafia, street violence and youth gangs. Removing elderly women from their spots outside the market, just for them to return as soon as the officers leave, is not at the top of the list for combating crime. Quite to the contrary, the many phone calls from the Insiders result in very few visits by police. Even if the police had been consistent in removing the old women, it would only be the tip of the iceberg, since most Outsider sales took place in disguise. Products were also sold from cars after dark (referred to by Pine (2001a) as "car-boot sales"; for comparison, see also Mincyte 2009) or by old women on bicycles. In Marijampolė, the urban yards were divided into different territories shared by a number of Outsiders who would have their own yards, where they came twice a week with their dairy products. There was also the option of selling products to neighbors and friends, all practices that classify as Outsider trade, as the products were not officially approved. Hence, most Outsiders are doing their sales in spaces very distinct from the marketplace. In this sense, the constructed non-EU space was created in different locations for short time periods. It appeared that the EU's product control mainly worked for those who were already embedded in the system and, by extension, embedded in the EU way of understanding production. The controls did not reach the groups of people who, according to the law, were the most obvious targets for legal interventions.

The Eight-Legged Pig

Creative interpretations of the law were likewise used by the salespeople whom I referred to as meat men (it was only men who sold meat). Due to their products and rules for production, they could not circumvent the law by changing space; instead they were, literally speaking, able to mix the categories of legal and illegal. The requirements for the meat men were that each and every pig had to be sent to the butcher and be certified for sale. Prior to 2004 they had been able to slaughter their pigs at home and sell them at the market but now, home slaughtering was only allowed if it was for one's own consumption. Pigs for sale could not be killed at home. Although beneficial for the butchers, this legal change was an unwelcome expense for the farmers.

I was made aware of the situation shortly after I started my fieldwork in 2006 and went to visit the family Jankauskas' neighbors. Their son, a young man of 27, worked as a veterinarian in the area and from time to time was sent to the market hall in Marijampolė to control the meat. He explained that the prohibition of home slaughtering had created difficulties, as many farmers could not afford to pay for the butcher. A common solution, he told me, was to send one pig to the butcher, where the animal was checked and then slaughtered under the prescribed rules. This gave the farmer a "certificate for sale." Meanwhile, he would slaughter another pig at home. As the certified pig was sent back from the butcher, the farmer would mix its meat with the meat from the home-slaughtered pig, and then sell both meats at the marketplace as meat from one (very big) certified pig. The veterinarian continued:

> I am sure that they [the farmers selling meat] get away with it more often than they should. If we come too late [to control the meat], they may already have sold enough of the animal, so we do not notice the cheating. They must think we are stupid and that we do not know what is going on. We know, but we cannot always prove it [...]. Sometimes we catch them, and then they are the ones who look stupid. "It certainly is a big pig you have there," I say to them. "And it has so many legs! Eight! Incredible! A very special pig you have." Then you see how they get red faces (laughing). I live in this village [Straigiai]. I am not very popular here, but I have to do my job.[9]

I once raised the topic when talking with a farmer who had previously sent meat to the market. He explained:

> The woman who cannot pay for being inside, she goes outside and sells her cheese. But that is cheese. We are selling pigs. Pigs! If we started to carry a couple of dead pigs out in front of the market; that would mean trouble. You can get away with a small cheese, but a pig, that is a big animal. So, either you sell [non-certified meat] straight from your farm to your neighbors and friends, or you take such chances with mixing the meat inside now and then.[10]

Just like the dairy women outside, the meat men were caught in dilemmas for which they had to develop intermediate strategies. It was not because they were, per se, in opposition to the EU, but they were bound by practical and economic

---

9 Interview, October 2006. The veterinarian spoke English.
10 Interview, April 2007; my translation from Lithuanian.

realities that made it difficult for them to profit from their production if they always followed the rules; this goes back to my argument about practical negotiations in the aftermath of the EU entrance. The meat men were already selling inside, had permission to do so, and preferred to stay as certified sellers. When negotiating around the rules, the meat men chose to keep the legitimacy of the spatial location and go around the rules by mixing the meat. As long as they were not caught, they did not lose any prestige. As the man from Straigiai explained, "When not caught, you are no thief." (*Nepagautas – ne vagis*).[11] As a way to legitimate his and others' actions, he declared the bending of rules acceptable, as long as it was not proven. The meat men, albeit running a risk, managed to incorporate outside strategies with inside locations, literally mixing the categories of legal and illegal into one.

Senses of Personhood

In an edited volume by Mandel and Humphrey (2002), it is shown how making profit from marketing was illegal during Soviet times and branded as immoral and in opposition to the state ideology of collectivism. During this period, individual trade was carried on outside the logic of the system and connected with shame and ambiguity. Due to Soviet policy rules, which evoked ambiguous and even negative feelings towards salespeople, sales were an activity connected with shame (Mandel and Humphrey 2002; for similar conclusions see Hann 1992; Wedel 1992; Hohnen 2003; Humphrey and Skirvskaja 2009). The transition to a market economy meant a radical change in this perception. In the official discourse, trade now symbolizes the very core of the system, seen as "civilized" and "modern" (Mandel and Humphrey 2002; for similar conclusions, see also Kaneff 2002 and Hohnen 2003). Whereas younger generations in present-day Lithuania quickly embodied the ideas of modern marketing and consumption, the older generations, who grew up with different perceptions of trade as promoted in the Soviet ideology, have had more difficulties in doing so. Thus, although markets are now incorporated into a capitalist system, they are still surrounded by misbelief and contested opinions (Mandel and Humphrey 2002).

Reflecting on the idea of person-making, I suggest that the emergence of EU products, EU regulated farms, and standard making are used by the Insiders to circumvent their mixed feelings about trade and to appear as legal and trustworthy salespeople. The often economically disadvantageous position inside the market hall, the sense of personhood and the negative feelings connected to those "out there" were strong incentives to keep the spot inside, although the competition was hard. The inside position not only reflected the kind of farms they were running, it also reflected which kind of persons they were.

---

11 Interview, April, 2007; my translation from Lithuanian.

Indeed, the Insiders reiterated the standard regime rhetoric in order to appear economically, socially and morally superior to the disadvantaged Outsiders. Although there were plenty of privileges obtained through exclusion, the Insiders connected legality with a certain pride. Being inside was thus both to be embedded in the EU-accepted trading system and perceived as a way to receive symbolic capital in terms of recognition and respect. It was also a way to distinguish oneself from the Outsiders and thus define oneself as a person in accordance with both the EU and the local environment. This was exemplified by their view of the Outsiders, who they saw as *prasti žmonės* (simple folks, lower class people) with little or no education. Jankauskaite, for one example, was the daughter of the previous agronomist of the collective farm in Straigiai, and it was certain that her father would never allow her to change space and stay with the "dubious" women in front of the market. Likewise, Petrauskienė, also coming from one of the richer families, valued her reputation as a law-abiding citizen and as an eager and devoted churchgoer. She often acquired new leaflets about the EU and believed it an honor to know about the latest production requirements and funding and program options.

The longer I stayed at the marketplace, the more I became aware of how the proclaimed distinctions between Insiders and Outsiders were challenged through practical and economic negotiations. Whether or not the women subscribed to law was highly dependent on circumstances and possibilities. The women were not only in the market hall as salespeople, they also bought products at the market, not only grocery products from the other stalls, but also products sold illegally within the market hall. This was especially true for illegally imported Belarusian alcohol or cigarettes. This kind of sale contested the inside market as being legally "pure." Ragged-looking men, dressed in big worn-out coats under which they hid a couple of plastic bags, would approach the Insiders discretely at their stalls. The mutual understanding of the meeting was clear from the very start and the exchange of money and products was surprisingly quick; a nod in the right manner and a bottle and a carton of cigarettes would be in the women's baskets, where they hid it under a piece of cloth. When asking about the men selling these products, I was never given much of an answer.

"Uh, he is such a... he is some bum [*bomž'as*],[12] smuggling and selling illegally, we do not talk with him," Petrauskienė once said after having bought a provision of goods from a man.[13] Whereas she distanced herself from the man by considering

---

12 *Bomž'as* is not originally a Lithuanian word, but comes from Russian and is "Lithuanianized" with the ending –as. The original Russian word is '*bomzh*' [*бомж*] which consists of the first letters of *bez opredelionnogo mesta zhitelstva* [*без определенного места жительства*]. In English: "[the one] without a permanent place to live."

13 From my field notes, February 2007; my translation from Lithuanian.

him as lower class (bum) and his actions as bad (smuggling and selling illegally), she still bought his products, quickly and covertly. Hence, she claimed, she had nothing to do with the man as such and did not wish to, either. Dealing with the "bum" was surrounded by contrasting feelings of disgust and immorality, yet still there was desire for his products. Whereas I knew the women liked to drink, although they would always deny it, the cigarettes puzzled me, as none of them smoked. Petrauskienė had always talked about smoking as being a bad habit of poor people. "Why did you buy cigarettes from him?" I once asked her. "Neither you nor your husband smoke." "Indeed we do not," Petrauskienė answered, "and we never did!" "But why did you buy them, then?" I asked, insisting on some kind of an answer. Petrauskienė waited a moment and replied, "Well, there is this man living down the street, not far from our house, and he sometimes comes and helps a bit at the farm, and I pay him with cigarettes."[14]

Indeed, by recirculating the illegal goods into the familiar sphere of networking, these goods lose their previous ambiguous status. Other things were also kept "under the counter." The women often brought baskets from home with food and alcohol, preferably vodka. While selling, the women would offer each other bread with cheese or meat, sweets and alcohol. They always brought a single shot glass along, which was repeatedly filled with vodka and passed around from the very moment they started to sell to the moment they left for home. Drinking was something they otherwise verbally rejected as the path to all evil, but here it underwent a different discourse. Drinking was a way to keep warm during the cold winter days in the market, or a way to celebrate someone's birthday (or recently had been) or someone's name day (or recently had been). To return home from the marketplace tipsy or even slightly drunk was nothing exceptional. Although they distanced themselves from the Outsiders' sales, the Insiders' own engagement in buying illegally imported products was understood within a frame of practicalities and reintegrated into an accepted social sphere through common friendly consumption (alcohol) or redistribution in the wider household economy (cigarettes). The norms they adhered to were not a simplified matter of right or wrong. Rather, one model of behavior would be rejected in one context and accepted in another. The proclaimed borders between inside and outside the law were not ultimate and once and for all.

This capability of renegotiating the situation and sense of personhood became clear to me as both Jankauskaite and Petrauskienė withdrew from the market hall. The reason was, that both of their families had applied for engaging in the EU's Early Retirement Program, which was offered to farmers above 55 (in the case of Jankauskaite, the retirement was granted to her father; in the case of Petrauskienė, she had recently had the farm transferred to her name from her husband's, as he

---

14 From my field notes, February 2007; my translation from Lithuanian.

was too old to apply for Early Retirement). The aim of the program was to reduce the amount of small-scale producers by paying them to withdraw from production. They were allowed to keep one cow and 2 hectares of land and produce solely for their own consumption. Indeed, a few weeks after Petrauskienė had obtained Early Retirement and was thus prohibited from selling her dairy products, I found her in the row of Outsiders she had previously despised. In her new renegotiation of the situation, she, like the other Outsiders, turned exclusion into an economic benefit by profiting from inflation and rising prices within the market hall. Hence, Insiders also had to make a daily living and when pushed, to renegotiate their legal status. As Petrauskienė explained:

> The cow gives too much milk for me and my husband to consume alone, and who am I to waste it? Mind you, my products are still the same quality as before.[15]

As this example shows us, morality is cultivated with pride as long as people, literally speaking, can afford to have such standards. Jankauskaitė, on her behalf, never did go outside the market hall to sell her products, and only jokingly would refer to this as an option. This did not mean that she stopped selling dairy products, but the sale was now to neighbors and other villagers who would come to Jankauskaite's house and ask for a cheese or a liter of milk. According to the law, this was no different than if she had actually moved outside the market hall. However, for Jankauskaite, the difference was significant. She was not lined up with the Outsiders coming from all sorts of disorderly farms, but had a safe and orderly place for sale – her home.

Geopolitics of Food and Fashion

Anthropologist Neringa Klumbytė (2009), in an article about consumption of sausages in Lithuania, has looked into a specific aspect of the market, which she refers to as "The Geo-Politics of Taste." Here she evaluates the opinions about and consumption of two different sausage brands in Lithuania: the Samsonas company, which produced a sausage with the brand name "Tarybinė" (Soviet), a supposedly "traditional" Soviet sausage; and the Biovela company, which had launched the new "Euro-Sausage." The preference of the consumers was clear: "Samsonas' profit skyrocketed after it began to produce 'Soviet' sausages [...]. In 2005 all 'Soviet' meat brands comprised more than 50 percent of Samsonas' production" (Klumbytė 2009, 130). According to Klumbytė, the Soviet sausage was perceived by her informants as familiar and part of the traditional Lithuanian

---

15 Based on my field notes, February 2007; my translation from Lithuanian.

cuisine of fatty – and thus, tasty – food. In addition, the Soviet sausage was recognized as a "natural" product without food preservatives. In comparison the distinct "Euro-sausage" – which fulfilled EU criteria and was low in fat – never gained the same kind of popularity, and was never characterized as being part of the Lithuanian traditional cuisine (Klumbytė 2009).

Klumbytė's study confirms my own observations in Lithuania; numerous times I have been told how no honey is sweeter than Lithuanian honey, no meat is tastier than Lithuanian meat, no milk is healthier, no cheese is fatter, and no vodka has the quality and taste the Lithuanian home-distilled has. My non-food gifts from abroad, such as perfumes, clothes and toys for the children were always valued as "good quality" and often not even used, but put on display in the living room. Contrary to that, my attempts to bring eatable gifts from abroad always failed. People politely consumed some, only to conclude that there could be no comparison in quality with the Lithuanian version of the same product; it was "synthetic," whereas the Lithuanian products were seen as "real" and "natural" (*tikri/ natūralūs produktai*). Homegrown food, it was argued, was the real food, not comparable with things you would obtain in the store (for comparison, see Caldwell 2009). A sausage, for example, should not be purchased in a store, wrapped in plastic, as it would taste like the wrapping. The "real" product was also free of "vitamin E," as some of my informants ironically referred to food preservatives, which are assigned codes known as E-numbers.

Frances Pine (2001a), in a work about consumerism in Poland, has shown how the understanding of goods imported from the West has changed during the past decades. From being the status symbol of Western culture during the socialist regime and, thus, in opposition to the socialist regime, the disappointments following the breakup of the Soviet Union made Western products the very symbol of betrayed hopes and promises. The result was a turnaround in consumption, which took form as the revival of national Polish products. In other words, Polish material culture and food products had a comeback, both as a way of voicing disappointment with the West, but also because many simply could not afford products imported from Western Europe (ibid.). In this way, consumption inevitably bears political connotations as an approval, or rejection, of changes and ideologies.

In the case of Lithuania, I found many mechanisms similar to what Pine described in her earlier work on Poland. The political, economic and social ups and downs, however, had not resulted in an altogether rejection of Western society by Lithuanians. Many people were still fascinated with the West, had hope for increased wealth in the future and aimed at adopting a modern and Western lifestyle with the EU membership being a reality (see also De Munck 2008). Visions of rich, famous and beautiful people were visibly displayed in the many glamorous TV shows and "docusoaps." Going down the main shopping street in

Kaunas, Laisvės Aleja, your attention is immediately drawn to the Lithuanian women with brightly bleached hair, shiny makeup, short skirts and high boots, waltzing down the avenue, mirroring the freedom to dress in what is considered hip and modern fashion. The same image of material fascination was conveyed through the many shopping malls that have been mushrooming all over Lithuania. Temptations were many and symbolized the "new" kind of society people now lived in. My informants managed to drag me from one shopping mall to another during my stay, often even against my will. It was far from always that people wanted to or had to buy something, most often they simply wanted to show me the mall, as it had a big indoor aquarium, a new ice skating hall, a fancy pizza place, a pet store with dogs in cages, or because it was newer and bigger than the one they had shown me the last time. Sometimes the malls were actually destinations of day trips, and even school excursions for kids now went to shopping malls instead of the castle of Trakai,[16] as they used to. The shopping malls reflected an angle of the new "modern" input in society, with imported goods, kitsch, fancy stores, clothes, pizza chains, pop music, pop colours, cinemas, commercials and slogans.

However, coexisting with expectations or hopes for increased wealth was a fear of a moral degradation of Lithuania by the quick modernization of industry, with low-quality products as a result. And it embodied a set of negative images: "fabrication" of animals and dairy products containing preservatives. In addition to a general individualization of society, broken families and immoral and promiscuous behavior were enforced by liberal sexuality. Such scary images circulated in a range of former socialist countries, intertwined with the celebration of the materialistic culture (Pine 2001a; Caldwell 2009).

If we relate these thoughts to the idea proposed by Pine that consumption is an expression of approval or rejection of current politics and ideology, I suggest that the coexisting and contradicting feelings about the West have resulted in both a desire for and rejection of Western products. Indeed, the counter-example to the consumption of (modern) Western-style (non-food) products is seen at the food market. When people went to buy food here, it was in order to *not* buy imported products; quite to the contrary, here they wanted what no import could outdo: "(home)made in Lithuania." EUrope was consumed with fancy "outer" products, Lithuania with digestive "inner" products.

Cheese Production and Conflicting Perceptions

The elevation of national products in contrast to the food safety policy backed by the EU resulted in conflicting opinions in daily life, raising a new awareness

---

16 A restored stone castle in the historic city and lake resort of Trakai. The castle is originally from the fourteenth century.

about what a safe and healthy food product actually was. An agricultural advisor argued:

> The basic issue is that [the Outsiders] do not have permission to sell. [P]eople buy from them because it is cheap. The problem is that when you buy from them, you never know what you get. There could be all kinds of bacteria. If an old woman milks her cow with dirty hands and fills a bucket which is not clean, well, then you see... That is why people need a special permission to sell at the marketplace. And to get permission means that you have to go to many offices and milk institutes, you need a bunch of papers. The milk has to have the right temperature, do not get me started on the requirements for storage. And there should be no residual antibiotics in the milk. It is all very difficult.[17]

Whereas the advisor had embedded his argumentation in the emerging discourse about food safety and hygiene, talking along standard- and person-making lines, not all Lithuanians had adapted to this way of thinking, and instead found inconsistencies in the new regulations. As has been shown in a study by Diana Mincyte (2009) about uncertified sales of raw milk in Lithuania, many Lithuanians prefer local dairy products from the market, and big foreign or Lithuanian companies have not managed to convince them otherwise, despite the growing awareness about food safety regulations. Indeed, women engaged in uncertified trade with raw dairy products, according to Mincyte, are capable of building markets outside the reach of EU supervision (ibid). While farm products were never out of fashion (for one reason, people were bound by economic realities and could not buy expensive imported food products from the store), they did not exactly experience a comeback like the one Pine (2001a) noticed with regard to Poland. However, one can argue that they were never seriously threatened by imports, as the natural-food wave appears to be even stronger after the EU entrance. A customer, a man is his early 50s, explained to me that for him, it would make no sense at all to buy products inside the market hall. He had been brought up in the countryside and his mum had given him dairy products "straight from the cow" all his childhood. He continued:

> [M]eanwhile, somebody in Brussels got this idea that my mum's milk is bad, because it has not been sent to a laboratory. If I would listen to that, I should stay away from the milk I have been drinking for the past 50 years, because what used to make me healthy is now a danger to my health.[18]

---

17 Interview, Kaunas municipal administration, November 2006; my translation from Lithuanian.
18 From my field notes, January 2007; my translation from Lithuanian.

The problem for officials was the persistent discontinuity between official discourse and everyday conceptualizations of what a good food product really was. New understandings of hygiene would often conflict with perceptions of healthy milk straight from the cow. The discursive conflicts about food safety became visible due to the moving around of salespeople after the EU entrance: former Insiders were outside all of a sudden. This confused many customers. The Insiders who stayed, however, argued that it now finally became visible who was a real farmer and who was not. Outsiders, on the contrary, argued that their cheese had not gone bad overnight. A woman who sold as an Outsider explained:

> I have always made cheese like this, and before me, my mother made cheese like this. It was always good cheese, and now it is no longer good enough. But you see, it is the same cheese. One day good, next day bad. This is the kind of talk I do not understand.[19]

The woman produced her cheese from uncontrolled milk, which she stored by sinking the bucket down into her well outside the house. She made her cheese from whole fat milk, meaning that she did not separate milk from cream with a distilling machine; the milk stood and soured in a pot in her kitchen and she finally produced the white cheese in her old bathtub, where it was also pressed into its right, egg-formed flat shape under a heavy piece of wood. The woman argued that her cheese had been made like this for generations. It remained the same cheese, but the understanding and perception of the cheese changed, as it was embedded in the discourse of EU's food culture. However, it was also revived within the new rhetoric about traditional Lithuanian food products, contesting the fabricated and imported foods.

Conformed Diversification

In a description of two competing French biscuit companies, Simon Roberts (2007) shows how a regional product becomes a product of heritage and tradition only by the commercialization of consciously "created" history. Roberts is interested in the moment, when the unspoken and previously taken-for-granted is made explicit. Thereby, the product gains its originality and heritage only as it becomes part of a commercial discourse. Here, its authenticity as a traditional product becomes a prerequisite for its quality, and the present regains new meaning in the light of an idealized past (ibid).

   If we relate these thoughts to homemade food products from Lithuania, such as the white cheese, we also follow a pattern by way of which it changes from

---

19 From my field notes, January 2007; my translation from Lithuanian.

being merely a food and becomes a consciously traditional Lithuanian product. I suggest that this idea about Lithuanian quality is an outcome of the massive import of foreign products. The present understanding of cheese as something distinct, original and traditional, with an emphasis on the right shape and distinct taste, is created in comparison with "synthetic" products imported from the West. As white cheese has never been imported, it gains specific substance in contrast with other kinds of cheeses that now emerge at the market; various kinds of yellow cheese, cream cheese, camembert and even presliced cheese, every slice being wrapped in plastic and ready to be put on toast. The synthetic versus the traditional is thus, I argue, related to a more complex understanding that goes far beyond cheese: the negative image of capitalism and a reflection of the ambiguity towards the EU, possibly representing a way to modernity, possibly a threat to the society due to "fake" values. In the words of Roberts:

> We are looking [....] at contemporary, self-conscious appeals to tradition in which elements of an exemplary, even idealized Arcadian past are explicitly evoked to form part of the life-world of the present. (Roberts 2007, 27)

For the women outside the market in Marijampolė, it does not suffice to ride on the natural-product wave in opposition to the giant foreign (or even national) food companies; for them it is also a question of competition with the Insiders, who essentially sell the same products, the only difference being that they are already legitimized as salespeople by the thorough tests of their milk. The Outsiders, however, have no official legitimization, and low prices alone do not suffice for them to keep customers. Indeed, as my ethnographic material suggests, they more than anybody have to formulate the quality of their products by representing heritage and continuation. The evocation of the Outsiders' cheese as even *more* natural and *more* original than that of the Insiders was mobilized through a conscious mystification of the Insiders' products in the daily talk outside the marketplace. Since the Insiders' products were now embedded in the EU system, it would suggest that the cheese had been subjected to other forms of production and consequently, that they were no longer selling the "original" products.

An interesting twist in this case is that the revival of national and original food products is also promoted by the EU and done with a trademark within the member countries. The EU has two key concepts regarding food production, one being "harmonization," the other being "diversification" (Dunn 2005; Welz 2007). Whereas harmonization refers to the standards set for food production, diversification refers to the options of getting different "regional" products from different countries. In reality, both concepts seem the same, as both harmonized and diversified products must be produced in ways meeting a set of common EU standards. Within this discourse, national products are preserved, approved and trademarked as specific for a certain region. As Gisela Welz (2007) rightly points out, the EU ratification process itself transforms the national product into something different than it originally was.

This invites us to take a further look into what one could call the construction of a new product evoking tradition and uniqueness by subjecting it to a firm set of rules. Diversity is conformed in the *preservation* of this very diversity and, with Roberts, we could add, the product is made a "conscious product" by the EU ratification process. Not only does this change people's perception of the product, since it now is something distinct and traditional, but it also changes the product itself, as all food production is submitted to the same strict legislation, which leaves little space for variety. As Gisela Welz concludes in her discussion of the topic, the preservation of tradition of EU products creates

> Produkte, die es ohne die EU nicht so geben würde weil ihre Materialität, ihre Nutzungsmöglichkeiten, ihre kulturelle Bedeutung [...] und natürlich ihr ökonomischer Marktwert in hohen Maße EU-europäisch infiziert sind.

> [Products, which would not even exist without the EU because their materiality, their application and their cultural meaning to a high degree are affected by the EU.] (Welz 2007, 334; my translation)

In my example of the white cheese, the production becomes an issue of control. Only those who follow EU legislation for cheese production can obtain the official sales certificate. People have to produce under new circumstances and are made aware of bacteria, hygiene, fat content, storage facilities and animal nutrition, and the cheese is accepted only after having passed through bacteriological control. In this way, the means of production were changed, and the cheese standardized and "improved," yet possibly making it a somewhat different cheese than it originally was, not to mention being endowed with a mythical reality of the impact from the EU giving body to stories spread by the Outsiders about the possibly damaging EU-supervised production.

Concluding Remarks

In this chapter I suggest that the links between standards and identity politics are moderated by socioeconomic calculations by people subjected to the new standard-regime, and by the re-evocation of the traditional products. Whereas the EU control is pervasive, it is restrained to certain spaces, at certain times, for certain producers. The main reason the standard policy appears so ineffective is, I suggest, because the EU project of making people (producers and customers) does not work out in practice. The links between standards and the making of persons are influenced both by options and restrictions in the nearby environment and by the calculations and practical negotiations of the actors. Although Lithuania formally operates with a zero-tolerance policy towards informal production of and sale of dairy products, it is, on a practical level, not perceived as a serious crime. Indeed, any given police officer could have been brought up on the same kind of cheese which now classified as illegal, and in most cases, the police cannot be bothered to go to the marketplace, even when called up by angry Insiders. While justification through EU blueprinting appears only stimulating for the producers who, from the outset, have the knowledge and capabilities to become EU-certified farmers – which is a minority – the EU unintentionally provided the Outsiders with a new frame of understanding for their production. They did not submit to the disqualification of the outside products, but operated with a new frame for their milk and cheese products. They, in the midst of the growing import of E-numbered products from the old member countries, reinvented the wheel – the authentic classic Lithuanian farm products now appear "traditional anew."

CHAPTER 6

"If you wish your son bad luck, give him your land": EUropeanization, Demographic Change and Social Security

One afternoon in the spring of 2007 I was invited for coffee by a couple in Straigiai. They were both in their late 60s and had lived and worked in the village their entire life. During the Soviet system, the husband had been employed as a tractor driver, and the wife as a milkmaid at the local collective farm. After independence, they had started to farm the 6 hectares they got during the privatization. Their son had moved to the city, where he worked as a security guard, but returned to the village from time to time to help at the farm. It was difficult without the son, the husband explained, as he himself no longer had the strength to work in the fields and in the stables. When I asked them if their son had ever thought about taking over the farm, the wife shook her head quietly. "Our son never considered that an option," she answered and continued, "he has seen how difficult life is in the countryside, how hard my husband and I have been working. Farming is not exactly what you could call a rewarding occupation. It is work, work, work, and for that you hardly make any money. Look at us, we are worn out." Her husband added, "Today, a farmer has to be a businessman. And do we look like businessmen to you, huh? I would not even wish for our son to come back to the village. As I say, if you wish your son bad luck, give him your land."[1]

In the following days, the husband's comment lingered in my head; if you wish your son bad luck, give him your land (*Jeigu linki savo sūnui blogo, duok jam savo žemę*). The sentence gave voice to the turnaround in property values in the years after independence and the insecurity connected with farming. The difficulties

---

1 Based on my field notes, January 2007; my translation from Lithuanian.

embedded in the cultivation of the land was one point that came across in the old man's remark, the other point was the (lack of) future perspectives for the new generation of semi-subsistence farmers (land equaling "bad luck"). The consequence was a massive emigration from the countryside that had severe consequences for family structures and options for obtaining social security. Urban life, with all its possibilities, seemed more attractive and promising than the often monotonous life in the countryside, and young people were drawn by the possibilities of working abroad in Western European countries. Although the parents did not necessarily wish for their children to stay if there were better possibilities for them in the cities or abroad, it proved to be difficult to do without them. The demographic restructurings in the countryside resembled what I choose to call unintended consequences of rural development and they were combined with other and related problems, such as land and property failing to provide "real value," aging land owners, insufficient options for retirement and changes in family structures. These changes were visible in everyday life in the villages. As Kostas, my landlord in Bilvytis, frequently reminded me, the countryside was now mainly populated by "pensioners, drunkards and a few farmers" (*pensininkai, pijokai ir keletas ūkininkų*). Although he exaggerated, there was a great deal of truth to it.

EUropeanization and Strengthening of Kinship Ties

The planned modernization of the agricultural sector by enlarging and specializing farms meant that future prospects for small-scale family farms were meager. Consequently, young people started to leave the countryside in search of jobs in the cities or abroad, as there are no or only very few alternatives to agriculture in the rural areas. This tendency for emigration entailed two problematic issues: First, it appears to be counterproductive to the goals set for the future of the agricultural sector, as it proves increasingly difficult to modernize the agricultural sector if the young people leave. The second and related problematic aspect is that the emigration from the countryside likewise affects family structures and patterns for obtaining social security, because young people leave the villages in great numbers. In this sense, it proves equally hard for aging parents to maintain their households.

When looking back at the past years in Lithuania as well as other formerly socialist countries, the aspect of *in*security played a dominant role as governments, politics and socioeconomic circumstances changed continuously. After the breakup of the Soviet Union and the privatization of collective farms, local networks regained importance in order to provide for one's family (for comparison with Ukraine and Azerbaijan, see Kaneff and Yalcin-Heckmann 2002; for comparison with Poland, see Pine 2002). This also relates to the fact that the continuously unstable situation marked by unfulfilled promises in the 1990s has reinforced a general feeling of insecurity and distrust of the system, leading people to approach institutional solutions and options with skepticism (Torsello 2003). If we pair this with the large-scale emigration from the countryside as experienced in recent years, we find a situation where people are, on the one hand, reluctant to turn to institutions for support and yet, on the other, cannot rely on their children to stay at home and take care of the parents when they grow old.

The aforementioned development was thereby not creating a straightforward "aging parents–emigrating children" situation; rather, the young people's pursuit of more independence and individualism paired with the reinforcement of kinship obligations, merged into new constellations of family structures and patterns for care and support. This was especially the case for people engaged in semi-subsistence farming, which was the majority of my informants. Subjected to an unsatisfying standard of healthcare in many rural communities, low pensions and little institutional care for the elderly, many aging people find themselves in vulnerable situations. Young people, consequently, face a dilemma as they, on the one hand, see no future in the rural areas and, on the other hand, still are responsible for their aging parents. This means that previous patterns of child-parental care are renegotiated under the changing circumstances, leading to new ways of upholding both work and kinship obligations. This created a specific situation, primarily with respect to urban migrants and their aging parents, where the youth engaged in "circular migration," a constant shifting between urban and rural life.

I noticed that the maintenance of small-scale farming is not equally shared between genders and generations; old women and young men appeared to carry the heaviest burdens under the changing circumstances. The reason is that both aging and work are highly gendered in rural Lithuania. Indeed, with a life expectancy of 66 years for males and 78 for females, Lithuania has the largest difference in age expectation between genders in the EU. Additionally, Lithuania also hits the record with the lowest male life expectancy in the EU. Women live longer, are in better health and are capable of handling their work even in later years. Men, due to a lower life expectancy and often bad health in their old age, are not equally capable of carrying out their work tasks in the fields, in the stables and in the woods, work which requires a lot of physical strength. Here, the young men come into the picture, as they have to step in and fulfill the work duties their fathers or fathers-in-law are unable to do. Consequently, the urban male migrants become ping-pong balls between the urban and the rural setting as they carry out their work in the city during weekdays and return to the countryside on weekends. While the pattern of urban settlers going to the countryside on weekends and helping family and kin on the farms was also common in the Soviet era, this pattern has been subjected to significant changes over the years. With a mass migration to Western Europe by mainly young men and with the national pattern of gendered aging, the need for young men particularly has increased significantly. This results in a situation where young men are in much greater demand by aging parents than young women are. Due to the general lack of "male hands," this also increases the pressure on sons who have not left the village. Both urban migrants and rural "stayers" are thus part of another form of circularity, what I call "the circulation of sons": due to the general shortage of (working) men in the countryside, those who either live in the village or come back frequently as part of their returning migration patterns, are further "circulated" around in the village to carry out extra work for those relatives, neighbors and friends who lack young men in the family. In this sense, young men are embedded in the wider exchange economy as a response to the demographic changes in society. These readjustments of work, cooperation and parent-child relationships suggest that the unintended consequences of rural development plans and their counterproductive influence on the further future modernization already have had significant impact on the composition and socioeconomic organization of rural Lithuanian families. Rather than looking to the state for support, aging parents supplement their pensions with sale of farm products, and uphold patterns of security by increasing the pressure on their children.

Aging Lithuania

It had been predicted that with the enlargement towards the East in 2004, a new wave of migration to the West would start under the label of free movement of labor. This created tension between new and old member countries, a tension that, in the heated atmosphere up to 2004, became a fear of an uncontrolled migration to the West (Górny and Ruspini 2005; Gruževskis 2004). However, governments in the new member countries were not looking upon the development with excitement either, as they experienced a prevailing fear of losing their skilled labor force (Pop 2004). Although the migration did accelerate, the fear in the old member countries of the great move from East to West turned out to be exaggerated (Kaczmarczyk 2005). Still, in the home countries the emigration rate was experienced as serious, as it often was skilled workers who were the first to leave the country, causing what EU terminology called "brain drain." The reason for the decrease in population was not only emigration, but also negative birth rates. The UN country data on Lithuania showed that population growth in urban areas had declined by 0.5 from 2000 to 2005, whereas it had been declining by 0.1 in the rural areas in the same period.[2] Even if the rural birth rate were to rise, it would not balance the

---

2 See UN data country profile Lithuania at: http://data.un.org/CountryProfile.aspx? crName=Lithuania (accessed 10 March 2010).

Table 6.1. Age distribution, Lithuania 2007.

Age group	Number	%
1 – 14	516,998	15.35
15 – 29	764,825	22.71
30 – 44	720,227	21.39
45 – 59	673,493	20.00
60 and above	690,814	20.59

Source: http://db1.stat.gov.lt/statbank/selectvarval/saveselections.asp?MainTable=M3010203&PL anguage=0&TableStyle=&Buttons=&PXSId=3766&IQY=&TC=&ST=ST&rvar0=&rvar1=&rv ar2=&rvar3=&rvar4=&rvar5=&rvar6=&rvar7=&rvar8=&rvar9=&rvar10=&rvar11=&rvar12= &rvar13=&rvar14= (accessed 10 March 2010).

demographic situation if the children continued to emigrate when they reached a certain age. Although birth rates are dropping all over Europe, it is the combination with mass-scale emigration in new EU member countries like Lithuania that make the long-time effects more severe. Statistics of the demographic structure in Lithuania show the following age distribution in 2007:

We can compare the general aging process at the national level with the age distribution in my two field sites.[3]

If we look at the overall picture from both villages, the situation reflects the national situation with the older generation of 61+ exceeding the young generation

Table 6.2. Age distribution, Bilvytis and Straigiai, 25% of all households.

Age	1–18	19–30	31–45	46–60	61 +	Total	%
Bilvytis 25 households	30	8	23	13	12	**86 citizens**	**27.74**
Straigiai 70 households	49	25	38	38	74	**224 citizens**	**72.26**
Total 95 households	79	33	61	51	86	**310 citizens**	**100.00**
%	25.48	10.65	19.68	16.45	27.71		

3 The table is based on the household survey. Following my informants' definition, I calculated one house as one household; however, I was aware that the lines between different households can be blurred, as will be discussed later in this chapter. See Chapter 1 for further description of the household survey.

by a few percentage points. Although I extended the group to include 18-year-olds, which makes the youngest group bigger, the 61+ still exceeds this group. If we look at the two field sites separately, there are important differences to point out.

In Bilvytis, the biggest age group is 1–18, followed by a decrease in the group of 19–30. In the brackets after that, there is a stable but steady decline, the smallest group being the 61+ pensioners. The drop occurs after 18, which is probably due to the children leaving for the cities or abroad to find work. The number of people decreases with age, the group of 61+ being the smallest. Taking into consideration that the national picture points to an overabundance of pensioners, I found the reason for the comparatively low number of elderly in Bilvytis to be the low living standards in the region, which in 2005 was estimated to be considerably below the average Lithuanian level.[4] According to a regional report, the area belonging to Graižiūnai had the highest mortality in the entire region in 2003, with 18 per 1,000 citizens.[5] In reports, the regional high mortality was related to the low living standards, lack of employment possibilities, which led to poverty, and poor nutrition. The situation in Straigiai differs, as the two largest groups are the 1–18-year-olds and the 61+, the latter being the largest. This follows the national picture of a high number of elderly. It also displays the same decrease from the group of 1–18 to the group of 19–30, though it is not as radical as in Bilvytis because of better options for employment and higher living standards.

While the statistics show the overall numbers in Lithuania, city and countryside included, my survey is limited to two villages, both of which are subject to regional conditions. In Bilvytis, the comparatively low number of elderly reflects the regional problem of high mortality, while the situation in Straigiai points more to the general situation in the rural areas, where elderly people are left behind as young people are emigrating. The uneven age structures in my two field site villages create specific problems for the maintenance of the farms. Here, I want to point to the older part of the generation again in order to provide a closer understanding of the position of aging people in current rural Lithuania. Furthermore, aging is not a unisex process, as men and women age in different ways and the circumstances for aging also affect the genders in different ways, with women's life expectancy being 12 years longer than men's.[6] Thus, we not only speak about an aging population, we speak about an aging population with a majority of elderly women. One reason is general health conditions: consumption of alcohol and cigarettes is widespread in the countryside and thus, has a serious impact on people's health. This is especially the case for men, who more often than women are heavy drinkers and smokers.

---

4 Dzūkija Rural Development Association and Partners (2006).
5 Ibid.
6 See UN data country profile Lithuania, online at http://data.un.org/CountryProfile.aspx?crName=Lithuania (accessed 10 March 2010).

Table 6.3. Age and gender distribution in Straigiai and Bilvytis, 2007.

Age	1–18	19–30	31–45	46–60	61 +	Total
Women	40	18	31	27	53	169
Men	39	15	30	24	33	141
All in all	79	33	61	51	86	310

In the frame of my research, this becomes clear when we look at the different life expectancies of men and women.

Although there are minor differences between the number of men and women from ages 1 to 60, the main difference strikes when looking at the category of 61+. Here we find a rapidly decreasing number of men in comparison with the number of old women. Lithuania is but one example of a country with an overabundance of old women; the life expectancy of women worldwide is higher than men's, while the socioeconomic conditions they live under in their retirement age is often worse than men's, as pension systems often favor men above women (Judd 1999). Hence, it would be safe to assume that those who live longer are also those who face the worst conditions. While the scheme here shows us a striking difference in aging and life expectancy, the question remains as to what the consequences of this are in the broader perspective of gender roles and provision of social care and security.

Gender Roles and Gendered Aging

In works about gender in socialist and postsocialist countries, it has been argued that there has been a return to "traditional gender roles" after the breakup of the Soviet Union. Instead of the Soviet-style emancipation, we now see women in less dominant roles on the labor market and in many cases, they are housewives (Buckley 1997; Kuehnast and Nechenias 2004). On a similar note, a study of Hungary after the collapse of the Soviet system voices that privatization secured greater influence for aging men, as they were the ones who primarily received land. Thus, property and resources were gendered during the privatization process leading to a "new power of old men" (Thelen 2003b).

When discussing the situation of rural Lithuania, I argue that this shift in gender roles has not been remarkable. Indeed, despite the Soviet policies of gender equality and full employment of women, which together with the institutionalization of care and support should do away with "bourgeois" family structures, it proved increasingly difficult to maintain such policies. Instead, the family became integrated into the Soviet system as an important social and economic building block that took over responsibility for care and support of the citizens (Haukanes and Pine 2005). As the function of the family was reevaluated in the Soviet system, the position of women became increasingly difficult; they were subjected to a double burden, as they had both full employment and responsibility for the household (for a similar argument with reference to Estonia, see Tedre and Tulva 1999). Although there were various communal establishments in the rural context that were to ease the women's burden, such as common dining rooms for lunch and day care for children, much responsibility remained with the women. Some of the women from Straigiai and Bilvytis told me that they and others had taken the children to work with them from time to time.

With regard to the rural areas, it is therefore a question of whether we can speak of a "return" to traditional gender roles or if such gender roles, in one or the other disguise, were in reality reproduced during the Soviet system. When employed at the collective farms, women often worked as milkmaids, in the cafeteria or as secretaries, thus occupying typically female work spheres, while still being responsible for the households. In contrast, men were working with the tractors, in the fields, repairing machinery, and it was men who were in charge of the collective farms, holding jobs as chairmen and agronomists, thus, also jobs that were typically "male." In this sense, a high employment of women should not overshadow the fact that the work they carried out belonged in the traditional women's domain and thus, gender roles had merely been institutionalized and camouflaged through a high employment rate. After independence, I argue, there was therefore no radical shift in work areas, as the institutionalized gender roles from the collective farms were implemented in the household, mirroring the same work divisions. Men kept working in the same areas as on the collective farms: cultivating the land, looking after the machinery, cleaning the stables, cutting hay, cutting winter wood, slaughtering pigs and cows. Women, however, were more often occupied with the household, cooking, cleaning, working in the vegetable garden, feeding the animals and milking the cows. This should not be confused with an assumption of women leading a life in the shadows of their men; rather, as I will argue, women were in many instances "pulling the strings" in the household.

The combination of gendered aging and gendered working spheres made old women and young men obtain central roles in rural Lithuanian households. Especially with regard to semi-subsistence farms with but a few resources, this specific combination became particularly important in terms of providing for the household. While women had a longer life expectancy than the men and often were in better health in their old age, they had a more central function in the household as caretakers after the breakup of the Soviet Union. Men had greater difficulties working long hours in the fields as they grew older; they often had health problems and aged faster than their wives. Elderly men, especially in the poorer families, which constituted a significant part of my informants, often went heavy on the bottle and/or were in bad physical shape, if they were not dead already.[7] It appeared that men were married in their old age, while the women often were widows. Due to gendered aging, old men often failed to fulfill the working tasks they had hitherto been responsible for, as long hours in the field were increasingly demanding for them. However, as the working tasks remained gendered, the young men were called upon to fulfill the tasks their fathers or fathers-in-law could not. However, the fact that old women did not take part in the work should not be confused with the assumption that they left it all to their sons. Instead, they took over responsibility for running the farms. Young men thus had to fulfill obligations on the farm, under the supervision of – not their fathers – their mothers.

As has been shown by Pine (2007) in a discussion of gender roles in rural Poland, women are associated with motherhood care, and the domestic domain. However, she suggests, motherhood and caretaking should, in this context not be viewed, as a repressed position of women; rather, motherhood entails its own agency and space for action. Hence, women's role as caretakers, also in the case of Lithuania, does not lead to a distinction of public and private domains, where women are at home; rather, as my focus on old women reveals, old women are often those who run the household, either by directly taking over the organization and supervision of work, or by controlling the household "from behind." The specific constellations for farming in the rural areas had given a particular importance to age and gender groups in household economies. Lack of machinery meant that the demand for physical work was high. Although the young women also returned to the countryside to help out their parents from time to time, it was not as often as the young men. When they had children, they found their primary obligations were to their own nuclear family. It would, however, not be uncommon that their husbands, the sons-in-law, would return to his wife's parents and help them carry out heavy work at the farms. Thus, young men had become a shortage in both my field site villages, leading to what I call a "circulation of sons," as the available young men had to fulfill tasks not only in their parents' households, but also for other kin members, neighbors and friends. That I choose to focus on the specific combination of old women-young men is not to undermine

---

7 Although several of my informants claimed that alcoholism had increased after independence, it appeared to me that the main change was that it had become more visible. Previously, people had been able to drink during work without it causing them to lose their job. After independence, many lost their jobs and the hitherto disguised alcoholism was taken "to the streets" and visibly displayed. The cause of the men's lower life expectation should therefore also be seen in relation to the policy that allowed drinking at the workplace during Soviet times.

the roles of old men and young women.[8] Rather, I wish to foreground that with reference to aging semi-subsistence farmers, this particular combination played a central role in order to maintain social security. However, while old women were central figures in households, the paradox emerged that they are in economically weaker positions than their husbands.

EUropeanization and Shifting Pension Arrangements

Currently, unstable and insecure situations for semi-subsistence farmers emerge as a result of the processes of EUropeanization I have previously called attention to: economic and political decisions made during Soviet times, the undoing of the very same after independence and the creation of new models under the EU. Indeed, previous arrangements and laws continue to influence the daily of the rural population. One central example, which proves to be valid for the majority of the people among whom I carried out research, is the inherent contradictions in planning for retirement years. The pension system emerged during Soviet times when there was full employment for all rural citizens on the collective farms. The idea behind the pension was that the monthly amount retired people would receive depended on the number of years they had been employed. All citizens thus had to "earn years" to their pension. As the Soviet system collapsed, rural citizens were instead encouraged to start farming individually, an occupation that due to its private character, did not add active working years to the pension and for many people, no years have been added since. As the economic shock therapy caused inflation and people lost their savings in rubles, many would rather rely on "concrete property" such as land and cows that should secure them in their old age, as people reasoned that the pension, due to the "lost" working years, would not be sufficient. Around the same time, the EU started supporting big-scale farming and seeking to retire the small-scale farmers, so that land and property lost value for semi-subsistence farmers who could not keep up commercial production. Consequently, this coexistence of initiatives from different political systems put aging rural citizens in vulnerable situations; people had initially planned ahead with the Soviet system in mind, not anticipating a total shift in governance and ideology, the path of which was flawed with confusion, contradictions and ever-changing conditions for farming and production.

---

8 For a general discussion of women in postsocialist countries, see Pine (1996, 2000, 2001b); Buckley et al. (1997); Kuehnast and Nechenias et al. (2004). For a discussion of older men and their positions in postsocialist Hungary and postsocialist Germany, see Thelen (2003, 2005).

Figure 6.1. Lithuanian wedding around 1970. Private photo.

While the coexistence of different systems had practical consequences for retirement options, it also left many citizens with skepticism, as past experiences taught everyone not to trust any system to have either duration or reliability. Shifting governments and the following disappointments of the 1990s affect comprehensions of institutional support to this very day.[9] Social security should therefore not only be understood as something material, there is also a strong emotional dimension to it (F. and K. von Benda-Beckmann 2007; Leutloff-Grandits, Peleikis and Thelen 2009). The ever-changing political and economic environments had reinforced a feeling of everyday *in*security, which, as F. and K. von Benda-Beckmann (2007) have argued, may be just as much a counterpoint to social order as open conflicts and disruption. I wish to foreground here that different time periods have in various ways had concrete impact on the present-day conditions in rural Lithuania, and that the many shifts and changes have likewise affected emotional aspects of social security, which in turn affects the decisions people make for the future. This proves crucial when attempting to understand why many rural citizens, rather than turning to institutions

---

9   This institutional distrust is so outspoken that, at the time of my research, Lithuania was
    the only EU country that did not have obligatory insurance for farms, meaning most
    farmers were not covered in case the harvest would fail. The LŪS (Lithuanian Farmers'
    Union) in 2007 tried to advocate the implementation of insurance, but this was met with
    broad protests.

for support or following a path of greater individualization of society, instead revive patterns of exchange and dependency on kin. As emphasized by Leutloff-Grandits, Peleikis, and Thelen (2009), it is not necessarily the economic outcome that gives people a sense of security, but just as much the social relations they can relate to in times of crisis. As kin and family play a central role in networks and support, such patterns are challenged when the children start emigrating from the countryside.

The State Pension

With the nationwide trend of more pensioners in the countryside, one type of income became increasingly important in the rural areas – the state pension. The amount of the pension varied from person to person; one pensioner would get close to nothing, whereas another could easily make a living from the state pension. The reason behind the uneven amounts is that the pension is closely linked to the number of years people have been employed by the state and/or a private company.

A pension is paid out when a person reaches retirement age. For men the retirement age is 62.5 years, for women, 60. During Soviet times, men and women would have already retired by the age of 55. The pension paid by the state consists of two parts: a base amount and an additional part. The basic pension was 266 litas (77 euro) in February 2007. The additional part of the pension depends on the social security contributions a person paid and on the number of years a person was employed. In order to receive more than the basic pension, it is required that the person has been working and has paid into social security for at least 15 years.

There are also additional premiums that are paid to select groups of pensioners. If a person was sent to Siberia during Soviet times, compensation will be paid as part of the pension. Women who give birth to three children or more can choose to retire earlier. In that case they are paid a special "many-children pension" (*daugiavaikės motinos pensija*). They can also choose the normal pension and continue working until they are 60. For disabled persons, the same rule is applied. The person can choose either a handicap pension or a normal pension. People will have to calculate which is more beneficial for them. It is normally estimated that a person should have worked 30–35 years in order to receive what one would call a normal state pension (basic plus additional), which is approximately 587 litas (170 euro).[10] If people are still healthy, they can work on the side to supplement the pension.[11]

---

10 Information from Lietuvos darbo birža in Vilnius (Lithuanian unemployment center).

11 Based on interviews with working pensioners in Straigiai (2007) and with municipality workers in Marijampolė and Graižiūnai (in 2006 and 2007).

Farmers and other self-employed workers receive no additional pension unless they sign up for a private pension fund, for which they have to pay monthly 50 percent of what they expect to receive every month when they retire. This is too high an expense for many of them, taking their daily costs into consideration. The same is the case for the unemployed and for people who work illegally in Lithuania and abroad. This means that many who already are in a weak position are not favored by the pension system. The self-employed find themselves in a situation of constant work, with no prospects for a reasonable pension. "We will work till we die" (*mes dirbsim kol numirsim*), as my landlord in Bilvytis said to me as he explained their unfortunate situation.[12]

The problem of employment occurred after 1990, when many shifted from state employment on the collective farms to a life as private small-scale farmers. As previously emphasized, this meant that they stopped "saving years" for their pensions. The problem for many older people today is exactly this lack of employment years, and this is more often the case for women than for men. Whereas men have had no interruption in their work, many women do not have the sufficient years of employment because they were at home with the children. Under the Soviet system, they were only to be given short maternity leaves because of the gender equality policy; in reality, however, many women did not return to the collective farm once they had children, because they thought they could return when the children were older and ready to establish families of their own. This was not insensible future planning at the time, as all social guarantees were embedded in the collective farms, and no one anticipated the collapse of the Soviet Union. When it happened, there was no workplace to return to, even if the women had so desired. If the women then became engaged in family farming, this did not add any additional years to their pensions, as it counted as a private business, not public employment. Although the collapse may have ended some careers, the majority of men had not had any interruption in their work during the Soviet system, and so they had a high pension of up to 800–900 litas (231–260 euro). The more years one had been working, the higher the additional premium became. Women, who had not had the minimum 15 years of work, received the minimum of 266 litas (77 euro). Other women who had only taken short maternity leaves were on the same level as men regarding their pension, but this was not the rule.

An important thing to bear in mind is that in general, older people depend on multiple incomes in order to compensate for the decrease in social security and state support experienced after 1990. Having different sources of income appears to be more important to women than men due to their lower pensions. For women who had not yet reached retirement age but foresaw that they would lack years of employment, certain precautions could still be taken in order to

---

12 From my field notes, April 2007; my translation from Lithuanian.

improve the situation. One option was to look for work in the city until they reached retirement age. This could be a part-time occupation for a few hours a day. It was not so important that they earned much money, although this was an extra benefit, but it was important that they were registered as working. Others came by the missing years in other ways. By pulling the right strings, some could get "employed" by a company in order to make additional years for their pension. This option was only accessible if one had friends in the right places, as the employment would be on paper only and merely had the function to add fictive working years to one's record.

For women who had already retired and had a comparatively low pension, there were other ways of adding to their monthly income. If one had a state pension, it would function as the base, with various additional monetary and nonmonetary resources added to it. This could be the (illegal or legal) sale of dairy products, calves, piglets, chickens and eggs. Cooperation with other households also offered stability and security, as people were further safeguarded through their networks and there was again extra security in the land and the animals, as people would be close to self-sustainable in terms of food. In this way, a wide variety of monetary and nonmonetary contributions supported elderly people. New possibilities from the EU were only further additions to the basic economic system, such as Early Retirement or Direct Payments for land. Hence, some incomes were lost with the EU entrance due to stricter rules for agriculture, but then others were gained. This was the strength of the multiple income system as the flow from many sources established an overall security. The aspect of seeing the diverse incomes pooled by different family members also reflects the wider social and economic organization in different families. It was not necessarily a rule that individual incomes would contribute to the family as such. Although I met families where money and resources were equally shared, it was just as often the case that the household was internally divided.

The women explained that the wife was the one who was responsible for most of the daily expenses, and many of them complained that the men only thought about alcohol and cigarettes, and they saw little if any of their husbands' pensions. This was a cause of frustration among the women who argued for a better-shared economy and thus took various contra-actions. One elderly woman was so suspicious of her husband that she always kept her money in her bra so that he would not take it. Another elderly woman removed most of the food from the kitchen and hid it in various places in the living room so that the husband would not find it. Eventually, he would start to buy food for the household as well, she reasoned, at least when he got hungry enough. But it turned out that every time she cooked, he managed to get some of the food anyway. In another household, the wife had to buy the hay and corn for the cows from her husband, since he argued that legally, the fields were his and the cows were hers.

I do not intend to give the impression that there were no exceptions from this rule of economic division. Rather, I want to emphasize that it was not necessarily the case that the husband's higher pension compensated for the wife's lower one. This tendency has also been exemplified by Frances Pine (1993) in an article with the very telling title "The Cows and Pigs are His, the Eggs are Mine". Pine shows how gender divisions in terms of status and working spheres are demonstrated through internal divisions of property in Polish rural households. Just like in the Lithuanian case, one could not take for granted that the household functioned as a whole, rather, property and work were gendered. Hence, the woman Pine quoted in the title of her article gave voice to different values attached to the men and women; clearly, cows and pigs had a much higher value than eggs. In the case I referred to previously, where the woman was in charge of the cows and the man of the fields, this both reinforces Pine's argument and shows an interesting development that has taken place in the years after the collapse of the Soviet Union. Whereas the cows in Pine's case had a considerably high value, inflation of production costs and the low milk prices mean that the cow no longer is such a valuable possession in Lithuania. This again emphasizes the need for multiple incomes, which, in the case of older people, would often be a mixture of pensions, Direct Payments for land, and sales of farm products.

European Engagement

With the situation of an increasing number of aging women in the countryside and a high-scale emigration of young people, it calls into question how previous patterns of kin-based support were upheld under the changing circumstances. If aging people were trapped in a difficult situation, it was likewise challenging for their children, who were faced with few perspectives for employment in the rural areas and with a remaining responsibility for their parents. This put them in a dilemma between changing conditions for work and persistent kinship obligations.

This leads us to how generation and demographic restructurings become central elements in determining new (old) ways of providing social security in the aftermath of the EU entrance, with a profound impact on everyday life arrangements for work, care and kin-based responsibilities, and how the youth understand and respond to processes of EUropeanization.

Victor de Munck (2008), in an article about the Westernization of Lithuanian society, analyzes such responses to the current developments with focus on the educated and English-speaking youth, the so-called "New Lithuanians," young people who feel competent as cosmopolitan actors on a global stage. The New Lithuanians have emerged from Lithuania's recent history of a sudden turn to the West and the rejection of the immediate past, which creates an expectation of wealth and access to a Utopian world in the immediate future. The grand number of young Lithuanians, eager to access Europe in this way, leads De Munck to speak about a secular and money-fixated (or money-obsessed) "Millenarian Movement" in Lithuania, where participants consciously try to transform themselves into Western Europeans by means of the acquisition of wealth, the consumption of Western goods and the development of what De Munck refers to as a "hybrid" Lithuanian–Western mind. Thereby, he understands young people who possess a certain crossbreed between a "Lithuanian mind" and a "Western mind." In this manner, he divides the Lithuanians into groups: those who are capable to access Europe and respond to the recent developments (the participants) and those who are incapable of doing so due to lack of education, including limited if any foreign language skills, lack of money and lack of vision (the so-called nonparticipants) (De Munck 2008). Whereas I well recognize the young generation De Munck describes as the New Lithuanians, and very well follow his thoughts about their Westernization, I find that the rough classification of his nonparticipants is based on superficial observations, which suffer from a lack of direct interaction with them. His description goes as follows:

> The boys I saw were loud and unruly, with short hair, hard faces, and tight shirts that prominently displayed their muscles; they smoked and drank beer daily (so it seemed). Not all of the boys and men were like this, of course, but these were the ones I noticed and sought to avoid. The exterior of the complex could be somewhat intimidating, with these little gangs of aimless youth and their 'I am dangerous, therefore I am' twist on Descartes. (De Munck 2008, 177)

Reading this short but precise description, I immediately thought to myself: these are my informants! Although De Munck carried out his research in the city and I in the countryside, there was nothing in this brief description which could determine whether these actually were city boys (who, regardless of this fact, would also be subjected to EUropeanization and changes), or whether they belonged to the group of circular migrants who every Friday return to the countryside to work on their parents' farms on the weekends. Although vividly descriptive, it appeared to me to be a very narrow picture that did not show any familiarity with their situation. De Munck points to two interconnected features, the one being their crudely displayed masculinity, obviously intimidating to the innocent observer, and the second, their being young "aimless" men unable to take active part in Europe-Lithuania. My observations of the gangs of "rough guys," suggest a different analysis.

In an article by German anthropologist Otto Habeck (2005) on gender and culture at the Siberian and Northern Russian frontier, he seeks to understand the reason behind displayed masculinity through an approach he frames as "the unsettled social roles of young men." The article starts out with his concern about perplexing behavior of young Siberian men, a behavior which he describes as macho, with reference to the performed masculinity, abusive language and drinking, underlined by the potential or actual use of physical violence, thus, similar features to what both De Munck and I observed during our fieldwork in Lithuania. Habeck sees these aspects of the young men's identity as a way to establish a role in the community. He is, however, attentive to the fact that such macho behavior is not generally displayed and accepted everywhere, but it is confined to certain places. In the case of Habeck's study, the display of macho behavior is exclusively acceptable in what he defines as an "uncultured space" – the tundra. However, the same behavior is not tolerated in the village, which falls under the definition of a "cultured space." In the latter setting, very different expectations of behavior and norms exist, which are to be followed (Habeck 2005).[13]

If we compare Habeck's study in Siberia with similar phenomena in Lithuania, we could likewise assume that the displayed masculinity is not accepted and well seen everywhere and furthermore, that it serves as a response to the strict obedience youth employ when together with their parents. In fact, I know of several young men who would be drinking and most likely fighting in the evening and the following morning would wake up at six o'clock and start working in the fields under the strict supervision of their mothers, aunts and other female family members (due to the increasing importance of old women, as emphasized earlier). Likewise, the same young men who made use of abusive language among their friends and used rough behavior as a way to show their role as "real men," would address their parents with *Jūs*, which is the Lithuanian polite form of address equivalent to the German *Sie*. While it would be masculine to display their strength in front of young women, it would undermine their masculinity if they opposed their mothers (rebellion against fathers would be more common). It would also be the same group of "tough young men" who could be seen following their mothers or grandmothers to town, carrying their grocery shopping around from one shop to the other without a word of complaint.

Contrary to De Munck, I found that the so-called nonparticipants had an important function in family life with regard to care and social security – the rough masculinity being but one aspect of a more complex gender role. The groups of young men I knew from my two field site villages were – although often unruly, loud, drinking, smoking and occasionally fighting – still in a process of bridging old expectations in a new setting, of finding ways to access new opportunities while being subject to unemployment, restructurings and difficulties. Without attempting to glorify the kind of gangs De Munck described (at first I was also struck by their unpleasant attitude

13 See also Ventsel (2007) for discussion on masculinity in Siberia.

and not the least their direct and rough language), I emphasize the need to tell a fuller story of their situation. I will discuss the issue of emigration, unemployment, and the parents' need for care based on three different narratives about young men, each of which points to the issues of circular migration and the circulation of sons.

The Urban Migrant

Donatas was 29 years old when I met him.[14] He had initially had six siblings: one older brother and two older sisters who were all in their 30s, two younger twin brothers in their late 20s and a much younger brother 16 years his junior. Tragically, the youngest had died at the beginning of 2007 due to heart failure. He was the second child who died; just the year before, one of the twin brothers had been killed in a car accident. There were five children left. The two older sisters lived with their husbands and children in other parts of Lithuania. One of the sisters was engaged in small-scale farming and dairy production, whereas the other was at home with the children, while her husband had a job in town. The oldest brother lived in Kaunas with his wife. He was a truck driver and she worked in the local kindergarten. The other twin brother lived just across the street from the parents' place with his teenage wife and their baby son. He worked in a bakery in a bigger town close to the village and his wife was at home with the child.

Donatas' mother had retired at the age of 50. She had chosen to take the so-called "many-children pension" (*daugiavaikės motinos pensija*) that was offered to all women with more than three children. This did not mean that she got more money than she would have with a normal pension, but it meant that she had been able to retire early. The father received state support for disabled persons (*invalidumas*) due to his poor health, and he spent most of his time in bed. The family had previously had a few cows, pigs and a horse, but during my fieldwork, the horse and all but one cow were sold. The mother supplemented her pension by selling the little extra milk she had and by preparing food for weddings and funerals.

The combination of farming and pension constituted their living. The natural resources on the farm were only potentials from the outset: if no one worked the land, it provided no crops; if no one planted potatoes or cultivated vegetables, they would not grow; if no one took care of the animals, milked the cow or slaughtered the pigs, no milk or meat would be provided. To keep even a small farm required hard labor and despite the many children, labor was scarce. As previously mentioned, two of the sons had died, the remaining children had left the house and the father was ill. The farm was primarily the mother's responsibility, but as an aging woman, she could not possibly carry out the heavy work on her own.

---

14 About Donatas' family, see Chapter 2.

She was dependent on her children. The daughters and the elder brother lived far away and had their own families to take care of. The brother across the street was working daily in a bakery, but would help out at the farm when he could. He was, however, drinking quite heavily, which had an impact of his ability to work. Then there was Donatas. Contrary to his siblings, he had no family of his own, which meant that his family obligations were towards his mother only. The problem was that he no longer lived in the village. He was employed both as a carpenter and a construction worker and he worked illegally in order to avoid taxes. This meant he moved around Lithuania, from city to city, from job to job.

To be an urban migrant with elderly parents in the countryside put Donatas in an uncanny situation. After five days of hard work in the city, he went back to his parents on Friday evening. The weekend was spent in labor on the farm, and in the evenings he was together with his friends in the village (the kind of young men that De Munck described to us, and Donatas was no exception) who had returned home on the weekend for the same reason, to work on the farms. In the evenings, they would hang out in front of the local store with beers or they would go down to the lake in the company of girls, would drink and smoke and some almost always got into a fight. As Monday arrived, Donatas left in the early morning in order to get back to the city. The summer was particularly demanding, as this was the season with the most work on the farms. During this period, the eldest brother would also come from Kaunas in order to share the workload, and his wife came along to collect potatoes or help the mother in the kitchen. In the winter, there were other tasks such as chopping winter wood and transporting it home, repairing equipment for the farm or renovating the house. During this period, Donatas only returned occasionally.

As the internal resources in the mother's household were few, the mother had to expand them with resources from other families. Donatas' mother would help on other farms and often, other women or men would work on her farm in return. When Donatas was at home, the neighboring women would often come over on the weekends and "borrow" him to work on their farms. The additional work Donatas carried out on other farms enabled the family to engage in a broader network, something the mother could benefit from when he was not there. I once asked Donatas if he would not rather stay in the countryside and work on the farm instead of always having to travel, but he replied, "Are you kidding, or what?!" (*Juokauji, ar ką?!*). Clearly, a countryside life was not to be preferred to his present situation.

Donatas' situation of was not exceptional, but reflected the situation for many young people. The countryside of Bilvytis offered basically no alternative work to farming, and it was becoming increasingly difficult to make a living off farming unless you had a lot of land or many animals. The situation demanded that young people found employment elsewhere. This was in itself not a sacrifice, as the small and remote villages were not attractive places to live. The problem was that the parents still counted on their children's support. The fact that the children no longer lived in the village did not change this expectation. In this we find the reason why the bus that arrived in Bilvytis on Friday at 5:30 p.m. and left from Bilvytis on Monday at 6:30 a.m. was always crowded with young people who travelled back and forth between the city and the countryside. It was, as a rule, young men in their 20s who had not yet married and still had primary obligations toward their parents. The prevailing work pressure of the urban–rural compromise, however, was further increased by the circulation of sons. Thus, the returning young men were further "circulated" in the village as an available labor force in case neighbors or friends needed additional help at their farms.

Although they officially had left their parents' house and as such, no longer counted as staying in the village, their frequent return pointed towards a circular migration. The situation of Donatas' family with the constellation of old woman/ young man (or young men) was one of many other examples I encountered during my fieldwork – the father being in poor health, the mother shouldering the main responsibility for the farm, the daughters caring mainly for their own families – while Donatas and, from time to time, his brothers, returned to the countryside to carry out hard labor at the parents' farm.

The EU Migrants

The other type of emigrant was the EU migrant, people who had left for other EU countries in western or northern parts of Europe after 2004. There were those who went abroad for educational reasons. However, the majority of EU migrants left in order to find work abroad. This was typically in factories, on farms, in fields picking berries and fruit or in greenhouses picking mushrooms. All of the young people I knew had arranged for jobs abroad through their networks. One of them was Tomas, a friend of Donatas' and a part of the same group of young men hanging out at the lake on weekends. Tomas was in his late 20s, from the countryside surrounding Bilvytis and had been working as a car mechanic in Lithuania ever since he left school. During my fieldwork, Tomas was offered a job abroad in a fish factory in Ireland. There was a line of people who had been forerunners for the job Tomas had now been offered. In 2001 a few young men left for Ireland to work in a factory, a job that had been arranged for them through an employment agency. As they arrived in Ireland, one of the men then arranged for a friend of his to get a job in the same place, and this friend in turn arranged a job for his girlfriend. The girlfriend arranged jobs for her father and her two brothers. One of the brothers was a friend of Tomas', and through him, Tomas got a job in the same factory.

Tomas continued making connections for new workers; as his younger girlfriend Regina finished high school, he arranged for her to come over to the same fish factory. Later on, Tomas also arranged for his mother to come to Ireland and work.

Tomas and Regina left with no immediate plans for how long they would stay, or when they would return to Lithuania. As long as they liked it and made enough money, they saw no reason to return home. The job abroad provided a good and stable income, and Tomas, who, through different more and less severe criminal activities, had been sentenced to fines of an overall amount of 10,000 litas (2,896 euro), was able to pay it all within one year and then go on to save some money for his and Regina's future. As Tomas' mother was relatively young, in her late 40s, he had taken care of securing a job for her instead of sending money home. There was no need for him to send money to his father, who had a job in town and managed well on his own. Instead, Tomas would send his younger sister money in order to support her studies.

However, there were also other ways of reacting to the current changes of emigration. Two brothers, Edmundas and Vilius from Straigiai, had left for Ireland, and, happy with their new and high incomes, they preferred to use the money to enjoy a new lifestyle. So now that they had money, they spent it. They spent it abroad, but primarily they spent it when at home in Lithuania. Their mother, Vilma,[15] and the father, Algirdas, had a tight budget and it was surreal for them to witness how the young men used money on alcohol, parties, girls, fancy clothes, iPods and music, not to mention their need for two cell phones each (one for their friends and one for their girlfriends, as they said). Although the mother did not ask them for money, she had hoped for generous gifts from abroad, and a box of chocolates from the airport ultimately did not satisfy her. When they were abroad in Ireland, the mother did not fail to praise them and their present course in life, but when they were at home, she shouted at them and threatened to throw them out every other day, because they were "useless" and worked too little on the farm. However, in some of the more fierce arguments with their father, it was made clear to them that being at home also meant carrying out work, not just on the parents' farm, but also on the aunt's farm. It was intriguing that there also were two daughters in the family. The oldest was in her early 20s, and she now studied in Kaunas. Although she helped out one time or the other, there were no such expectations of her as of the brothers, as she had to take care of her studies. As for the youngest daughter, a girl of 16, she was free from work as long as she did well in school.

The one person who compensated for the lack of (working) children at Vilma and Algirdas' farm was Vilma's nephew, Rolandas, a bachelor in his mid-30s who had never left the village and had no family of his own. Rolandas was a tall man with uncombed red hair, always wearing working clothes. Rolandas was known in the village for having had severe learning problems in school and for his rough and dirty appearance, which became linked to his difficulties in finding a (decent and sober) woman. Not least was he known for his occasional disappearances, when he

---

15 Vilma was likewise mentioned in Chapter 3.

took his mother's old bicycle and rode off in order to drink with his pals. On these occasions, his angry mother would make a tour around the entire village to search for her bicycle (and her son) while complaining to all the villagers who would listen to her. This general image of Rolandas in the village set aside, he actually served a central function at several farms. He not only took up the main part of the work on his mother's farm and her sister Vilma's farm, but also at his uncle's, who likewise had a farm in Straigiai. Thus, he was covering the working spheres of the other absent sons in the family, which left him with a very heavy workload. Consequently, he, like Donatas from Bilvytis, was "circulated" around in this village due to the general lack of young men. Due to this arrangement, Edmundas and Vilius were obligated to work at their aunt's farm (Rolandas' mother's farm) when they were home on vacation, as compensation for the work Rolandas carried out in their absence. Rolandas, however, never seemed particularly thrilled when his cousins came over to his mother's farm to help; they were flashing their new cell phones, bragging about their many girlfriends and the excitement abroad, mocking him for not having any women and never having been abroad. As a return "favor," Rolandas would let them carry out the heaviest work tasks, although he could have done it better and faster himself. At least that kept them silent. The times Rolandas was thus "burdened" with his cousins' help, he tended to be tense and cranky. Once, after the cousins' departure, he made an exaggerated gesture of wiping sweat from his forehead with his hand, before shaking his thick, uncombed, red hair, his eyes turning to the sky.

> "Thank God they left!" he said. "Frankly speaking, I would rather work extra hours at my aunts' place than having them come here to work. It is much nicer without them, don't you think, huh?"[16]

Diplomatically, I left the questioned unanswered, although I perfectly understood his point; turning their experience as EU migrants into mockery at the home stage, was neither well seen nor accepted in the rural community.

As has been shown by Lithuanian anthropologist Liubinienė (2009), EU migrants, despite many negative experiences in their everyday life as construction workers or factory workers, still tend to idealize the country where they now reside, while Lithuania is thought of as an increasingly ambiguous place: both as a place of nostalgic memories of "home" and viewed with increasingly negative feelings when compared with the highly idealized country of residence (for comparison see Čiubrinskas 2004 and 2005). I observed these features reproduced in the home setting, however, the idealization of abroad used as a way to create new social status at home.

---

16 Based on my field notes, June 2007; my translation from Lithuanian.

Despite the image given when at home, I was well aware that Edmundas and Vilius were under just as much work pressure abroad as their urban counterparts were at home. Indeed, such labor migrants who accessed Europe through hard work were not accessing a Utopian dream. They were employed in factories and hotels or on farms abroad, working many hours a day. But the image they wished to portray of themselves in Lithuania was not the downside of being abroad, but the more glamorous and adventurous side of it. When the migrants were home in the village, they would display their relative wealth with different material items, and some underlined their migrant status by wearing sweatshirts or T-shirts saying "London," "I heart Dublin," "Sweden," or the like. They would speak extensively about their experiences and compare the excitement abroad with the miserable life in Lithuania. Some of them also dropped different English words into their daily vocabulary, telling their friends that they had mastered the language, something that they gladly demonstrated for their non-English-speaking audience. In my presence, however, they seemed less eager to show their language abilities. The eagerness to demonstrate their migrant status did not fit with the norms and fulfillment of kinship obligations, such as working at the farm and being circulated among relatives in the village.

The Villager

With the increasing emigration from the village, the pressure on the young men who stayed greatly increased. The family Jankauskas was living in Straigiai as farmers.[17] The parents were above the retirement age and both were in poor health; the mother had a bad heart and the father had recently had his leg amputated. Then there was the youngest daughter, a schoolteacher, her husband and their small children who lived in the house. The son in the family had left for Ireland in 2004, and the oldest daughter lived in Marijampolė with her family. The oldest daughter was home with the children while her husband was engaged in trading cars from Germany. The husband hardly ever visited his parents-in-law in Straigiai, nor did he ever help out on the farm. As he never offered to help with anything on the farm, he was perceived by the old parents more as a stranger than family.

As the workload on the farm became too heavy, the parents applied for, and got, EU's Early Retirement. The farm was formally transferred to the youngest daughter and the family could therefore continue farming just like before, although minor changes were made to lessen the workload. As they still tried to keep up commercial production of wheat and vegetables, the days were long and demanding on the farm. The situation put extra pressure on the youngest daughter's husband, Mindaugas, a man in his early 30s. He was not the De Munck type of rough guy; rather, Mindaugas was immediately likeable, friendly and with a subtle

---

17 About the family Jankauskas, see Chapters 2, 4 and 5.

sense of humor. He had his own business, buying cars in Germany and selling them in Lithuania, but still spent most of his time working on the farm. Although Mindaugas counted as a "stayer" in the village, his private income still came from the monthly ride to Germany, where he, with a mixture of his few German and English phrases, managed to make an additional income for his family.

Mindaugas was, however, not satisfied living with his wife's parents. He felt that their house would never become his real home and it bothered him that he could not live an independent life. Even his children were raised as much, if not more, by their grandparents than by him. Last, but not least, he had never wanted to be a farmer. When he had married his wife, he thought that living with the parents-in-law would be a short-term solution, whereas his wife was happy that they could stay in her old home. "I married my wife! I did not marry the farm,"[18] Mindaugas once said to me with frustration in his voice. After a lot of consideration, Mindaugas decided to move out. His mother had acquired an old school building in the nearby village after 1990. She could not use it and so she had given it to Mindaugas. He was determined to rebuild the old school and move in there with his family. This did not make him popular. If Mindaugas and the daughter moved out, it would be close to impossible for the parents to keep the farm. This was very hard, especially on the mother, and Mindaugas' house was a taboo in the family; one was not to mention it, out of respect for the mother's nerves. Mindaugas could not understand why he was made responsible for the continued existence of the farm. Instead of making life difficult for him, he argued, the parents could make their son come home from Ireland. The daughter was torn by the circumstances. On the one hand, she understood her husband and his wish to have his own house. On the other hand, she could not leave her parents. The daughter shifted between thoughts of divorce and thoughts of following her husband.

Mindaugas still pursued his idea with the house in the nearby village and started the project. The money he made with his car business was all put into restoring the old school, and he spent all his free time working on the old building that he slowly transformed into a house. The mother did not want to confront Mindaugas directly, but knew that they could not afford to lose him. Therefore, she pulled other strings to stop the project. She contacted Mindaugas' friends and asked them to talk him back to his senses, and she let the story "slip" in the village, which put Mindaugas under social pressure from all sides. Furthermore, she went to see Mindaugas' mother. She knew that although Mindaugas made his own money, he still needed to borrow from his mother in order to finish the project. She convinced Mindaugas' mother of the severe consequences of his project. This was an efficient move, as it definitely ended the money flow from Mindaugas' mother.

---

18 Original in English. As mentioned earlier in the section, Mindaugas did speak a bit of English.

The story of Mindaugas and his house raises questions about the understanding of family and family obligations in rural Lithuania. The parents viewed the marriage with the daughter as socially and economically binding to their family unit. Hence, in their perception, to marry the daughter was indeed to marry both them and the farm (not literally speaking, of course). Not only would they face a difficult situation without Mindaugas, his leaving would also have been an act that displayed his lack of sensitivity for the family's difficult situation. The situation reflected more than anything the upper limit of how many young people a family could afford to lose. It was not that the Jankauskas family clung to their children, but with the oldest daughter and the only son gone, they could not afford to lose the last daughter and her husband. Furthermore, this case story is again another example of the specific pressure put on the young men and the central role the older generation of women played in sustaining the household. Indeed, it was the wife in the Jankauskas family who had made the necessary arrangements that eventually prevented Mindaugas from leaving the household. The father, although being the head of the household, was in such poor health that he could no longer take the main responsibility.

Preventing Mindaugas from moving out was done via social pressure and the family's network, but it was another use of network that was displayed, one that did not involve helping each other out with the work on the farm. The Jankauskas family had never cooperated much with other villagers. They knew such exchanges would be too uneven, as the father's education as an agronomist and their relative wealth set them in a more advantageous position, meaning that there would be by far more "outgoing" than "incoming" favors. In all the years they had been farming, there had been many internal resources at the farm, which meant that they did not need to expand the resources with additional cooperation from outside. The other villagers had been used to the Jankauskas family being a closed unit that would only ask others for help in very rare situations. This model had functioned as long as they were all healthy and present, but as the internal resources weakened, the situation became more subtle. This did not mean that they now went out and engaged more with other families; they wanted things to continue as before, as a family cooperation.

EUropeanization, Individualism and Parental Expectations

The three case stories, each in their own way, illustrate the way young men experience increasing pressure under the changing circumstances. Emigration and gendered work and aging reinforce the need for young men to work on the farms. This analytical perspective mainly emphasizes how large-scale emigration from Lithuania coupled with the lower life expectancy of their fathers, have created a general shortage of men in the rural areas. Young women, on their behalf, would form other roles with regard to the maintenance of work. As displayed in the case about the Jankauskas' family, the youngest daughter was still helping out on the farm and, by marriage, secured additional male help to the farm. In such instances, the woman would stay and help her parents, while forming a link to the much-needed young males. In other instances, young women who had left the village would return when certain seasonal work was due, such as the yearly collection of potatoes in the fields. Some young women from my research villages, also made extra income by helping and nursing elderly widows, who in return paid them parts of their pension or, if they had no children of their own, made promises that they would be the sole heirs to whatever property they might be in possession of. While aging women shouldered the main responsibility, young women could in such cases contribute by other means.

De Munck recognizes and distinguishes the inequalities that prevent some from taking part in processes of Westernization. However, I argue that there is no "either/or" with reference to European engagement; rather, there are different ways and different degrees of engagement. In accordance with my definition and understanding of EUropeanization, *everybody* is inevitably engaged in and shaped by the EUropean project, and especially the rural population that has been subjected to so many and so pervasive restructurings of daily life in the light of the EU preparations and the EU entrance. Thus, the young, and in many instances, uneducated people from the rural areas, are already actively engaged in processes of EUropeanization and respond to the EU impacts, as do their aging parents. Young rural citizens may respond by becoming labor migrants in Western EU countries and thus in a very concrete "hands-on manner" make use of the new possibilities that came along with the EU entrance, although they do not count as having "hybrid minds." In a similar manner, the tendency of other young people from rural areas move to cities to find work is closely linked to the current restructurings of the countryside: the small-scale agricultural production their parents engage in no longer pays off and the countryside offers few if any alternative jobs. Their response in the manner of circular migration deeply embeds them in overcoming the obstacles they faced in the aftermath of EU integration. Even when working in the cities, they still have to adhere to their parents' needs for support, as the expectations of the youth did not change, despite the changed practical circumstances. The young people in my study were bound by changes in structures and new options for work paired with parental expectations and obligations. However, these restraints (or their appearance for that sake) did not put the young people in nonparticipatory roles in Europe. It is here, I argue, that we get a better insight into what EUropeanization comes to mean for the majority of young people from the rural, and likely, the urban areas, as the envisioning of a cosmopolitan life is only an option for the minority. The youth staying behind in Lithuania are forced into a concrete relationship with changed circumstances, which they have to cope with on the home stage. Thus, in other and probably more concrete ways than the New Lithuanians, they participate in the presently changing society. My point is that only when refraining from persistently formulating the EU as an elite project and from setting specific requirements for what kind of engagements and activities count as "active participation in Europe" are we able to analyze how those people, who are otherwise excluded or alienated, actively correspond to and implement the changes and, thus, engage themselves in the EUropean project.

Kinship Obligations and Emigration

The demographic restructurings did not enforce much change in the parents' ways of obtaining security. For many years, they had based their living on a system of multiple incomes and had expanded resources with neighboring households. New opportunities for extra incomes such as Direct Payments for land, Early Retirement or other possible extra incomes from the EU were embedded into the old system by some, while others relied on past experiences and refrained from participation in any form of institutionalized support due to their inherent skepticism of official arrangements. The youth's emigration did not change this system, it rather reinforced the importance of it. In this regard, other features also came into play, such as gendered aging and gendered work, which merged with specific constellations of demographic changes and new family structures, namely, quickly aging or dying men, leaving a majority of old women (or widows, more specifically) in the rural areas, resulting in increasing pressure on young men, either forcing them to stay, to migrate circularly from city to countryside or, coping with the shortage of men, to be further circulated within the village. Due to the unruly years in the 1990s, people have difficulties trusting the state alone for support, and rightly so. The overlap between the disintegration of one union and integration into another had resulted in what F. and K. von Benda-Beckmann have called "no longer, not yet" ([1994] 2000, 24). There was no longer a system of collective farming, which had employed basically all villagers and supported the old, and it had not yet been replaced by sufficient state support and/or alternative work places for the youth. Many of these features have lasted until the present day, even being reinforced by EU-supported development of the agricultural sector, as large-scale farming was to replace the semi-subsistence farming that had been the main occupation for most villages. On top of this, past experiences had taught people not to rely too strongly on institutions, but instead create their own means of support, such as cooperation with kin, neighbors and friends. The general response was balanced between change and continuity, as both older and younger had to make choices corresponding both to current changes and persistent needs in the family. As Haukanes and Pine (2005; see also Tedre and Tulva 1999;

Brandtstädter 2003) have argued in their contribution to the debate about care and postsocialism, the emergence of individualized lifestyles and increasing urbanization does not undermine existing patterns of kinship obligations; rather, they are reproduced under the new circumstances and with specific consequences and outcomes for gender relations. Indeed, the dual existence between emigration and circular migration is the form of EUropeanization fitting the majority of young people from the rural areas (and very likely also many young people from the urban areas), and it is, as such, a predominating pattern, questioning ideas about increasing individualism and decreasing kinship relationships.

As the Lithuanian case shows, the EU influences much wider functions of everyday life than mere production; it stimulates changes in relations between genders and generations and reinforces new patterns of obtaining social security among small-scale farmers and their children. Instead of seeing this as Europeanization, and thus a process of fulfilling desires and dreams or adapting to certain lifestyles, EUropeanization coins the consequences that EU integration has in people's everyday life, such as demographic changes, circular migration and responses to persisting demands under a changed structure. Far from being the road to an increasingly cosmopolitan life, EUropeanization may, for many, mean increased pressure and responsibility on the home front.

CHAPTER 7

"They told us we would be getting up on the high mountain": Concluding Remarks

One day toward the end of my fieldwork, I was sitting at the bus stop in Bilvytis, waiting for the bus to arrive. Next to me sat an old man who only looked for shelter from the sun while drinking his beer. Although I had not talked with him before, rumor had him well informed about me and my research. During our talk, I stressed the fact that I was very interested in the changes in people's lives that came about with the EU. He laughed to himself, shook his head and said to me, "What changes? Nothing has changed." He took a sip of his beer and continued, "They said we would be getting up on the high mountain. Well, I am still sitting here! [*Jie sakė, kad mes pakilsim į aukštą kalną. Na, aš vis dar sėdžiu čia*]."[1]

The old man's remark was straight to the point. For many people, the outcomes of the EU entrance were nothing to hooray about. There had been no money pouring down from the sky, as intimated by infomercials prior to the EU referendum, and for the small-scale farmers – the majority – no higher living standards had come about. The visions of wealth (the high mountain) and him "still sitting here" was literally as well as metaphorically the old man's summary of the gap between promises prior to the entrance and everyday reality.

That day at the bus stop was not the first time I heard such sarcastic remarks. When I asked people in Straigiai and Bilvytis what they felt had changed after the EU entrance, I was often met with the statement that "nothing had changed" followed by further ironic comments such as "Oh, but my hair got grey," "Well, the children grew up," "My house caught fire," or, as a villager from Bilvytis bitterly remarked, "What changed after the EU? My wife ran away! That's what's changed!"[2] All comments reflected a preoccupation with the close and nearby

---

1 From my field notes, August 2007; my translation from Lithuanian.
2 From my field notes, 2006–2007; my translations from Lithuanian.

environment, not with the larger geopolitical framework. When people said that "nothing had changed," it was not to be taken strictly at face value. These remarks underlined the fact that things had not changed in the ways it was supposed to, or the way they had been promised. Ironically, the villagers, who showed less excitement about the EU entrance, and who stated that "nothing had changed," were among the people who most thoroughly had been targeted by the changes which came about with the EU membership. Furthermore, due to their sheer numbers, they had proven to be determining in the process and the outcomes of EUropeanization. Recalling the evening of 1 May 2004, when I had been sitting in Straigiai listening to barking dogs while there had been fireworks in the capital, it appeared to me that the unfulfilled promises did not exactly come as a shock to the villagers. Rather, they had anticipated it.

Going West?

Anthropologist Monica Heintz (2006, 19–21), in her study of Romania, notices a very positive attitude among Romanians towards Western Europe. Heintz distinguishes four components through which Romanians express their "longing for the West": imitation, Western superiority, Western migration and Romania's image. The first component, imitation, is in reference to consumption, clothing and TV shows, as people tend to buy Western products, watch Western television shows and eat in expensive fast food restaurants rather than in cheaper Romanian restaurants. She sees this as an uncritical attempt to adopt a similar lifestyle as they imagine is practiced in Western Europe. The second component Heintz dwells on is that the Romanians nurture ideas about Western superiority, a component that is closely related to the first-mentioned point about imitation. Here she looks at how people view everything coming from Western Europe or the United States to be of higher standards than in Romania; hence, her informants argue, "civilization" and "culture" are only found in the West. The third component is migration to Western European countries, which Heintz sees as the most concrete symptom of the Romanians' desire to become Europeans. Finally, the fourth component is in reference to the national level, where she reflects upon the effort to give Romania a good image in the eyes of the EU and NATO, even if it entails decisions that are not well seen nationally (Heintz 2005). My concern with these four components is that even when summed up as a general pattern, they shed light on a particular and limited aspect of the broader picture. I can best evaluate this by comparing Heintz's four components to Lithuanian conditions.

Imitation: While in Lithuania, I noticed, just as Heintz had noticed in Romania, that the Lithuanians took a liking to American B-movies and Mexican and South American soap operas, not to forget the high popularity of the German crime serial "Kommissar Rex" about an intelligent and brave police dog (the latter is also seen in the fact that several dogs in the countryside have been named "Reksas" – the Lithuanian version of "Rex"). On the same note, I also paid attention to the exploding number of shopping malls and the mushrooming of fast-food restaurants in the country. However, this should not lead us to conclude that we solely witness imitation of Western societies and/or an uncritical consumption of Western goods. First, it is pertinent to consider whether these features alone reflect Western societies or if they are not simplified stereotypes prompted by the diverse, complex and multifaceted lifestyles of Western Europe. Here we also find a preoccupation with organic food and "slow food" movements, a wide variety of artistic movies (not only soap operas) and anticapitalist demonstrations, to mention but a few examples. Second, this said, we can consider whether the preoccupation with consumerism and Western products in the former socialist countries really is a one-dimensional "longing for the West." However, perhaps we should consider this in a broader context and pay attention to how increasing Westernization led to a stronger need to redefine what is truly national. To give one example from my research: importing of food from other countries and the increasing number of fast food restaurants led to the reinvention of authentic, natural and healthy Lithuanian food products as opposed to Western European products, the latter being seen as unhealthy and filled with preservatives and likely to cause all kinds of diseases. This gives voice to the idea that it is not only a question about imitation, but it is also a question of national reinvention, both of which are coexisting processes.

Western superiority: This overlaps with the following point about what Heintz finds is an exaggerated respect for everything Western. Viewed from one angle, I could say that similar patterns are found in Lithuania, and that the notion of "the West" is still embedded with a certain air of modernity, and that young migrants in the villages take pride in the fact that they have been abroad. This being said, I could come up with just as many counter-examples where Lithuanians would raise a critical voice toward the West. One example is the treatment of older people in Western Europe (instead of taking care of the elders at home, they are "put away" in nursery homes). "Immoral" sexual behavior with multiple partners and a high divorce rate are other points of criticism, I often overheard. Another example is the idea, which flourishes among many Lithuanians, that Western Europeans are spoiled, soft, whiny and incapable of coping with shortages and hard times (see also De Munck 2008). Homosexuality as an unwanted "import" is likewise a central point of criticism.[3]

---

3 Homosexuals were strongly repressed during the Soviet regime and if discovered, were put away in prison or in mental hospitals. Therefore, they were not visible in society, which led many people to conclude that they had not existed at all. Villagers in my fields of research argued that since homosexuals only had appeared after the Soviet dissolution, the only explanation for their appearance was that "mentally sick people" got "inspired" by homosexual ideas, movies and images deriving from Western Europe and/or the United States.

Concerned Lithuanians found that Lithuania's first gay pride parade in Vilnius in the year 2010 displayed "diseased behavior," a concern which is shared by many people working in the Lithuanian government who tried to make a ban against all information about homosexuality in Lithuanian society. Such sentiments do not match the official position of EU laws, which state that it is the duty of all member countries to protect the rights of minorities. In my research, none of the above-mentioned examples are seen as an expression of "Western superiority" by Lithuanians; quite to the contrary, many expressed fear of that such "demoralization" would emerge in Lithuania and undermine national values.

Migration: The third point relates to Western migration, where Heintz refers to the exceeding numbers of Romanians who have migrated to work abroad, mostly higher-educated people. Migration is the central point where people define their will to become Europeans, she argues. But is it really so? In Lithuania many if not the majority of all migrants did not have a higher education, but went abroad to make money through labor on farms or in factories. As has been argued by Neringa Liubinienė in a study about Lithuanian migrants in Ireland, those in the Lithuanian diasporas often keep together in groups and thus, only speak Lithuanian, celebrate Lithuanian festivals and make it a noble act of keeping Lithuanian traditions, maybe even more so when abroad than when at home (Liubinienė 2009). Only when returning home is the opposite image displayed, namely, their internationalism and cosmopolitanism. Taking the great number of Romanian migrants arriving in old EU member countries, I strongly doubt that their case is radically different and that they mainly represent the higher-educated parts of the population.

International image: The final point made by Heintz was that the Romanian's struggle to look good at a national level was an attempt to achieve both membership in NATO and EU, which in the case of Lithuania and Romania happened in 2004 and 2007, respectively. But could we conclude from this that it only is a question about appearing good? In 2003, a year when neither Romania nor Lithuania had joined the EU or NATO, the two countries, together with Albania, Bulgaria, Croatia, Estonia, Latvia, Macedonia, Slovakia and Slovenia, caused much debate as they signed the Vilnius letter, where they showed support for the United States in the Iraq War and sent troops to Iraq.[4] This was an act that evoked harsh criticism from other European governments, as it went against the political climate in many of the existing EU member countries.[5] Hence, we cannot reduce the attempts to join the EU

---

4 The Vilnius letter can be read online at http://www.novinite.com/view_news.php?id=19022 (accessed 29 September 2009).

5 The opposition toward the Iraq War was most strongly led by Germany and France. However, Italy, Spain, Portugal, Britain and Denmark likewise sent troops to Iraq.

as an uncompromising will to appear good. Rather, leaders in the formerly socialist countries not only want to be imbedded in the EU and follow orders, they also want to define the EU, contribute to what it means to be European and demonstrate the values EU should stand for.

My systematic counter-argumentation to Heintz's ideas emerges from the concern that claiming such an eagerness to be Westernized proves little attention to the work done by postsocialist scholars. In order to sum up my alternative, I will return to the four points laid out in the introduction, namely: (1) the coexisting processes of disintegration from the Soviet Union and integration into the EU; (2) the reconceptualization of history and identity; (3) the EU attempt to create the new member countries as metonyms of the larger entity that resulted in the emergences of locally produced EUs; and finally (4) how EUropeanization targets everyday life of the people furthest from the decision-making institutions.

Coexisting Processes of Disintegration and Integration

First, I would like to call attention to the fact that the actual entrance into the EU was not such a big step for rural citizens. New laws and legislation did, in most cases, not arrive with the membership, but had been in the making many years before that. Integration into the EU started shortly after Lithuania regained independence and from 1995 onward, the requirements for the preparations grew year by year. The rapid destruction of the Soviet societal structures took place at the same time as Lithuania started to receive advice and to adopt laws from the *Acquis*. Such continuous interrelations led to new hybrid constellations between the Soviet system and the system of the EU. On these grounds I suggest it would be more accurate to see this as coexisting processes of disintegration from the Soviet Union and integration into the EU. In light of this coexistence, people were not wrong to say that nothing had changed because of the EU entrance, since the integration into the EU had been in the making for a number of years before that. The villagers of my research likewise reflected this in their statements about the double union-ness, with remarks such as "Lithuania has always been in a union" or "We are going from one union to the other."[6]

Furthermore, the discourses about the EU as a return to the historical belonging became inflicted with difficult paradoxes. The message surfaced that although returning to the right geopolitical constellation, the EU was still not for all.

---

6 From my field notes 2006–2007; my translation from Lithuanian.

Reconceptualization of History

> Is it really the case, I pondered, that I have got away from that swamp of
> idiocies, vulgarity and lies that is Soviet ideology, only to be forced to plunge
> head into the even more idiotic, vulgar and lying marsh of anti-Sovietism?
> (Zinoviev [1982] 1985, 59)

EU integration affected Lithuanian national images and the re-creation of history
and invention of the "new society" and the "new man." Consequently, image
resources were set into the frame of the past in the "right" way, namely, occupation,
poverty, lack of freedom and imprisonment, while the freedom fighters (*partizanai*)
became the symbol of the true Lithuanian spirit. In addition, belonging to the EU
was promoted as a return to the geopolitical entity to which Lithuania rightfully
belonged. Thus, the creation of the nation's future was grounded in an unambiguous
recreation of the Soviet past as a time of evil.

If it appears that I put the situation slightly on the edge, we can consider an
event in Lithuania that was a part of the program "Vilnius – European capital
of culture 2009". I here point to the interactive theater performance *1984 in the
Bunker (Back to the USSR)*, referencing George Orwell's novel *Nineteen Eighty-
Four*, in which he describes life under a totalitarian regime (Orwell [1949] 1982).
The cultural show – which is not recommended for people with heart problems –
is a conscious attempt to evoke positive feelings about the present time. This is
done by letting people re-experience selected negative parts of the Soviet past. In
the theater play, the audience is under the command of actors dressed in Soviet
uniforms and has to follow instructions, march in rows and obey orders. The
audience is furthermore humiliated, threatened and harassed by an actor playing
the part of the Soviet KGB agent (Klumbytė 2008). According to the organizers,
the idea behind the show is to "cure" those Lithuanians who are "diseased" with
Soviet nostalgia by reviving the past that they seemingly have forgotten (ibid.).
1984 in the Bunker is an example of the publicly accepted – and EU-supported –
history-making taking place in present day Lithuania as an attempt to do away
with "false" memories and feelings in order to help people reestablish a "correct"
historical narrative. The curious thing about *1984 in the Bunker* is that it is not
interactive at all. The idea behind interactive theater is that the structure is open
and can be influenced by the audience, making the outcome of the play open for
various endings and interpretations. However, in this case, the structure of the play is
determined beforehand as the audience has no influence on it, leading the structure
to contradict the content. Sadly, the play ends up as the exact kind of propaganda it
warns against, as there is only one acceptable narrative about the past that is valid.[7]

---

7 Links about and pictures of *1984 in the Bunker (Back to the USSR)* are available online at
   http://www.sovietbunker.com/en/ (accessed 24 January 2012).

While "the Bunker" was a show put into being for a specific purpose at a specific event, the message it conveys in nonetheless clear; only by doing away with the contested past can the present be embraced and the future anticipated as something new and better than what was before.

The Locally Produced EUs

Rather than small EU metonyms, I argue that we find a production of diverse local EUs in the candidate countries. The vertical encompassment the new member states were subjected to as a prerequisite for their geopolitical incorporation into the EU should ideally have resulted in greater compatibility between the old and the new member states. Furthermore, Lithuania and other new member states were to be incorporated in the spatial construction of the techno-zone. Many of these goals were reinforced through law, making the *Acquis* a cornerstone in the EU enlargement process. However, instead of materializing, the EU legislation became transformed into something else, as the local environment and the continued influence of the past had significant impact on the process. The EU was just as much integrated into Lithuania as Lithuania was integrated into the EU.

As my ethnographic material from the two field sites confirms, differences in such EUs do not require large distances, but can appear even in neighboring regions. The semi-subsistence farmers from my study were thus engaged in circumventing the EU. While neither rejecting the EU nor being capable of complying fully with its demands, the farmers found intermediate solutions between what was required and what was possible. I referred to this as "practical negotiations of the situation." These proved especially relevant with regard to the sale of farm products in Lithuania. With the increased controls and strict requirements for sales, more people were impelled to sell illegally or semi-legally. Practices that were well known before the entrance were thus strengthened. Other areas, for which we have witnessed interrelations between change and continuation, regard social security and care. Indeed, while urbanization and migration provided new opportunities and sources of security, as young people earning higher salaries can provide their parents with money and material goods, it also cut into and undermined other forms of social security. As has been observed by Leutloff-Grandits, Peleikis and Thelen (2009), the migrants failed to fulfill work obligations at home, and thus the youth staying behind have to assume more responsibility for providing practical and emotional support for their parents in daily life. As my ethnographic data suggests, this leads to patterns of circular migration, especially for the urban migrants, as young people employed in the city have to return continuously to their parents in the countryside. As the work pressure is especially targeting the young men due to gendered work and gendered aging, they find themselves caught between urban work on the weekdays and work at the farms and support for their parents on the weekends. And, they not only work for their parents, but also for neighbors and relatives who likewise need help on their farms. The circular migration is thus extended by the circulation of sons, as sons or sons-in-law are "circulated" in the village to compensate for the general shortage of labor on the farms. The urbanization and changed family patterns have thereby not resulted in the emergence of increased individualized lifestyles and the establishment of small nuclear families. Rather, expectations of parental care and kinship obligations are revived under the new circumstances, leading to a reproduction of recognizable patterns of care and security, albeit in a different form as hitherto. This leads me to my final point.

How Do We Understand Processes of EUropeanization?

Aging semi-subsistence farmers have increasingly been viewed as a remnant of the Soviet past, and were consequently made into an obstacle to the intended modernization due to their inability to adapt to the required practices. Despite their own feelings of being dis-integrated from the changes or set apart from the developments, the intriguing point that came across in my study was that aging farmers in the rural outskirts still had a central position in determining the way of the development, due to their sheer numbers and the resources they had at hand as a result of the EU-supervised development in the 1990's. In accordance with this understanding, I would say, although the majority of people in my two field sites were not recognized as New Lithuanians, they were the ones who experienced the greater impacts of the EU, despite the fact that (and this is where the "nothing has changed" answer entered the picture) they did not always recognize such changes as emerging from the EU. Indeed, the ideal formulations of what the EU should be and who can participate overshadow the factual outcomes and make them unrecognizable, because the outcomes do not reflect how things were supposed to be. If the EU is associated with wealth and money and the realization of this fails to materialize for the citizens while a range of other anticipated or not anticipated changes take place, it should not solely be seen as "the EU gone wrong." Rather, it should be viewed as *actual* processes of EUropeanization. Instead of viewing what the ideal outcome of the EU should be concerning the establishment of technoscientific zones, we should view the impacts in terms of who they affect, and how they affect them. I suggest that we work with an elaborate and wide concept of EUropeanization of the new member states as their specific background and socioeconomic and legally hybrid constellations led to new and other forms EU than originally intended. We might as well witness a return to familiar patterns than the adaptation of something "new."

Final Remarks

The question about EU membership and its consequences continues to be a central topic for Lithuanians. For the Eurovision Song Contest 2010, the group InCulto was selected to represent Lithuania. InCulto's song reflects many of the sentiments that Lithuanians have experienced in the aftermath of the EU, questioning how equal and European they actually became with the membership, or if it opened up new forms of work exploitation. The lyrics go as follows:[8]

> You've seen it all before/ We ain't got no taste we're all a bore/ But you should give us chance/ Cause we're just victims of circumstance/ We've had it pretty tough/ But that's OK, we like it rough/ We'll settle the score/ We survived the Reds and two World Wars/ Get up and dance to our Eastern European kinda funk!/ Yes Sir we are legal we are, though we are not as legal as you/ No Sir we're not equal no, though we are both from the EU/ We build your homes and wash your dishes/ Keep you your hands all soft and clean/ But one of these days you'll realize Eastern Europe is in your genes.[9]

8 The Eurovision commission first needed time to consider whether the song should be allowed at the Eurovision song contest, as it was seen as being too political. It was suggested that InCulto might have to change the lyrics in order not to offend other (Western European) countries. Finally the song made it to the contest in an unrevised version, yet, the Lithuanians never made it to the finals. Source: http://www.lrytas. lt/-12682150641267689621-inculto-dainos-%C5%BEod%C5%BEiuose-eurovizijos-ekspertai-ie%C5%A1ko-politikos-papildyta.htm (accessed 3 October 2010).

9 Source: http://www.lrytas.lt/-12682150641267689621-inculto-dainos-%C5% BEiuose-eurovizijos-ekspertai-ie%C5%A1ko-politikos-papildyta.htm (accessed 3 October 2010).

BIBLIOGRAPHY

Abrahams, Ray, 1996. "Introduction: Some thoughts on recent land reforms in Eastern Europe." In *After Socialism: Land Reform and Social Change in Eastern Europe*, ed. Ray Abrahams, 1–22. New York and Oxford: Berghahn Books.

Alanen, Ilkka (ed.) 2004. *Mapping the Rural Problem in the Baltic Countryside: Transition Processes in Rural Areas of Estonia, Latvia and Lithuania.* Aldershot: Ashgate.

Alanen, Ilkka, Jouko Nikula, Helvi Põder and Rein Ruotsoo (eds). 2001. *Decollectivisation, Destruction and Disillusionment: A Community Study in Southern Estonia.* Farnham: Ashgate.

Alexander, Catherine. 2002. *Personal States: Making Connections between People and Bureaucracy in Turkey.* Oxford: Oxford University Press.

Ališauskiene, Rasa, Rita Bajaruniene and Birute Sersniova. 1993. "Policy mood and socio-political attitudes in Lithuania." *Journal of Baltic Studies*, Special Issue: Public Opinion in the Baltic States 24 (2): 135–48.

Anderson, Benedict. 1982. *Imagined Communities: Reflections on the Origins and Spread of Nationalism.* London: Verso.

Anderson, David G. and Frances Pine (eds). 1995. *Surviving the Transition: Development Concerns in the Post-socialist World.* Cambridge: University of Cambridge, Department of Anthropology.

Asad, Talal. 2003. *Formations of the Secular: Christianity, Islam and Modernity.* Stanford: Stanford University Press.

Ågh, Attila. 1993. "Europeanization through Privatization and Pluralization in Rural Hungary." *Journal of Public Policy* 3 (1): 1–35.

Bafoil, François. 2009. *Central and Eastern Europe: Europeanization and Social Change.* New York: Palgrave Macmillan.

Barry, Andrew. 2001. *Governing a Technological Society.* London: Athlone Press.

Bateson, Mary Catherine. 2001. *Full Circles, Overlapping Lives: Culture and Generation in Transition.* New York: Ballantine Books.

Bellier, Irene and Thomas M. Wilson. 2000. "Building, Imagining, and Experiencing Europe: Institutions and Identities in the European Union." In *An Anthropology of the European Union*, ed. Irene Bellier and Thomas M. Wilson, 1–27. New York: Berg.

Benda-Beckmann, Franz von. 1992. "Introduction: Understanding Agrarian Law in Society." In *Law as a Resource in Agrarian Struggles*, ed. Franz von Benda-Beckmann and Menno Van der Velde, 1–22. Wageningen: Pudoc.

———. 1997. "Citizens, Strangers and Indigenous People: Conceptual Politics and Legal Pluralism." *Law & Anthropology* 9: 1–43.

Benda-Beckmann, Franz von and Keebet von Benda-Beckmann. [1994] 2000. "Coping with Insecurity." In *Coping with Insecurity: An "Underall" Perspective on Social Security in the Third World*, ed. Franz von Benda-Beckmann, Keebet von Benda-Beckmann and Hans Marks, 7–34. Yogyakarta, Indonesia: Pustaka Pelajar.

———· 2006. "The Dynamics of Change and Continuity in Plural Legal Orders." *Journal of Legal Pluralism and Unofficial Law* 53–54: 1–44.

———· 2007. "Where Structures Merge: State and Off-State Involvement in Rural Social Security on Ambon Indonesia." In *Social Security between Past and Future: Ambonese Networks of Care and Supply*, 205–35. Münster: Lit Verlag.

Benda-Beckmann, Franz von, Keebet von Benda-Beckmann and Anne Griffiths. 2009. "Introduction." In *Spatializing Law: An Anthropological Geography of Law in Society*, ed. Franz von Benda-Beckmann, Keebet von Benda-Beckmann and Anne Griffiths, 1–29. Farnham: Ashgate.

Borneman, John and Nick Fowler. 1997. "Europeanization." *Annual Review of Anthropology* 26: 487–514.

Brandtstädter, Susanne. 2003. "The Moral Economy of Kinship and Property in Rural China." In *The Postsocialist Agrarian Question: Property Relations and the Rural Condition*, ed. Chris M. Hann, 419–40. Münster: Lit Verlag.

Bridger, Sue and Frances Pine. 1998. "Introduction: Transition to post-socialism and cultures of survival." In *Surviving Post-Socialism Local: Strategies and Regional Responses in Eastern Europe and the Former Soviet Union*, ed. Sue Bridger and Frances Pine, 1–15. London: Routledge.

Bourdieu, Pierre. [1977] 2000. *Outline of a Theory of Practice*. Cambridge: Cambridge University Press.

Buchowski, Michal. 2003. "Redefining Social Relations through Work in a Rural Community in Poland." Max Planck Institute for Social Anthropology Working Paper No. 58.

Buckley, Mary. 1997. "Victims and agents: Gender in post-Soviet states." In *Post-Soviet Women: From the Baltic to Central Asia*, ed. Mary Buckley, 3–17. Cambridge: Cambridge University Press.

Caldwell, Melissa. 2009. "Introduction: Food and everyday life after socialism." In *Food and Everyday Life in the Postsocialist World*, ed. Melissa Caldwell, 1–28. Bloomington: Indiana University Press.

Cartwright, Andrew. 2003. "Private Farming in Romania: What Are the Old People Going to Do with Their Land?" In *The Postsocialist Agrarian Question: Property Relations and the Rural Condition*, ed. Chris M. Hann, 171–88. Münster: Lit Verlag.

Clemens, Walter C. Jr. 1991. *Baltic Independence and Russian Empire*. New York: St. Martin's Press.

Čiubrinskas, Vytis. 2000. "Identity and Revival of Tradition in Lithuania." *Journal of Danish Ethnographic Society* 42: 19–40.

———· 2004. "Lithuanian Transnationalism: Constructed, Imagined and Contested Identity of Lithuanian Americans." In *Beginnings and Ends of Migration: Life Without Borders in the Contemporary World*, 33–50. The Lithuanian Emigration Institute, Vytautas Magnus University/Versus Aureus.

———· 2005. "Transnacionalinis Identitetas ir Paveldas, Lietuviškumas Diasporoje." *Sociologija, Mintis ir Veiksmas* 16 (2): 41–54.

Connerton, Paul. [1989] 1998. *How Societies Remember*. Cambridge: Cambridge University Press.

De Munck, Victor C. 2007. "First, Second and Finally Third Order Understandings of Lithuanian National Identity: An Anthropological Approach." *Sociologija. Mintis ir Veiksmas* 1 (19): 51–73.

————. 2008. "Millenarian Dreams: the Objects and Subjects of Money in New Lithuania." In *Changing Economies and Changing Identities in Post-socialist Eastern Europe*, ed. Ingo Schröder and Asta Vonderau, 171–91. Berlin: Lit Verlag.

Dunn, Elizabeth C. 2004. *Privatizing Poland: Baby Food, Big Business and the Remaking of Labor*. Ithaca, NY: Cornell University Press.

————. 2005. "Standards and Person-Making in East Central Europe." In *Global Assemblages: Technology, Politics and Ethics as Anthropological Problems*, ed. Aihwa Ong and Stephen J. Collier, 173–93. Malden, MA: Blackwell Publishing.

Dzūkija Rural Development Association of Partners (Dzūkija LAG). 2006. *Case Study of Rural Area and Drafting of Integrated Pilot Strategy for Improving the Quality of Life in Rural Area of Alytus County*. Dzūkija: Dzūkija LAG.

Ehrlich, Eugen. [1936] 2002. *Fundamental Principles of the Sociology of Law*. New Brunswick, NJ: Transaction Publishers.

Eidson, John and Gordon Milligan. 2003. "Cooperative Entrepreneurs? Collectivisation and Privatisation in Two East German Regions." In *The Postsocialist Agrarian Question: Property Relations and the Rural Condition*, ed. Chris M. Hann, 47–92. Münster: Lit Verlag.

Ferguson, James. [1990] 2003. *The Anti-Politics Machine: "Development," Depolitization, and Bureaucratic Power in Lesotho*. Minneapolis: University of Minnesota Press.

Ferguson James and Akhil Gupta. 2002. "Spatializing States: Toward an Ethnography of Neoliberal Governmentality." *American Ethnologist* 29 (4): 981–1002.

Fernandèz, Javier. 2002. "The Common Agricultural Policy and EU Enlargement: Implications for Agricultural Production in the Central and East European Countries." *Eastern European Economics* 40 (3): 28–50.

Firlit, Elzbieta and Jerzy Chlopecki. 1992. "When Theft is not Theft." In *The Unplanned Society: Poland after Communism*, ed. Janine R. Wedel, 95–109. New York: Columbia University Press.

Fox, Katy. 2009. "Confusion, Secrecy and Power: Direct Payments and European Integration in Romania." In *Annuaire Roumain d'Anthropologie* 46 (special issue), ed. Thomas Sikor and Stefan Dorondel.

Frohberg, Klaus and Monika Hartman. 2000. "Baltic Agricultural Competiveness and Prospects under the European Union Accession." In *Agriculture and East-West European Integration*, ed. Jason G. Hartell and Johan F. M. Swinnen, 33–65. London: Ashgate.

Getty, J. Arch, Gábor Rittersporn and Victor N. Zemskov. 1993. "Victims of the Soviet Penal System in the Pre-War Years: A First Approach on the Basis of Archival Evidence." *American Historical Review* 98 (4): 1017–49.

Giddens, Anthony. [1979] 2003. *Central Problems in Social Theory Action, Structure and Contradiction in Social Analysis*. Basingstoke: Palgrave Macmillan.

————. 2007. *Europe in the Global Age*: Cambridge: Polity Press.

Giordano, Christian and Dobrinka Kostova. 2002. "The Social Production of Mistrust." In *Postsocialism: Ideals, Ideologies and Practices in Eurasia*, ed. Chris M. Hann, 74–92. London: Routledge.

Goodman, David. 2003. "The quality 'turn' and alternative food practices: Reflections and agenda." *Journal of Rural Studies* 19 (1): 1–7.

Górny, Agata and Paolo Ruspini. 2005. "Forging a Common Immigration Policy for the Enlarging European Union: For Diversity of Harmonization." In *Migration in the New Europe, East-West Revisited*, ed. Agata Górny and Paolo Ruspini, 247–78. New York: Palgrave Macmillan.

Gorton, Matthew, Phillip Lowe and Anett Zellei. 2005. "Pre-Accession Europeanization: The Strategic Realignment of the Environmental Policy Systems of Lithuania, Poland and Slovakia towards Agricultural Pollution in Preparation for the EU Membership." *Sociologia Ruralis* 45: 202–23.

Government of Lithuania (Lietuvos Respublikos Vyriausybė). 1991. *On the Procedure and Conditions of Restorations of Ownership to the Existing Rights.* 18 June.

———. 1991. "The Goal of Land Reform." *Law on Land Reform, Number 1-1607*, chapter 1, article 2, 25 July. Lietuvos Respublikos Aukščiausioji Taryba, Atkuriamasis Seimas.

———. 2003. *Nutarimas dėl Tipinių Pieno Pirkimo-Pardavimo Sutarties Sąlygų Patvirtinimo*, no. 726, 4 June, Vilnius.

Government of Lithuania (Lietuvos Respublikos Vyriausybė) (in cooperation with Lithuanian Ministries). 2004. *Single Programming Document 2004–2006.* Vilnius.

Grabbe, Heather. 2005. *The EU's Transformative Power: Europeanization through Conditionality in Central and Eastern Europe.* New York: Palgrave Macmillan.

Gruževskis, Boguslavas. 2004. "Labour Migration in Lithuania." In *New Patterns of Labour Migration in Central and Eastern Europe*, ed. Daniel Pop, 70–7. Cluj-Napoca: Open Society Foundation.

Habeck, Joachim Otto. 2005. "Gender and Kul'tura at the Siberian and Northern Russian Frontier." In *Generations, Kinship, Care, Gendered Provisions of Social Security in Central Eastern Europe*, ed. Haldis Haukanes and Frances Pine, 189–206. Bergen: University of Bergen.

Hann, Chris M. 1992. "Market Principles: Market Place and the Transition in Eastern Europe." In *Contesting Markets: Analyses of Ideology, Discourse and Practice*, ed. Roy Dilley, 244–59. Edinburgh: Edinburgh University Press.

———. 1994. "After Communism: Reflections on East European Anthropology and the 'Transition.'" *Social Anthropology* 2 (3): 229–49.

———. 2002. "Farewell to the Socialist 'Other.'" In *Postsocialism. Ideals, Ideologies and Practices in Eurasia*, ed. Chris M. Hann, 1–11. London: Routledge.

Hann, Chris M. and the Property Relations Group. 2003. "Introduction: Decollectivization and the Moral Economy." In *The Postsocialist Agrarian Question: Property Relations and the Rural Condition*, ed. Chris M. Hann and the Property Relations Group, 1–47. Münster: Lit Verlag.

Harboe Knudsen, Ida. 2010a. "Who Represents Who? A Critical Approach to Current Lithuanian Identity Discourse." In *Identity Politics: History, Regions and Borderlands*, Acta Historica Universitatis Klaipedensis XIX, Studia Anthropologica III, ed. Čiubrinskas, Vytis and Sliužinskas. Rimantas, 59–69. Klaipeda: Klaipeda University Press.

———. 2010b. "Effects of Legal Changes in the Lithuanian Countryside after the Entrance to the EU." PhD dissertation, Max Planck Institute for Social Anthropology, Halle, Saxony-Anhalt, Germany.

Haukanes, Haldis and Frances Pine. 2005. "Introduction." In *Generations, Kinship, Care: Gendered Provisions of Social Security in Central Eastern Europe*, ed. Haldis Haukanes and Frances Pine, 1–22. Bergen: University of Bergen.

Heintz, Monica. 2006. *Be European, Recycle Yourself! The Changing Work Ethics in Romania.* Münster: Lit Verlag.

Hohnen, Pernille. 2003. *A Market out of Place? Remaking Economic, Social and Symbolic Boundaries in Post-Communist Lithuania.* Oxford: Oxford University Press.

Hudson, Ray. 2000. "One Europe or Many? Reflections on Becoming European." *Transactions of the Institute of British Geographers*, new series, 25 (4): 409–26.

Hugh, James, Gwendolyn Sasse and Claire Gordon. 2005. *Europeanization and Regionalization in the EU's Enlargement to Central and Eastern Europe. The Myth of Conditionality.* New York: Palgrave Macmillan.

Humphrey, Caroline. 1995. "Introduction." In "Surviving the Transition: Development Concerns in the Post-socialist World," ed. David G. Anderson and Frances Pine, *Cambridge Anthropology* (special issue) 18 (2): 1–12.

———. [1998] 2001. *Marx Went Away – But Karl Stayed Behind.* Ann Arbor: University of Michigan Press. (Updated edition of *Karl Marx Collective: Economy, Society and Religion in a Siberian Collective Farm,* pub. 1983.)

———. 2002. "Does the Category Postsocialist still Make Sense?" In *Postsocialism: Ideals, Ideologies and Practices in Eurasia,* ed. Chris M. Hann, 12–14. London: Routledge.

Humphrey, Caroline and Vera Skvirskaja . 2009. "Trading Places: Post-socialist container markets and the city." *Focaal – European Journal of Anthropology* 55: 61–73.

Ilonszki, Gabriella (ed.) 2009. "Perceptions of the European Union in the New Member States: A Comparative Perspective." *Europe Asia Studies* (special issue) 61: 6.

Judd, Karen (ed.) 1999. *Ageing in a Gendered World: Women's Issues and Identities.* Santo Domingo: Instraw.

Kaczmarczyk, Pawel. 2005. "Future Westward Overflow from Accession Countries: The Case of Poland." In *Migration in the New Europe: East-West Revisited,* ed. Agata Górny and Paolo Ruspini, 65–92 . New York: Palgrave Macmillan.

Kalb, Don. 2002. "Afterword: Globalism and Post-socialist Prospects." In *Postsocialism: Ideals, Ideologies and Practices in Eurasia,* ed. Chris M. Hann, 317–30. London: Routledge.

Kaneff, Deema. 1996. "Responses to 'Democratic' Land Reforms in a Bulgarian Village." In *After Socialism: Land Reform and Social Change in Eastern Europe,* ed. Ray Abrahams, 85–114. New York and Oxford: Berghahn Books.

———. 2002. "The Shame and Pride of Market Activity: Morality, Identity and Trading in Postsocialist Rural Bulgaria." In *Markets and Moralities: Ethnographies of Postsocialism,* ed. Ruth Mandel and Caroline Humphrey, 33–52. Oxford: Berg.

Kaneff, Deema and Lale Yalcin-Heckmann. 2003. "Retreat to the Cooperative or the Household? Agricultural Privatization in Ukraine and Azerbaijan." In *The Postsocialist Agrarian Question: Property Relations and the Rural Condition,* ed. Chris M. Hann and the Property Relations Group, 219–56. Münster: Lit Verlag.

Klimašauskas, Erikas and Gindra Kasnauskienė. 1996. *Land Reform in Lithuania. Results and Problems of Privatization.* Vilnius: Vilnius University/Lithuanian Institute of Agrarian Economics.

Klumbytė, Neringa. 2006. "Biographic Citizenship: Memory, Subjectivity, and Politics in Post-Soviet Lithuania." PhD dissertation, University of Pittsburgh.

———. 2009. "The Geo-Politics of Taste: The 'Euro' and Soviet Sausage Industries in Lithuania." In *Food and Everyday Life in the Postsocialist World,* ed. Melissa Caldwell, 130–53. Bloomington: Indiana University Press.

———. 2010. "Post-Soviet Publics and nostalgia for Soviet times." In *Changing Economies and Changing Identities in Postsocialist Eastern Europe,* ed. Ingo W. Schröder and Asta Vonderau, 27–47. Münster: Lit Verlag.

Komulainen, Tuomas and Lauri Taro. 1999. "The 1998 Economic crisis in Russia and Finland's Foreign Trade." *Bofit Online* 3: 4–11.

Kuddo, Arvo. 1996. "Aspects of Restitution of Property and Land in Estonia." In *After Socialism: Land Reform and Social Change in Eastern Europe,* ed. Ray Abrahams, 157–68. Providence, RI: Berghahn Books.

Kuehnast, Kathleen and Carol Nechemias. 2004. "Introduction: Women Navigating Change in Post-Soviet Currents." In *Post-Soviet Women Encountering Transition: Nation Building, Economical Survival, and Civic Activism*, ed. Kathleen Kuehnast and Carol Nechemias, 1–23. Washington DC: Woodrow Wilson Center Press.

Kuodytė, Dalia. 2002. *Laisvės Paslaptis yra Drąsa*. Vilnius: LGGRTC.

Kuodytė, Dalia, Eugenijus Peikštenis and Dalius Žygelis. 2007. *Už Laisvę ir Tėvynę*. Vilnius: LGGRTC.

Lampland, Martha. 2002. "The Advantage of Being Collectivized: Cooperative Farm Managers in the Postsocialist Economy." In *Postsocialism: Ideals, Ideologies and Practices in Eurasia*, ed. Chris M. Hann, 31–56. London: Routledge.

Lange, Bettina. 2007. "How to Conceptualize Law in the European Union Integration Process: Perspectives from Literature and Empirical Research." In *European Ways of Law*, ed. Volkmar Gessner and David Nelken, 255–76. Oxford: Hart Publishing.

Ledeneva, Alena V. 1998. *Russia's Economy of Favors: Blat, Networking and Informal Exchange*. Cambridge: Cambridge University Press.

———. 2006. *How Russia Really Works: The Informal Practices that Shaped Post-Soviet Politics and Business*. Ithaca, NY: Cornell University Press.

Lerman, Zvi. 1998. "Does Land Reform Matter? Some Experiences from the Former Soviet Union." *European Review of Agricultural Economics* 25 (3): 307–30.

Leutloff-Grandits, Carolin, Anja Peleikis and Tatjana Thelen. 2009. "An Introduction." In *Social Security in Religious Networks: Anthropological Perspectives on New Risks and Ambivalences*, ed. Carolin Leutloff-Grandits, Anja Peleikis and Tatjana Thelen, 1–22. New York and Oxford: Berghahn Books.

Lithuanian Institute of Agrarian Economics (Lietuvos Agrarinės Ekonomikos Institutas). 2005. *CEEC Agro Policy, Agro Economic Policy Analysis in the New Member States and the Countries of the Western Balkans: Monitoring on Agricultural Policy, Market and Trade Developments in Lithuania*. Project no. 513705. Vilnius: Lithuanian Institute of Agrarian Economics.

Lithuanian Ministry of Agriculture (Lietuvos Respublikos Žemės Ūkio Ministerija). 2000. *Agriculture and Rural Development Plan 2000–2006*. Vilnius: Lithuanian Ministry of Agriculture.

———. 2004. *Rural Development Plan 2004–2006 Lithuania*. Vilnius: Lithuanian Ministry of Agriculture.

———. 2007. *Lithuanian Rural Development Program 2007–2013*. Vilnius: Lithuanian Ministry of Agriculture.

Liubinienė, Neringa. 2009. "Migrantai iš Lietuvos Šiaures Airijoje: 'Savo Erdvės' Konstravimas." PhD dissertation, Vytautas Magnus University, Kaunas.

Long, Norman. [1977] 1982. *An Introduction to the Sociology of Rural Development*. Boulder, CO: Westview Press.

———. 1989. "Encounters at the interface: A perspective on social discontinuities in rural development." Wageningen Sociologische Studies 27.

———. 1996. "Globalization and Localization: New Challenges to Rural Research." In *The Future of Anthropological Knowledge*, ed. Henrietta L. Moore, 37–59. London: Routledge.

LVLS (Lietuvos Valstiečių Liaudininkų Sąjunga). 2007. "Lietuvos Valstiečių Sąjunga – Lietuvos Ateičiai." Vilnius: LVLS.

Mahmood, Saba. 2005. *Politics of Piety: The Islamic Revival and the Feminist Subject*. Princeton: Princeton University Press.

Mandel, Ruth and Caroline Humphrey. 2002. "The market in everyday life: Ethnography of post-socialism." In *Markets and Moralities: Ethnographies of Postsocialism*, ed. Ruth Mandel and Caroline Humphrey, 1–16. Oxford and New York: Berg.

Mincyte, Diana. 2006. "Small-Scale Farms, Large-Scale Politics: The Changing Landscape of Rural Lithuania." PhD dissertation, University of Illinois, Urbana-Champaign.

———. 2009. "Self-made Women: Informal Dairy Markets in Europeanizing Lithuania." In *Food and Everyday Life in the Postsocialist World*, ed. Melissa Caldwell, 78–100. Bloomington: Indiana University Press.

———. 2011. "Subsistence and Sustainability in Post-industrial Europe: The Politics of Small-scale Farming in Europeanising Lithuania." *Sociologia Ruralis* 51 (2): 101–19.

Moore, Sally Falk. [1978] 2000. *Law as a Process: An Anthropological Approach*. Hamburg: Lit Verlag.

Ong, Aihwa and Stephen J. Collier (eds). 2005. *Global Assemblages. Technology, Politics and Ethics as Anthropological Problems*. Malden, MA: Blackwell Publishing.

Orwell, George. [1945] 1989. *Animal Farm*, London: Penguin.

———. [1949] 1982. *Nineteen Eighty-Four*. Bungay: Penguin.

Pawlik, Wojciech. 1992. "Intimate Commerce." In *The Unplanned Society: Poland after Communism*, ed. Janine R. Wedel, 78–94. New York: Columbia University Press.

Pine, Frances. 1993. "The Cows and Pigs Are His, the Eggs Are Mine: Women's Domestic Economy and Entrepreneurial Activity in Rural Poland." In *Socialism: Ideals, Ideologies and Local Practices*, ed. Chris M. Hann, 227–42. London: Routledge.

———. 2000. "Kinship, Gender and Work in Poland." In *Gender: Agency and Change*, ed. Ana Victoria Goddard, 86–100. London: Routledge.

———. 2001a. "From Production to Consumption in Postsocialism?" In *Poland Beyond Communism: "Transition" in Critical Perspective*, ed. Michal Buchowski, 209–24. Freiburg: Universitätsverlag Freiburg/Schweiz.

———. 2001b. "Who Better Than Your Mother? Some Problems with Gender Issues in Rural Poland." In *Women after Communism: Ideal Images and Real Lives*, ed. Haldis Haukanes, 51–66. Bergen: Bergen University Press.

———. 2002. "From Production to Consumption in Postsocialism?" In *Markets and Moralities Ethnographies of Postsocialism*, ed. Ruth Mandel and Caroline Humphrey, 209–24. Oxford: Berg.

Pop, Daniel (ed.) 2004. *New Patterns of Labour Migration in Central and Eastern Europe*. Cluj-Napoca: Open Society Foundation.

Priban, Jiri. 2007. "Is there a Spirit of the European Ways of Law? Critical Remarks on the EU Constitution Making and Political Culture." In *European Ways of Law*, ed. Volkmar Gessner and David Nelken, 233–54. Oxford: Hart Publishing.

Rausing, Sigrid. 2004. *History, Memory, and Identity in Post-Soviet Estonia: The End of a Collective Farm*. Oxford: Oxford University Press.

Roberts, Simon. 2007. "Order and the Evocation of Heritage: Representing Quality in French Biscuit Trade." In *Order and Disorder. Anthropological Perspectives*, ed. Keebet von Benda-Beckmann and Fernanda Pirie, 16–33. New York and Oxford: Berghahn Books.

Roepstorff, Andreas and Aušra Simoniukštytė. 2005. "Cherishing the Nation's Time and Space: Lithuanian Identity and the Maintenance of Tradition." In *Tradition and Agency: Tracing Cultural Continuity and Invention*, ed. Poul Pedersen and Ton Otto, 157–93. Aarhus: Aarhus University Press.

Schimmelfennig, Frank and Ulrich Sedelmeyer. 2005. "Introduction: Conceptualizing the Europeanization of Central and Eastern Europe." In *The Europeanization of Central and Eastern Europe*, ed. Frank Schimmelfennig and Ulrich Sedelmeyer, 1–29. London: Cornell University Press.

Schöpflin, George, A. 2000. *Nations, Identity, Power. The New Politics of Europe*. London: Hurst.

Schwartz, Katrina. 2006. *Globalizing the Ethnoscape, Nature and National Identity after Communism*. Pittsburgh: University of Pittsburgh Press.

Scott, James C. 1985. *Weapons of the Weak: Everyday Forms of Peasant Resistance*. New Haven: Yale University Press.

_____. 1990. *Domination and the Arts of Resistance: Hidden Transcripts*. New Haven: Yale University Press.

_____. 1998. *Seeing Like a State. How Certain Schemes to Improve the Human Condition Have Failed*. New Haven: Yale University Press.

Sedelmeyer, Ulrich and Helen Wallace. 1996. "Policies toward central and eastern Europe." In *Policy-making in the European Union*, ed. Helen Wallace and William Wallace, 353–87. Oxford: Oxford University Press.

Senior Nello, Susan. 2002. "Preparing for Enlargement in the European Union: The Tensions between Economic and Political Integration." *International Political Science Review*, "Enlarging the European Union: Challenges to and from Central and Eastern Europe" 23 (3): 291–317.

Senn, Alfred Erich. [1990] 2002. *Lithuania Awakening*. Berkeley, Los Angeles, Oxford: University of California Press.

_____. 1994. "Lithuania's first two years of independence." *Journal of Baltic Studies* 25 (1): 81–8.

Sewell, William H. Jr. 1992. "A Theory of Structure: Duality, Agency, and Transformation." *American Journal of Sociology* 98 (1): 1–29.

Smigielska, Joanna. 1992. "There's the Beef." In *The Unplanned Society: Poland after Communism*, ed. Janine R. Wedel, 110–21. New York: Columbia University Press.

Smith, David J., Artis Pabriks, Aldis Purs and Thomas Lane. 2002. *The Baltic States, Estonia, Latvia and Lithuania*. London: Routledge.

Sovietų Socialistinių Respublikų Sąjungos Konstitucija (pagrindinis įstatymas) [*Constitution of the USSR (main law)*]. 1936 [1940]. Moscow: Svetimomis Kalbomis Literatūros Leidykla [The Publishing House of Literature of Foreign Languages].

Spoor, Max and Oane Visser. 2001. "The State of Agrarian Reform in the Former Soviet Union." *Europe-Asia Studies* 6: 885–901.

Stead, David R. 2007. "The Mansholt Plan Forty Years On." *EuroChoices* 6 (3): 40–5.

Swain, Nigel. 1992. *The Rise and Fall of Feasible Socialism*. London: Verso.

_____. 1996. *Rural Transformation in Central Europe*. Budapest: Central European University Press.

Tarybų Socialistinių Respublikų Sąjungos Konstitucija (pagrindinis įstatymas) [*Constitution of the USSR (main law)*]. 1977 [1983]. Vilnius: 'Mintis' Publishing House.

Tedre, Silva and Taimi Tulva. "Older Women in Transition in Estonia: Continuing Caregivers." In *Ageing in a Gendered World: Women's Issues and Identities*, ed. Karen Judd, 199–214. Santo Domingo: Instraw.

Thelen, Tatjana. 2003a. *Privatisierung und soziale Ungleichheit in der osteuropäischen Landwirtschaft. Zwei Fallstudien aus Ungarn und Rumänien*. Frankfurt and New York: Campus Verlag.

———. 2003b. "The New Power of Old Men: Privatisation and Family Relations in Mesterzàllàs (Hungary)." *Anthropology of East Europe Review* 21 (2): 15–21.

Thelen, Tatjana, Andrew Cartwright and Thomas Sikor. 2005. "Local State and Social Security in Rural Communities: A New Research Agenda and Example of Postsocialist Europe." Max Planck Institute for Social Anthropology Working Paper No. 105.

Torsello, Davide. 2003. *Trust, Property and Social Change in a Southern Slovakian Village.* Münster: Lit Verlag.

Trotskij, Lev. [1924] 1957. *Literature and Revolution.* Brasted: Russell & Russell.

Vebra, Rimantas. 1994. "Political rebirth in Lithuanian 1990–1991: Events and Problems." *Journal of Baltic Studies* 25 (2): 183–8.

Vėliūtė, Rūta Gabrielė. 2009. *Partizanai.* Vilnius: LGGRTC.

Ventsel, Aimar. 2007. "Pride, Honour, Individual and Collective Violence: Order in a 'Lawless' Village." In *Order and Disorder: Anthropological Perspectives*, ed. Keebet von Benda-Beckmann and Fernanda Pirie, 34–53. New York and Oxford: Berghahn Books.

Verdery, Katherine. 1991. "Theorising Socialism: A Prologue to the Transition." *American Ethnologist* 18 (3): 419–39.

———. 1996. *What Was Socialism and What Comes Next?* Princeton: Princeton University Press.

———. 2002a. "Seeing Like a Mayor, or How Local Official Obstructed Romanian Property Restitution." *Ethnography* 3 (1): 5–33.

———. 2002b. "Whither Postsocialism?" In *Postsocialism: Ideals, Ideologies and Practices in Eurasia*, ed. Chris M. Hann, 15–31. London: Routledge.

———. 2003. *The Vanishing Hectare. Property and Value in Postsocialist Transylvania.* Ithaca, NY and London: Cornell University Press.

Vonderau, Asta. 2007. "Yet Another Europe? Constructing and Representing Identities in Lithuania Two Years after EU Accession." In *Representations on the Margins of Europe, Politics and Identities in the Baltic and South Caucasian States*, ed. Tsypylma Darieva and Wolfgang Kaschuba, 220–42. Frankfurt and New York: Campus Verlag.

———. 2008. "Models of Success in the Free Market: Transformations of the Individual Self-Representation of the Lithuanian Economic Elite." In *Changing Economies and Changing Identities in Postsocialist Eastern Europe*, ed. Ingo Schröder and Asta Vonderau, 111–29. Münster: Lit Verlag.

Waal, Clarissa de. 1996. "Decollectivization and High Scarcity in High Albania." In *After Socialism, Land Reform and Social Change in Eastern Europe*, ed. Ray Abrahams, 169–92. New York and Oxford: Berghahn Books.

Wallace, William V. 2000. "Enlarging the European Union, an Overview." *Perspectives in European Politics and Society* 1: 1–18.

Wedel, Janine R. (ed.) 1992. *The Unplanned Society: Poland during and after Communism.* New York: Columbia University Press.

Welz, Gisela. 2007. "Europäische Produkte: Nahrungskulturelles Erbe und EU-Politik. Am Beispiel der Republik Zypern." In *Pradikat "Heritage" Wertschopfungen aus kulturellen Ressourcen*, ed. Dorothee Hemme, Marcus Tauschek and Regina Bendix, 323–36. Münster: Lit Verlag.

Young, Craig and Sylvia Kaczmarek. 2008. "The Socialist Past and Postsocialist Urban Identity in Central and Eastern Europe." *European Urban and Regional Studies* 15 (1): 53–70.

Zinoviev, Alexander. [1982] 1985. *Homo Sovieticus.* Boston and New York: The Atlantic Monthly Press.

Internet Resources

"Danų antropologė: Lietuvos kaimo žmones charakterizuoja kančia ir skundas, kad sovietmečiu buvo geriau."
  http://www.delfi.lt/news/daily/lithuania/article.php?id=11011434 (accessed 27 September 2011).

Demographic statistics on age distribution in Lithuania.
  http://db1.stat.gov.lt/statbank/selectvarval/saveselections.asp?MainTable=M3010203&P
  Language=0&TableStyle=&Buttons=&Pxsid=3766&Iqy=&TC=&ST=ST&rvar0=&rv
  ar1=&rvar2=&rvar3=&rvar4=&rvar5=&rvar6=&rvar7=&rvar8=&rvar9=&rvar10=&
  rvar11=&rvar12=&rvar13=&rvar14= (accessed 16 November 2011).

General information about Lithuania.
  http://lt.wikipedia.org/wiki/Lietuva (accessed 24 November 2011).

"'InCulto' dainos žodžiuose Eurovizijos ekspertai ieško politikos (papildyta)."
  http://www.lrytas.lt/-12682150641267689621-inculto-dainos-
  %C5%BEod%C5%BEiuose-eurovizijos-ekspertai-ie%C5%A1ko-politikos-papildyta.htm
  (accessed 3 October 2010).

Lietuvos Valstiečių Liaudininkų Sąjunga.
  http://www.lvls.lt/en.php/news/,nid.545 (accessed 16 November 2011).

Lithuanian EU referendum.
  http://www.electoralgeography.com/new/en/countries/l/lithuania/lithuania-eu-
  membership-referendum-2003.html (accessed 16 November 2011).

"Lithuania's Rural Development Plan."
  http://europa.eu/rapid/pressReleasesAction.do?reference=MEMO/07/369&format=
  HTML&aged=0&language=EN&guiLanguage=en (accessed 17 March 2012).

Michail Golovatov.
  http://lt.wikipedia.org/wiki/Michailas_Golovatovas
  http://www.bbc.co.uk/news/world-europe-14202371
  http://en.rian.ru/analysis/20110722/165330536.html (all accessed 16 November 2011).

"Statement of the Vilnius Group Countries" – the Vilnius letter.
  http://www.novinite.com/view_news.php?id=19022 (accessed 29 September 2009).

"The Lights are going out over Europe," by John Laughland.
  http://www.propagandamatrix.com/the_lights_are_going_out_over_europe.html
  (accessed 4 March 2010).

The Lithuanian national paying agency.
  www.nma.lt (accessed 16 November 2011).

"The Move towards Independence 1987–91" – Lithuanian country brief.
  http://www.country-data.com/cgi-bin/query/r-8286.html (accessed 16 November 2011).

"The Russian Crisis of 1998."
  http://www.twnside.org.sg/title/1998-cn.htm (accessed 16 October 2011).

Transparency International report on Lithuania.
  http://www.transparency.org/policy_research/nis/nis_reports_by_country (accessed 16 November 2011).

"The 2004 enlargement: The challenge of a 25-member EU."
http://europa.eu/legislation_summaries/enlargement/2004_and_2007_enlargement/e50017_en.htm (accessed 24 November 2011).

UN data country profile for Lithuania.
http://data.un.org/CountryProfile.aspx?crName=Lithuania (accessed 16 November 2011).

"Lithuania: Voters Likely to Approve EU Membership in Weekend Referendum."
http://www.globalsecurity.org/military/library/news/2003/05/mil-030509-rfel-171853.htm (accessed 4 March 2010).

"Žinios apie tikruosius ūkininkus – miglotos."
http://verslas.delfi.lt/archive/article.php?id=11734086 (accessed 17 March 2012).

1984 in the Bunker (Back to the USSR).
http://www.thetravelmagazine.net/i-2823--vilnius-back-to-the-ussr-the-bunker-experience.hml
http://www.sovietbunker.com/en/ (both pages accessed 17 March 2010).

INDEX

A

Acquis Communautaire 6, 16, 26, 56, 63, 167, 169; *see also* EU, laws
actualized history 17–18, 82; *see also* "annihilation of the past"; "reversibility of events"
Adamkus, Valdas 18, 53, 61
Afghanistan 49
age 23, 31, 42, 65–6, 75, 82, 84, 91–2, 99, 102–103, 105, 137–8, 142–4, 157; *see also* retirement
distribution 139–41
Agenda 2000 55
aging 2–4, 19, 21–3, 28, 31, 52, 58, 60, 62, 65, 69, 74–5, 84–5, 88, 91, 99, 101, 108, 109, 123, 136–44, 147–9, 159–69, 170; *see also* paradoxes of aging
farmers 2–4, 16, 21–3, 28, 31, 52, 65, 69, 71, 74–5, 78, 91, 125, 170
rural population 2, 137, 138, 140–2, 144, 149, 160–1
state representatives 23, 65, 75, 78, 84–5
agricultural 11, 43, 65, 71–2, 89, 90–1
advisor 2, 8, 70, 75, 78, 80, 101, 129
companies 12, 43–4, 85
enterprises 2, 12, 42–4
gigantism 22
production 11–12, 22, 30, 40, 56, 66, 98–9, 160
sector 1, 5, 16, 22, 24, 28, 34, 38–9, 40–1, 51–2, 56, 58, 63, 66, 67 (university), 69–70, 87–8, 91–3, 100, 136, 161
Agricultural Affairs, Office of 89
Agricultural and Rural Development Plan 2000–2006 57
Agricultural and Rural Development Strategy 57

agriculture 12–13, 16, 17 (model for), 49, 52 (subsidies), 57–8, 81, 85, 88, 94, 99, 108–9, 136, 146, 148
Albania 46, 166
alcohol 1, 36, 82, 124–5, 140, 148, 155
Alexander, Catherine 69
alienation 5, 30, 52, 98, 161
alliances, situational 72–4
Animal Farm (Orwell) 19
"annihilation of the past" 17; *see also* actualized history; "reversibility of events"
anticorruption 55–6
anti-Soviet 22, 23, 48, 168
"armchair farmers" (*fotelio ūkininkai*) 89–90
Armenia 39
Asad, Talal 27
asmeniniai ūkiai (private farms) 41; *see also* farms, private
Aukštaitija 10
Auštrevičius, Petras 60–1
Azerbaijan 28, 39, 136

B

Bafoil, François 6
Baltic states 18, 39, 59–61
Barry, Andrew 24
Bateson, Mary Catherine 1
Belarus 11, 39, 114–15, 124
Benda-Beckmann, Franz and Keebet von 26, 29, 51, 64, 79, 120, 145, 161
bendrovė (agricultural company) 43
"blat" 80
Bourdieu, Pierre 26–7, 69–70
Borneman, John 5
Brazauskas, Algirdas 37–9, 53, 155

Buchowski, Michal 106
Bulgaria 22, 39, 44, 46, 51, 55–6, 166

C

Common Agricultural Policy (CAP) 57, 89
Cartwright, Andrew 34
cheese 103, 105, 111, 115–18, 122, 125–7, 130–3
China 49
"circular migration" 137, 152, 154, 160, 162, 169–70
circulating sons 138, 143, 152, 154, 170
collective farms 21, 25, 28, 33, 35–6, 41, 46, 48, 50, 100, 102, 104, 124, 135, 142, 144; see also farms
  chairmen of 36, 43, 45, 50, 78, 87, 142
  privatization of 2, 16, 17, 28, 33–4, 36, 38–40, 42–6, 51, 65, 97, 102, 135–6, 147, 161
Connerton, Paul 17
consequences, unintended 31, 136, 138
consumption 50, 92, 109, 112, 121, 123, 125–8, 140, 150, 164, 165
contracts 66–70, 94–5, 108
Copenhagen Criteria 54–5
corruption 2, 53, 55–6, 62, 78, 101
Croatia 166
Cyprus 1, 55
Czech Republic 43, 55, 61

D

dairies 58
dairy; see also milk
  cows 49, 57, 91, 96
  farms 99, 109, 122
  farmers 12, 96
  producers 91–2
  products 11, 58, 101, 105, 107, 111–12, 114–19, 121, 126, 128, 129, 133, 148, 152
  sector 57, 88, 95
daugiavaikės motinos pensija: see pension, "many-children pension" (daugiavaikės motinos pensija)
democratization 37
demographic restructurings 29, 136, 149, 161
demography 3, 26, 91, 138–9, 161–2

deportations 35, 103; see also Gulag camps
de-Sovietization 2, 33–6, 38–9
Direct Payments (DP) 89–90, 93, 97–8, 148–9, 161
distrust 1, 20, 25, 29, 53, 62, 69–70, 78, 87, 97, 101, 137, 145, 161; see also trust
diversification (EU concept) 130–1
Dunn, Elizabeth C. 23–4, 112–13
Dzūkija 2, 10, 12, 14, 66

E

Early Retirement 31, 88, 90–2, 96–108, 125–6, 148, 157, 161; see also retirement
Eastern Europe 3, 4, 54, 91, 171
EEC: see European Economic Community (EEC)
European Coal and Steel Community (ECSC) 6
European Economic Community (EEC) 6, 54, 91–2
Ehrlich, Eugen 25
emigration 5, 28–9, 136–40, 146, 149, 152–5, 157, 159, 161–2
Estonia 55, 61, 142, 166
EU (European Union) 1, 10, 14–15, 28–9, 40, 57, 66–7, 70, 73–6, 80–2, 92, 94–5, 102, 105, 111, 125, 130, 137, 139, 144, 148–9, 154, 156–7
  development plans/reports 3, 5, 22
  enlargement 5–6, 16, 23, 54, 56, 58, 91, 138, 169
  entrance 24–5, 29–30, 54–6, 62–3, 66, 88–9, 93–4, 112, 117, 123, 129–30, 148–9, 160, 163–4, 167
  funds 26, 49, 51, 56, 64, 80, 85, 97
  integration 3–4, 23–5, 30–1, 34, 52, 62, 91, 113, 160–2, 167–70
  laws 3, 22–3, 25–6, 57, 66, 68, 112, 114, 119, 166 (see also Acquis Communautaire)
  legislation 6, 16, 27, 56, 58, 62, 65, 68, 71, 88, 113, 120, 132, 167, 169
  market 16, 24, 31, 62, 113, 117, 119, 120–4, 128–9, 131, 133
  membership 1, 3–8, 16, 18, 23–4, 30–1, 34, 39, 54–6, 58–64, 77, 86, 89, 91, 98, 109, 127, 164, 166, 167, 169–71

migrants 154–7 (*see also* migrants)
programs 2, 5, 8, 22, 52, 54, 56, 58, 62,
  75, 88–9, 91, 93, 96–9, 104, 106–7,
  109, 124
referendum 59–60, 93, 163 (*see also*
  Maxima referendum)
requirements 22–4, 30, 55, 62–4, 74, 88,
  111–13, 124, 161, 167
standards 7, 22, 24, 31, 52, 55, 56,
  58, 63, 86, 98, 109, 112–14, 123,
  129, 131–2
Europe 1–7, 11, 17–20, 23–4, 30, 43, 48,
  51–2, 54, 55, 56, 58–64, 66, 68, 80, 82,
  86, 89, 91, 92, 113, 115, 127, 136, 138,
  139, 149, 150, 154, 157, 160–1, 164–8,
  171; *see also* Eastern Europe; Western
  Europe
EUrope 4, 62–3, 75, 128, 160–1
"Europe-building" 23–4, 52, 63–4, 66,
  68, 86
Europeanization 5, 6, 7, 8
EUropeanization 3, 8, 4, 5, 6, 8, 16, 17, 23,
  25, 29, 30–1, 66, 136, 144, 149, 150,
  159, 160, 162, 164, 167, 170
Eurovision 171

F

Farmers' Farm Register (Ūkininkų Ūkio
  Registras) 89–90, 92
farming, subsistence 10, 39
  semi-subsistence 13, 51, 136, 144, 169–70
farms 1–3, 5, 8, 10, 12–4, 16–17, 22, 27–8,
  33, 49, 52, 58, 62–4
  collective (*see* collective farms)
  family 2, 16, 28, 31, 35, 38–9, 40–1,
    51, 56–7 (*see also asmeniniai ūkiai*
    (private farms))
  private 17, 22, 44 (*see also asmeniniai
    ūkiai* (private farms))
  state 33
Ferguson, James 22–3
folk
  clothes 81
  simple (*prasti žmonės*) 118, 124
  songs 76, 81
fotelio ūkininkai: see "armchair farmers"
  (*fotelio ūkininkai*)
Fowler, Nick 5

G

gender 5, 137, 140, 147, 149, 150–1, 162
  roles 137, 141, 142–3, 151
gendered
  aging 138, 141–3, 161–2, 169 (*see also*
    age and gender distribution)
  work 137, 142, 147, 149, 159, 161, 169
    (*see also* old women and young men)
geopolitical 17, 54, 65, 68, 126, 164, 167–9
  belonging 4
  construction 6
  history 15
  reconceptualization 19
  return to Europe 23, 63
  roots 18
Germany 6, 11, 33, 39, 49, 103, 114, 150–1,
  157–8, 164
Giddens, Anthony 24, 26
Giordano, Christian 17, 21, 51, 82
glasnost 37
Golovatov, Michail 37n6
Gorbachev, Mikhail 37–8
Government of Lithuania 17, 28, 38, 40, 57,
  88, 90, 93, 109, 166
Grabbe, Heather 6, 54, 56
grietinė (sour cream) 103, 115–18
Grybauskaitė, Dalia 18n10
Gulag camps 35–6
Gupta, Akhil 23

H

Habeck, Joachim Otto 150–1
Hann, Chris M. 28
harmonization (EU concept) 5–6, 23–5, 31,
  113, 131
Health Agency 112
Heintz, Monica 69, 164–7
"hidden transcripts" 27
history, reconceptualization of 4, 17, 167–9
Homo Europaeus 21
Homo Sovieticus (*Homosos*) 19–22, 82
homosexuality 35, 165–6
Homosos: see *Homo Sovieticus*
Hudson, Ray 7
Humphrey, Caroline 123
Hungary 39, 43–4, 46, 55, 141

I

Ignalina 56
illegal 47, 67, 115, 121, 123, 133, 147, 153;
    see also legal
    activities 25, 123–5
    migrants 49
    producers 25, 114
    sale 5, 24, 71, 73, 102, 108–9, 111,
        119–21, 124–5, 148
    sellers 31, 108, 112, 169
    trade 48
Ilonszki, Gabriela 29–30
"imagined community" 23
International Monetary Fund (IMF) 16,
    48, 54
"immutable mobile" 24
InCulto 171
independence 1–2, 4, 14, 22, 31, 34,
    36–40, 42–4, 46–51, 53, 70, 75, 78–80,
    97, 100, 104, 135, 142, 144, 167
    declaration of 33, 37
Insiders, 31, 112, 116–17, 119, 121, 123–6,
    130–1, 133; *see also* Outsiders
instrumentalism 3
"interface encounters" 64, 72–4; *see also*
    "multiple faces on the encounter"
invalidumas (disabled persons) 152; *see
    also* pension for disabled persons
Ireland 6, 103, 154–5, 157–8, 166

K

Kaliningrad Oblast 11
Kazakhstan 49
kinship
    obligations 5, 31, 137, 143, 149, 153, 154,
        156–7, 159–60, 162, 169–70
    relations 5, 29, 161–2, 70, 146, 162
Klumbytė, Neringa 78, 126–7
Kostova, Dobrinka 17, 21, 51, 82

L

land 2, 11–12, 14, 16, 22, 33, 35, 37,
    40–4, 46–52, 57, 63, 65, 67, 70, 75, 81,
    87–97, 102, 104, 106–8, 126, 141–2,
    144, 148–9, 152–3, 161; *see also*
    žemžudystė ("land murder")
    consolidation 2, 16, 57, 99

distribution 37, 41, 44, 48, 50
    equalizing "bad luck" 135–6
    measurements 89–90
    murder (*see žemžudystė*)
    plots 33, 35, 39, 41–4, 50, 57, 88–90
    quality 41, 90
    reform 40–2, 44, 56–7
Landsbergis, Vytautas 37, 39, 53
Latour, Bruno 24
Latvia 51, 55, 61, 166
law 2, 3, 5, 7, 22, 23, 25, 26, 31,
    39–44, 46–8, 50, 54–6, 63–4, 66,
    68, 70, 74, 76, 83, 86, 88–90, 109,
    112–14, 116, 119–21, 124–6,
    144, 166–7, 169
Law on Agriculture and Rural
    Development 57
Law on Privatization of the Assets of
    Agricultural Enterprises 42
LDDP: *see* Lietuvos Demokratinė Darbo
    Partija (LDDP)
LDP: *see* Lietuvos Darbo Partija (LDP)
Ledenova, Alena V. 86
legal; *see also* illegal
    arrangements 25
    categories 120–1
    changes 66, 75, 101, 122
    compatibility 16
    conflicts 119
    cooperation 6
    documents 57
    effects 25
    functions 68
    influences 3
    orders 26, 112
    outcomes 5
    pluralities 25–6
    power 7
    procedures 24, 44
    requirements 88
    rights 66, 121
    sale 123, 148
    sellers 31
    status 126
    structures 27
    systems 25, 77, 120
liberal capitalism 22, 29
Lietuvos Darbo Partija (LDP) 53

Lietuvos Demokratinė Darbo Partija (LDDP) 38–9, 52–3
Lietuvos Rytas 85
Lietuvos Ūkininkų Sąjunga (LŪS) 78, 80, 85, 90
Lietuvos Valstiečių Liaudininkų Sąjunga 77; *see also* Valstiečių Sąjunga
life expectancy 137, 140–2, 159
Literature and Revolution (Trotskij) 19
Lithuania; *see also* "New Lithuania"
 Communist leadership 37–8
 diasporas 166
 elite 2, 21, 30, 65, 77
 festivals 81–2, 166
 government (*see* Government of Lithuania)
 identity 4, 17–19, 51
 independence (*see* independence)
 products 58, 99, 111–12, 114–19, 121, 124–32, 165, 169
 society 17–19, 21–3, 25, 51, 77, 81, 112, 128, 138, 149, 161, 166, 168
 traditions 21–2, 81–2, 112, 126–7, 130–1, 166
Lithuanian Farmers' Union: *see* Lietuvos Ūkininkų Sąjunga (LŪS)
Lithuanian Ministry of Agriculture 40, 47, 56, 58, 90
Lithuanian parliament (Seimas) 39, 53, 56–7, 78
lonely-cow phenomenon 95–7
Long, Norman 64
land-parcel identification system (LPIS) 89
LŪS: *see* Lietuvos Ūkininkų Sąjunga (LŪS)

M

Maastricht Treaty 6
Macedonia 166
Mahmood, Saba 27
Malta 1, 55
"Man of the Future" 19–20
Mansholt Plan 91; *see also* "Mini-Mansholt"
Mansholt, Sicco 91
Marijampolė 10–13, 31, 59, 70–4, 98–9, 101, 103, 111–12, 114–15, 119, 121–2, 131, 157

Marijonų Vienuolynas 11
marketplace 10, 31, 107–8, 111–17, 119, 121–2, 124–5, 129, 131, 133
masculinity 81, 84, 150–1
Maxima referendum 58–62; *see also* EU referendum
Mažoji Lietuva 10
Mickevičius-Kapsukas, Vincas 11
migrants 30, 49, 51, 53, 137–8, 150, 152–7, 160, 165–6, 169
migration 138, 154, 164, 166, 169; *see also* "circular migration"; emigration
"Millenarian Movement" 150
milk 49–50, 57–8, 70, 91–2, 94, 96–7, 99, 101–2, 107–9, 111, 116–18, 126–7, 129–31, 149, 152; *see also* dairy
 price policy 31, 92, 96, 116
 products 11, 107, 116, 130; *see also* cheese; *grietinė* (sour cream); *varškė* (curd)
 quality 92–3, 96, 126–7
 quotas 71–2, 88, 92, 96, 100, 103, 106–7, 109
 raw 112, 115–16, 129–30, 133
 uncertified sale of 112, 114, 129
Mincyte, Diana 24, 52, 112, 129
"Mini-Mansholt" 90–2; *see also* Mansholt Plan
močiutės ("grandmothers") 120
Moore, Sally Falk 25
multiple faces on the encounter 64, 74–6; *see also* "interface encounters"
Munck, Victor C. de 149–51, 153, 157, 160
mutual stealing 46

N

NATO (North Atlantic Treaty Organization) 164, 166
Netherlands, the 6, 43
"New Lithuania" 4, 19, 21, 62, 149–50, 161, 170
"New Lithuanians": *see* "New Lithuania"
"new society" 19, 21, 168
Nineteen Eighty-Four (Orwell) 168
"no longer, not yet" 51, 161
norms 25–6, 64, 79, 86, 114, 125, 151, 157

O

OECD (Organisation for Economic
Co-operation and Development)
16, 54
Off-State 64, 79–81; *see also* On-State
old women and young men 137, 142
On-State 64, 79–81, 85; *see also*
Off-State
Orwell, George 19, 168
Outsiders 31, 112, 116–21, 124–6, 129–33;
see also Insiders
"overcoming the past" 65, 75, 82

P

Paksas, Rolandas 18n10
paradoxes of aging 65–6, 74–5, 144
partizanai (freedom fighters) 18, 168
Pawlik, Wojciech 46
pension 13, 43, 50, 69, 87–8, 92, 98, 100,
103–5, 116–17, 136–8, 140–1, 144,
146–9, 152, 160
"many-children pension" (*daugiavaikės
motinos pensija*) 146, 152
pension for disabled persons 146, 152; *see
also invalidumas* (disabled persons)
perestroika 37
"person-making" 113, 123, 129
pig 2, 102, 108–9, 148–9, 152
eight-legged 122
slaughter of 14–15, 121–2, 142, 152
Pine, Frances 29–30, 46, 121, 127–9, 143,
149, 161
Poland 12, 24, 29, 39, 43, 45, 49, 55, 106,
112, 127, 129, 136, 143, 149
pollution 2
populism 21, 76, 77, 84
post-socialism 3–4, 28, 55, 78, 119, 141,
162, 167
post-Soviet 13, 17–18, 22, 51; *see also*
Soviet, pre-Soviet
practical negotiations 27, 88, 108–9, 120,
123–5, 133, 169
practice theory 26
prasti žmonės: see folk, simple (*prasti
žmonės*)
pre-Soviet 18–19, 21–2, 76–7, 81–2; *see
also* Soviet, post-Soviet

privatization 2, 17, 22, 28, 34, 36, 39–44, 46,
48, 51, 56, 58, 63, 101–2, 135–6, 141;
see also *žemžudystė* ("land murder")
processes of 2, 16, 31, 47, 57, 141
rapid 17, 33–4, 38
property 2, 20, 33, 35–6, 38–40, 80, 96,
101, 104, 135–6, 141, 143, 149, 160
abuse of 44–8
administration of 45–6
cooperative/*kolkhoz* property 44
distribution of 34, 37, 42, 47
personal 44, 96
restitution (law of property restitution)
40–1, 44, 47–8, 104
socialist 44
state 41, 44

R

resistance 18, 27, 109
retirement 2, 13, 25, 52, 57, 60, 65, 68–9,
74–5, 94, 99–100, 102–3, 105, 107,
118, 125, 136, 141, 144–9, 152, 157,
161; *see also* age, Early Retirement
"reversibility of events" 17, 51, 82; *see also*
actualized history; "annihilation of the
past"
Roberts, Simon 112, 130–2
Romania 34, 39, 45–8, 55–6, 69, 89, 164,
166; *see also* urban, Romania
runkeliai (rural dwellers, "turnips") 21
rural 1, 8, 10–12, 14, 30, 39, 48, 52–3, 63,
77, 84, 87, 108, 137, 140–2, 154, 156,
159–60, 170
areas 3–4, 12, 22, 27–30, 33, 36, 39,
41, 52, 58, 77, 88, 90, 99, 136–8, 140,
142–3, 146, 149, 160–2
birth rate 138
citizens 1, 14–15, 21, 25, 30, 37, 42–3,
52, 59–60, 64, 68, 86, 88, 90, 116, 138,
144–5, 160, 167
development 56–8, 99, 136, 138
life 88, 93, 137
*Rural Development Plan 2004–2006
Lithuania* 57–8, 99
Rural Development Program 2007–2013
99, 109
Russia 17, 20, 39, 46, 49, 53, 58, 78,
101, 150

S

Sąjūdis 37–9, 48, 52–3
Scott, James 27, 47
Seimas: *see* Lithuanian parliament
(Seimas)
seniūnija (administrative body) 11
Siberia 35–6, 103, 146, 150–1
Slovakia 43, 55, 61, 166
Slovenia 55, 61, 166
social
memory 17
security 3, 5, 28–30, 41, 51, 53, 69, 101,
136, 144–7, 149, 151, 162, 169
Soviet; *see also* de-Sovietization, pre-
Soviet, post-Soviet; Soviet Union
breakup 3–4, 22, 28, 82, 127, 136, 141–2
countries 4, 7, 39, 54
communism 19, 21
industrialization 2
man 19–21, 82 (*see also Homo
Sovieticus*; "Man of the Future")
-minded 4
nostalgia 14, 18, 168
occupation 14, 40, 42, 77
power structures 16
practices 22, 75
times 11, 14, 17, 19, 41, 44–5, 50, 65, 70,
78–9, 96, 102–4, 123, 144, 146
Soviet Union 1, 3–5, 28, 31, 36, 38, 52, 62,
85, 127, 136, 141–2, 147, 149, 167
*Sovietų Socialistinių Respublikų Sąjungos
Konstitucija* 44
space
constructions of 7, 23, 119–21, 132
"cultured" 151
non-EU 121
"uncultured" 151
"spatial idiom-shopping" 120
Spindelegger, Michael 37n6
Stalin, Josef 35
"suprastate" 23, 63
Suvalkija 2, 10–13

T

"targeting the wrong audience" 65
*Tarybų Socialistinių Respublikų Sąjungos
Konstitucija* 44

tėvynė (fatherland) 21
Tėvynės Sąjunga (Union of the
Fatherland) 79
"The Geo-Politics of Taste" (Klumbytė) 126
Thelen, Tatjana 46, 146, 169
Transparency International (TI) 55
total social factor 28
Trakai 128
transition 3–4, 34, 38, 48–51, 123
Trotskij, Lev 19–20
trust 65, 70, 78, 123; *see also* distrust
TV tower event 37

U

Ūkininkų Ūkio Registras: *see* Farmers'
Farm Register (Ūkininkų Ūkio
Registras)
unemployment 38, 106, 147, 151–2
Union of the Fatherland; *see* Tėvynės
Sąjunga (Union of the Fatherland)
urban
citizens 60, 90
life 3, 136–7
migrants 137–8, 152–3, 169
residents 90
Romania 69
urban–rural compromise 154
urbanization 162
workers 39, 53, 169–70
working class 53,
yards 105, 121
urbanization 162, 169–70
USSR: *see* Soviet Union

V

valstiečiai (farmers) 76–7, 79–84
Valstiečių Sąjunga 10, 76–83, 85; *see
also* Lietuvos Valstiečių Liaudininkų
Sąjunga
varškė (curd) 115–17
Verdery, Katherine 45–8
"vertical encompassment" 23, 63, 169
Via Baltica 11, 114
Vilnius 1, 7–8, 37–8, 47, 78–80, 98, 166
as "European capital of culture 2009" 168
letter 166
Vonderau, Asta 21

W

"weapons of the weak" 27
Wedel, Janine 46
Welz, Gisela 132
West, the 19, 127–8, 131, 138, 149, 164–5
Western 17, 20, 22, 30, 127, 150, 160, 164
    migration 30, 138, 154, 160, 164, 165–6
    products 24, 127–8, 150, 164–5
    societies 19, 127, 149, 165–6
    superiority 164–6
Western Europe 2–4, 17, 20, 24, 51, 61, 80,
    92, 113, 115, 127, 136, 138, 150, 164–5

Westernization 19, 30, 149–50, 165, 167
World Bank 2, 16, 40, 48, 54
World Trade Organization (WTO) 89

Y

Yeltsin, Boris 38

Z

Žemaitija 10
žemžudystė ("land murder") 43
Zinoviev, Aleksandr 20–1, 82

Lightning Source UK Ltd.
Milton Keynes UK
UKOW041403020613

211590UK00002B/7/P